On Quakers and Pastors

Derek Brown

BARCLAY PRESS
Newberg, OR 97132

On Quakers and Pastors
©2019 by Derek Brown

All rights reserved. No part may be reproduced for any commercial purpose by any method without permission in writing from the copyright holder.

Barclay Press, Inc.
Newberg, Oregon
www.barclaypress.com

Cover design by Mareesa Fawver Moss.

Printed in the United States of America.

ISBN 978-1-59498-062-6

To my loving wife, whose patience and loving-kindness epitomizes the serene beauty of a Quaker soul.

Table of Contents

Introduction 7
Chapter One: Defining Terms 15
Chapter Two: A Brief History 41
Chapter Three: Quakerism and the Pastoral System 51
Chapter Four: Quaker Pastoral Theology 93
Chapter Five: Pastoral Expectations 109
Chapter Six: Theology, History, and Leadership 131
Chapter Seven: Gender 145
Chapter Eight: Proclamation 153
Chapter Nine: Leadership 211
Chapter Ten: Pastoral Care 245
Conclusion 267
Index 269
Endnotes 281
Bibliography 321

Introduction

In 2009, I spent ten days touring Israel with a group of pastors from the Calvary Chapel denomination. Unfamiliar with the movement, I was informed that the pastors wielded considerable authority in their churches and were considered the conduit by which vision and leadership were granted to the church (i.e., the Moses Model).[1] As a Quaker, I was horrified. But when pressed to offer the pastoral theology of the Friends church, I found myself at a loss. It was then that the desire to explore the ecclesiology and pastoral leadership of evangelical Friends was born.

Though I have never pastored in a Friends church, my PhD work focused on the exploration of American Quakerism through the lenses of ecclesiology and organizational theory. My dissertation explored the development of the pastoral role in Kansas Yearly Meeting (1873–1978). In addition, I serve as the professor of pastoral ministry at Barclay College, where I am also the vice president for graduate studies. Even though I educate and train pastors from various denominations represented in the student body, my mission and mandate is to faithfully train future Friends pastors in the framework of Christ-centered Quakerism.

Problem

My years of teaching practical theology in a Friends context made me highly aware of the lack of a unified, articulated pastoral theology. I was often forced to play it by ear, instructing students on the historical, theological, and pastoral principles I gleaned from historical and contemporary Quaker writings and my personal observations. The first part of this book articulates my main argument: the pastoral system was never properly integrated into American Quakerism. This occurred because of a lack of a unified theological and practical understanding of the expectations of pastoral ministry, coupled with the recruitment of pastors from outside the Friends movement who brought their own pastoral understandings into the local meetings.

During my interactions with other Friends churches and yearly meetings, I have discovered that I am not alone in recognizing the deficiency of common expectations for pastors. This lack of unity has several implications for American Quakerism. First, as mentioned above, a deficiency in common expectations makes it difficult for educational institutions, and even the yearly meetings themselves, to educate and train pastors. Second, pastors and churches are hindered by a lack of common understanding regarding the duties and authority of the pastor, which can create conflict, demoralize pastors, and hamper a church's mission. Third, even if a pastor finds success at their current pastorate, there is no guarantee that those same principles will work at other churches, for both the broad and the minute expectations of the pastor may vary wildly from church to church (that is, greater than the standard differences found in all churches). Finally, the ethos of Quakerism is weakened and diluted because many pastors do not know or understand enough of Quakerism to foster it in their local congregations. It is this last issue that is the most troublesome but also the most promising avenue of resurgence for Friends.

Untapped Potential

The diminishment of Christianity in America has led to recognition that the church may have an identity crisis.[2] Compounding the problem is the belief, both inside and outside the church, that "the church itself is the chief hindrance to Christian faith in our time."[3]

In response to this diminishing influence of Christianity in America, many church leaders have followed the erroneous idea that the answer lies in organizational efficiency. Gregory Liston describes this seductive yet dangerous strategy as thinking that by "being more organized and pragmatic—by simply *doing better* in some way—the western church can recover."[4] The other belief is that the recovery of Christian hegemony is to simply make Christianity "cool" again.[5] These attitudes, though prevalent, are misguided. Rather, one should view this time as an opportunity to rediscover the ways of Christianity that have been marginalized in the zealous (and failed) pursuit of American church growth. Quakerism is one such path, waiting to be rediscovered. I believe that there is untapped potential regarding the spread of Christ-centered Quakerism in America. The distinctive testimonies of Quakerism offer many a solution to those searching for authentic Christian living that is differentiated from the bland evangelicalism that is growing increasingly ineffective. Yet Quakerism in America is basically unknown, save for some literary references and pop culture iconography (e.g., Quaker Oats).[6] However, we have not made use of one of the most effective ways to spread the gospel through the Friends movement—word of mouth.

Word of mouth has been shown to be the deciding influence in up to half of all purchasing decisions.[7] In advertising, word of mouth has been found both more persuasive and more targeted—reaching the right people with the most effective message.[8] It is a hidden force, which costs nothing, yet outperforms traditional methods of advertising. In terms of evangelism and church growth, the biggest draw to a Friends church will be an invitation from a friend or acquaintance, evidence of an authentic excitement and connection to the movement or culture that the church represents. Herein lies the problem: because there has not been an articulated pastoral theology and ecclesiology which articulates the testimonies of Quakerism in contemporary context, Friends project either an anemic culture or one that is indistinguishable from surrounding churches and denominations. By articulating and embracing an ethos of Christ-centered Quakerism, churches could live out a community and culture that is truly distinct, and when asked, members could clearly and concisely explain what makes Friends "Friends." An articulated culture creates a strong movement, which creates strong ties to its members. Such members do not have to be pressed to share their faith, but cannot wait to tell others what God is doing through this authentic Christian community.

Creating a Quaker Pastoral Theology

The second part of this book addresses a problem that every organization faces—"Spreading constructive beliefs and behavior from the few to the many."[9]

Because a Christ-centered Quakerism is (or at least should be) rooted in the spirit and truth of a Trinitarian God revealed through scripture, its pastoral theology should be based on the testimony of scripture, illuminated by the Holy Spirit. In addition, Christ-centered Quakerism recognizes that God has chosen to speak through this stream of Christianity, and thus should embody the testimonies by which historic Quakerism lived out its faith and spread the gospel. By treating the example of early Quakerism seriously, we avoid the anachronism of judging seventeenth-century believers by our narrow, twenty-first-century standards—which allows us to take the testimonies of the early Friends and apply them to our contemporary predicament.[10]

Unfortunately, the biblical foundation and historical Quaker precedent for these pastoral elements do not guarantee that they will be accepted or adopted by pastors serving in Friends churches today. It is an unfortunate fact that, given the anxiety caused by the perceived decline of Christianity in America, the response has been to seek the pragmatic methods of church leadership which produce results, regardless of their fit or effect on the local church or denomination. While it is quite easy (and most satisfying) to rail against those who would sell their ecclesiological birthrights for a small stew of success, it is more prudent to recognize the reality of our situation and respond accordingly.

How to Read this Book

This book can be broken into two distinctive sections. The first five chapters provide a historical and theological overview of pastoral theology, a brief summary of Quakerism, and the circumstances and consequences of their convergence. The last five chapters provide a practical introduction to a Christ-centered Quaker pastoral theology.

Chapter 1 contains definitions and explanations of the theological terminology. This vocabulary provides both a foundation for understanding the concepts explored, and also helps prevent confusion. Chapter 2 provides a brief history of the Friends movement, with a focus on the events leading up to the adoption of the pastoral system. Chapter 3 explores whether pastoral ministry is compatible with the historical principles of Quakerism, while chapter 4 explores a related question: even if a formal pastoral theology is compatible with Quaker theology, is it necessary? Chapter 5 articulates the pastoral expectations revealed in the literature of the various yearly meetings.

Chapter 6 discusses the various domains found within pastoral theology, while chapter 7 delves into issues of gender within Quakerism (and Christianity as a whole). Chapter 8 is the first leg of the pastoral theology triumvirate, exploring the concept of the pastor's role to proclaim. Chapter 9 explores the expectation of the pastor to lead, while chapter 10 considers the pastor as shepherd.

Goal

My hope is to create a solid case for each pastoral element presented in this book, and in the process, formulate a brief, introductory, Christ-centered Quaker pastoral theology for use by pastors, churches, and yearly meetings. Yet this is not the only goal. Given that there will always be pastors who are unfamiliar with the Friends movement, this book can be foundational for acclimating and acculturating outside pastors into the ethos and mission of Christ-centered Quakerism. Also, there is the hope that this work will jumpstart other academic endeavors regarding all of the Christ-centered streams of Quakerism. Finally, this book might help pastors spur on individual Quakers and their local churches to recognize their unique testimony of Christ to the world, and to live out that testimony fearlessly as witnesses for the gospel.

This book can be viewed as the culmination or the beginning of a journey (or both). As a culmination, this book is the product of years of research, theorizing, and conceptualizing a Christ-centered Quaker pastoral theology. Though not finalized in the sense of a finished text (a pastoral theology, while rooted in key principles/traditions, should always be open to adaptation), it is the first formalized pastoral theology for Friends churches and yearly meetings.

This book can also be considered the beginning of a journey. The theology articulated in this book is not fossilized or immutable, but is an ecclesiological conversation piece that helps frame and guide future discussions of Friends faith and practice, as yearly meetings and churches seek to adapt to the needs of the ever-changing mission field of twenty-first-century America.

Chapter One

Definition of Terms

On account of the wide range of academic disciplines and concepts explored in this book, a definition of key terms is necessary. This chapter, however, should not be understood merely as a primer for the book, but also for understanding the Friends movement. While, on the surface, many Friends churches appear quite similar to other Protestant faith communities, the Society of Friends has its own distinct vocabulary that has been built up over three and a half centuries. Because this vocabulary is most familiar to those within the Friends movement, it can be confusing to new members (and sadly, to existing members as well). This is especially true of pastors coming into a Friends church from another denomination. Short explanations of key Quaker terms related to ecclesiology and pastoral ministry should help.

Quaker Terms

Friend vs. Quaker

The purpose of this book is to articulate a theology for American pastoral Quakerism that upholds the tenets of Christianity and emphasizes the distinct testimonies by which the Friends movement lives out its Christian faith. The main obstacle to understanding and adopting a Christ-centered Quaker pastoral theology is the lack of familiarity with Friends terms and concepts; this is especially true of those entering the movement from other denominations. Two major terms that set the table for further discussion are "Friend" and "Quaker." The explanation of these terms is complicated by the perceived tension between the two, especially during the last century.

Both "Quaker" and "Friend" are terms used to denote a member of the Religious Society of Friends. The term "Friend" emerged from the different titles the early movement had for itself, including "Children of the Light" and "Friends of the Truth," which was taken from John 15:15: "I have called you friends."[11] The term "Quaker" was initially a pejorative utilized by adversaries who witnessed the early worshipers physically shaking, or quaking, while experiencing the power of God during worship meetings.[12] According to Errol Elliott, "Quakerism was a quaking movement, a trembling under the *power* of the Lord, as Friends admonished others to *quake*, to tremble at the *word* of the Lord."[13] For most of the movement's existence, one could call any member either a Friend or a Quaker. However, the two terms began accruing differing connotations, which have built up over time and have caused a rift between the two terms (and the followers who utilize those terms).

It can be argued that the separation arose from perceived theological differences. The main difference was between those who held that Quakerism was a Christian movement and those who are Quaker but do not wish to be identified as exclusively Christian.[14] There were mutual accusations that each side had lost a key element of what it means to be a Quaker.[15] This divergence began with the slow separation of evangelical Friends from other Friends in terms of certain theological views, outreach and missions work, and cooperation with other denominations.[16] It now mirrors the split between conservative and liberal Christianity in contemporary America—a divide that emerged from the battle between the fundamentalists and proponents of the social gospel.[17] Many who sought to distance themselves from the liberal stream of Quakerism began using the term "Friend" exclusively. The terms then became a means by which one could get a vague generalization of another person's place in the historic Friends stream.

Much like the conservative/liberal split, the perceived gulf between the terms "Friends" and "Quakers" revolves around each side distancing itself from its opposing straw man. On one side, the Friends accused Quakers of having neglected the truth of the gospel for an incoherent faith supported by a vague spirituality. This vague mysticism utilized scripture irresponsibly, and diminished the historical person of Christ into a mere spiritualizing influence.[18] This neglect of the scriptures led to a diminishment of missionary zeal and a subsequent dampening of spiritual influence.[19] Thus without a general repentance and return to its Christian foundations, the movement will be unrecognizable when compared to the early Friends movement.

On the other hand, to the Quakers, evangelical Friends disregarded their godly heritage, sloughing it off like so much refuse, to revel in self-righteousness, hunkered safely in churches, away from the ills of the world.[20] This was aggravated by the creation of the evangelical Friends church. Since the adoption of the pastoral system, there was perceived, in evangelical meetings, that "not only is the traditional Quaker organisation absent, but the traditional Quaker values are being lost in what can become just another variety of mainstream protestantism."[21] Without a general repentance and return to its foundational testimonies, the movement was viewed as being close to unrecognizable compared to the early Friends movement.

It has been opined that the current divergent trajectories of the evangelical and liberal Friends movements are unsustainable and require a dramatic change of course or repentance.[22] For while these separations were once viewed as necessary, it must be noted that the division separated churches and yearly meetings who may have been similar in Christian theology. Within Friends United Meeting (FUM), there are many churches who proclaim orthodox, trinitarian theology. But since they are members of FUM, rather than Evangelical Friends Church International (EFCI), there is a perceived gulf and perhaps even a hint of suspicion (for example, a gentleman who attended an evangelical Friends church expressed genuine surprise that there were Bible-believing churches in FUM, for he had heard that this was not the case). Quaker churches who are evangelical may not be able to support one another because of a difference of affiliation.

And therein lies the danger: if Quakerism is to remain and reemerge as a decidedly Christian movement, it will take the cooperation of like-minded churches to create, enact, and sustain it. However, even though many, if not most, Friends churches in America are Christian, such cooperation does not occur because of the separation and distrust engendered by the separation of "Friend" and "Quaker," as well as between "Friend" and "Evangelical Friend." To overcome the baggage that accompanies these terms, a new term may be necessary—one that will describe a Friends church according to its theological beliefs and actions rather than its organizational affiliation. Thus, Christ-centered Quakerism.

Christ-centered Quakerism

Christ-centered Quakerism is not meant to be the title nor philosophy of a new organization, a new rival to EFCI and FUM. This is not an issue of denomination but of language. Rather than get caught up in the present tension over Friends/Quaker language (with all the corresponding baggage that accompanies those terms), this book hopes to unite Christian Friends churches everywhere.

Christ-centered Quakerism is a term meant to represent Quakerism in a way articulated by Elton Trueblood, not as "an odd little sect with a peculiar vocabulary, but a revolutionary effort to represent the Gospel of Christ without distortion."[23] At first I thought my name for this endeavor, Christ-centered Quakerism, was an original contribution, but I soon discovered that Seth Hinshaw had promoted, in general, the notion of Christ-centeredness as the key to Quakerism; he understood that "to be Quaker is to be a Christian."[24] This understanding is echoed by others as well.

The assumptions of Christ-centered Quakerism are built upon the fact that the early Friends movement was a Christian movement. Though the language may differ from contemporary Christian terminology, early Quakers believed in conversion through a personal experience of Christ, made evident by transformation through the Holy Spirit.[25]

These Christian origins are undeniable. Thus, when John Punshon spoke of evangelical Friends, he recognized that this stream of Quakerism "retains much of the pristine fervour, theological certainty, and passion which characterized the early Quaker movement—and more of its theology than those of us who do not belong to it can readily admit."[26] By emphasizing the lordship of Christ, revealed through the scriptures and experienced through the Holy Spirit, Christ-centered Quakerism recovers the heritage and inheritance of Christianity as the foundation and compass of Quakerism—thus, *Christ-centered* Quakerism.

The choice of Quakerism, instead of Friends, for the title emerged from the hope that Christ-centered Quakerism will not forget its historic roots—the testimonies of radically changed lives that preached loudly the love of God even if no words were spoken. Unfortunately, many of these testimonies have atrophied or been abandoned by the Friends movement over the centuries. This was especially true during the evangelical split-off of the late nineteenth and early twentieth centuries in which Quaker testimonies, alongside the social gospel and liberal politics, were viewed as something unfit and unbecoming of an evangelical faith. While space does not allow for a full articulation of Quaker testimonies, one major point must be made here: that the testimonies of the Friends movement are not alien to Christianity but are an attempt to take the teachings of Jesus (and scripture) seriously. The testimonies exist to help us individually and corporately live out a sound interpretation of scripture—and to have one's entire life be a witness to God. Thus, as a reminder of our opportunity to proclaim the kingdom of God through the vessel of Friends—Christ-centered *Quakerism*.

Unintentionally, the term *Christ-centered* could lead to a form of unitarianism, focusing solely on Christ the Son at the expense of other members of the Trinity.[27] However, this danger is relatively small. Christ-centered Quakerism is a new way to think about the Friends movement in America, a paradigm that builds or reinforces connections between Christian Friends congregations and categorizes the resurgence of American Quakerism that is apologetically Christian and unapologetically Quaker.

Other Significant Quaker Terms

Many of the theological, ecclesiological, and organizational terms utilized by the Society of Friends are unique to the movement.

Monthly Meeting

The smallest organizational unit in this study is the monthly meeting. Its Protestant counterpart is the local church. The term emerged in the time of George Fox, who gathered the various gatherings into monthly meetings to streamline the organizational life of the movement, as well as guard against heterodox teachings and ministry.[28] These meetings met monthly to conduct necessary church business. The monthly meeting has been defined as the "monthly gathering for the conduct of church business."²⁹ However, this definition is much too narrow, as the monthly meeting encapsulates all aspects of the community of faith, much like the word *church* encapsulates the work and worship of the local community of faith.³⁰ The ultimate purpose of the monthly meeting is to gather for worship and for fellowship.³¹ Thus, while the term *monthly meeting* speaks of the community of faith which gathers regularly for worship and engages in ministry and fellowship, at other times it also speaks of the administrative function of the leadership of the church, seeking to enact organizational leadership and stewardship.³² While historically, several congregations could reside under the administrative umbrella of a single monthly meeting, the common understanding in contemporary Quakerism is that "monthly meeting" refers to a single congregation—if the term is used at all.³³ When speaking of contemporary congregations in American Quakerism, the term "church" is most often used, while monthly meeting has fallen out of favor.

Quarterly Meeting

Several monthly meetings in the same general geographic area can be combined into a quarterly meeting.³⁴ A quarterly meeting is a "regional gathering of Friends from a number of monthly meetings for the conduct of business meetings, worship, and mutual support."³⁵ Quarterly meetings gather once a quarter to conduct necessary church business. However, these meetings not only convene to address business, but are also social gatherings, which organically lead to group cohesion as members from various churches come together at regular intervals and interact.³⁶

Yearly Meeting

The yearly meeting is the highest level of organizational autonomy, comprised of the monthly and quarterly meetings within a geographical area.[37] Yearly meetings are defined as "regional bodies that are responsible to adopt the book of discipline and delineate the faith and practice of the members of that body."[38] The closest comparison to a typical Protestant administrative body would be a denomination. Concordant with monthly and quarterly meetings, the term "yearly meeting" reflects the practice of gathering once a year to conduct denominational business. While the yearly meetings are connected by larger organizations (e.g., EFCI, FUM, FGC), they are functionally and philosophically autonomous. The business of decision-making occurs at a yearly gathering of representatives from the quarterly and monthly meetings (this is also called the yearly meeting). There, under the guidance of a presiding clerk, the group seeks to make collective decisions regarding theology, praxis, and administrative issues facing the yearly meeting.[39]

According to the Kansas Yearly Meeting, "Each denominational body has its own system of government, and rules for the transaction of its business and for individual observance by its members."[40] Each yearly meeting, because of geographical and cultural differences, will have, in addition to traditional Quaker aspects, unique nuances that separate it from other yearly meetings.

Yearly Meeting Minutes

The vehicle for recording and communicating the dialogue and conclusions of the yearly meeting sessions are the yearly meeting minutes. These minutes are written in real time by the recording clerk, who then compiles them, along with any other documents, into completed yearly meeting minutes. These minutes are then printed by the yearly meeting and distributed to the various churches and members. Because these are minutes of sessions occurring over a series of several days, there are different speakers at different times providing content that is recorded. However, not only are the speakers/presenters often not identified, but the purpose of the yearly meeting minutes is to communicate the *vox populi* of the yearly meeting *in toto*.

Faith and Practice

A yearly meeting's faith and practice (historically known as the discipline) is a combination of history, theological beliefs, and "guidelines for [Friends'] religious practices and concerns."[41] These documents helped codify beliefs and praxis in order to curb abuses of either, while also providing instruction regarding ecclesiological structures and organizational efficiency. While the various faith and practices have differences, Walter Williams highlighted that most contain "a brief history of Friends; Doctrines believed; Testimonies; Advices; Queries; Functions of the monthly, quarterly, and yearly meetings, with definitions of duties of officers, boards, and committees."[42] This document should be understood as representing the common wisdom of the yearly meeting, replacing a physical spiritual leader of the individual yearly meeting.

Ministers

Quakers believed that the spoken ministry was a spiritual gift bestowed upon certain members of a local congregation. According to Kansas Yearly Meeting:

> We believe that gospel ministry is not of man, but by the revelation of Jesus Christ. Holding it to be a doctrine truly Christian, that the Spirit of God is the foundation of all true knowledge in relation to that duty which we owe to Him, and one to another, we earnestly exhort, that those among us who apprehend that they are called to the ministry of the gospel may, in their public services especially, attend closely to their several and peculiar gifts, waiting for that divine ability by which they may faithfully and availingly minister the Word.[43]

These ministers, once recognized as having the spiritual gift of preaching, would be recognized as ministers by being officially recorded as such. These ministers would sit in the place of honor with the elders and would be expected to speak during worship meetings if the Spirit led them to. It is through ministers that the gospel was preached regularly to the congregation. If a minister is recognized as having an effective, eloquent, and faithful ministry, they are often promoted to greater ministry endeavors in their local area and beyond. As one minister related his early success at preaching, "This was a great encouragement to me and opened the way for other service among them. Meetings were appointed for me in three neighborhoods to the northwest."[44]

Another aspect of ministry that, while not unique to Quakers, highlights the sense of pastoral duty, is the traveling ministry. Because some congregations may not have anyone with the gift of preaching, other monthly meetings would liberate their ministers to travel and preach for a time. Sometimes this liberation would last months or years and would cover a general geographic area. In this way, those churches that have an abundance of recorded ministers could distribute the spiritual wealth to those with a deficit. Traveling ministry was an inconvenience, as a minister would have to leave profession, home, and family in order to make this journey. While some meetings sought to help maintain the farm or business of the traveling minister while he or she was away, as well as contributing voluntary financial support, this did not always occur.[45]

Recording

The Friends movement differs from other denominations and religious movements in its nomenclature regarding the official recognition and ordination of its clergy. Because of the movement's emergence as a protest of hierarchical religious organization (especially of the Anglican Church), its vocabulary avoided any hint of centralized authority.[46] Rather than ordain a minister in the service of the church, Quakers record a minister for service in the church.[47] This recording is a recognition of the gift of ministry (from the Holy Spirit) and an acknowledgment of the minister's role in the Friends movement.[48] The term emerged from the early years of Quakerism, with a clerk writing down, or recording, the names of official ministers.[49] Thus, officially recognized clergy are deemed recorded ministers, or later on, recorded pastors.

Friends did not bestow the status of minister, but simply recognized the divine gift that had been given by God. However, even at the beginning, ministers were not considered recorded unless they had been recognized as such by the monthly and quarterly meetings. There were levels of accountability and discernment regarding ministerial standards. Later, various requirements were added, including a multi-year process of vetting before a person could be recorded.

Pastor/Pastoral System

While ministers in the Friends church engaged in pastoral activities, it is imperative to distinguish them from pastors. The term "pastor" in this book denotes the "singular, paid position of leadership and authority in a local Friends meeting/church." While there may be many recorded ministers within a congregation, at the time of the shift into the pastoral system, there would have been only one pastor.

When the term "pastoral system" is mentioned, it is referencing the paradigm of "a paid, professionalized clergy." The term is not a common one in ecclesiological literature. This research will explicitly distinguish between the ministers and their ministry, and pastors found within the pastoral system.

Elders

In addition to ministers whose ministry could be classified as prophetic (i.e., preaching and teaching), the Friends movement also called upon spiritually mature people to engage in pastoral shepherding of the congregation.[50] These people were called elders. Indiana Yearly Meeting gives this advice to its congregations regarding eldership: "Monthly Meetings are advised to appoint some serious, discreet, and judicious Friends, who are not ministers, tenderly to encourage and help young ministers, and advise others as they in the wisdom of God see occasion."[51] When the meeting chooses an elder, "Age or wealth is not to be an inducement in the choice; but let such be appointed as fear God, love his truth in sincerity, are sound in Christian faith and doctrine, and are of clean hands."[52] These elders are instrumental in maintaining order among the congregations.

An exploration of Quaker pastoral theology, specifically pastoral leadership and authority during the first years of the pastoral system, must include the oversight of the elders. Because the prophetic ministry was not linked to authority and leadership in the congregation, the elders were considered the final authority in matters of faith and practice. Any transition toward an ecclesiological system that moves authority and leadership into the hands of someone other than the elders would surely be disruptive and find resistance. Research into the evolution of the pastoral role must consider the role of elder as well.

Unprogrammed Worship

In response to the highly-structured liturgy of the Church of England, worshipers in the Friends movement eschewed the requirement of any specific element in their worship, except for silence, out of which any number of elements may organically arise.[53] Typically, an unprogrammed service was marked by extended periods of silence, where worshipers would center down and wait for the Holy Spirit to speak to them. If a worshiper felt compelled, they would stand and share the message that the Lord laid on their heart. The meeting would end with a handshake by a presiding elder to the person next to them, signaling to the rest of the congregation that the service had ended.

The only element of hierarchy in the service was the facing bench, where the elders and recorded ministers would sit, facing the rest of the congregation. The services were extremely egalitarian. Anyone, without regard to age, race, or gender could stand and share. The poly-participatory nature of these services was dramatically different from the pulpit-centered aspect of a programmed service. Any move toward a pastoral system would have to account for the changes from an unprogrammed service to a programmed service, to avoid any ambiguity in the leadership and authority of a pastor.

Programmed Worship

As congregations grew from the evangelical revival that occurred during the nineteenth century, the unprogrammed worship style, which was unfamiliar to many of the new converts, was replaced with a programmed style with prayer, preaching, and singing (which was familiar even to the new converts from their experience at revival meetings).[54] This programmed worship began spreading throughout the American yearly meetings during the late nineteenth century and early twentieth century. Because of the focus toward the pulpit (where both the song leader and the preacher would stand) and away from the facing bench (where a multitude of elders and ministers sat), it is assumed that there was a symbolic shift in the authority of those occupying the pulpit (namely, the pastor).

Theological Terms

To understand the process of articulating a pastoral theology of Christ-centered Quakerism, one must first separate the concept of "pastoral theology" from theology proper. Because theology has been viewed and understood as primarily a discipline of abstraction and theory, it is easy to question its relevance to the practical matters of the church. Lewis Mudge and James Polling ask the question, "What is the relation between 'theology' as an academic discipline and living, worshiping, serving communities of faith?"[55] Theology should be, according to John Macquarrie, "the attempt to state as clearly as possible the beliefs or doctrines that belong to the Christian way of life."[56] Knowledge about God is no substitute for a life-changing experience of God, and theology is itself incomplete without a connection to real life.[57] According to Christopher Hall, for the early church fathers, "Any split between mind and heart, theology and spirituality, study and sanctuary would have been met with scant toleration."[58] Thus, "In theology, mind and heart—study and prayer—are both important."[59] A goal of theology is describing God and his work along with its practical implications in the life of a Christian.[60]

To know about God (theology) provides the impetus to shape one's life to please God through one's daily activities.[61] Theology not only shapes the actions and attitudes of the congregation, but is of utmost importance to clergy to effectively preach, shepherd, and evangelize.[62] As people grasp a knowledge and understanding of theology, they may still need guidance to put this knowledge into action. One then moves from theology proper to practical theology.

Practical Theology

Like many theological terms, "practical theology" has several different meanings, based on context, though they are conceptually linked.[63] Gisjbert Dingemans has written that, historically, "Practical theology was mainly a means for educating ministers for leadership in the church . . . [and] was taught in seminaries."[64] It was a term reserved as the subject heading of professional ministry educational courses. This perspective broadened in the twentieth century, especially in the United States, to include the practical application of theology as a more holistic concept.[65] This slightly broader definition understood practical theology as "critical reflection on the church's life in both corporate and individual expressions."[66] The domains, in this broadened understanding, included the internal functions and the external mission of church.[67] Unfortunately, until recently, the academic discipline of practical theology has been perceived as a secondary and substandard field of theology proper.[68]

The aim of practical theology is to provide "an understanding of how faith can guide action in contemporary circumstances."[69] In this definition, practical theology is moved from mere practical tips for ministers and into the broader intersection of Christian theory and praxis for members of the church.[70] It also allows theology, an oft-abstracted discipline, to be explored in conjunction with other fields, such as leadership and stewardship.[71] While formally relating to both clergy and lay faith leaders, the trickle-down effect of such interplay is that practical theology is useful to anyone who is curious about "those who work within Christianity with concerns about the relationship of theology to practice."[72] Practical theology, properly explored and applied, achieves the dual aims of moving theology into the realm of real life, as well as strengthening the individual believer and communities of faith with actions, attitudes, and outlooks enriched by godliness.[73]

Pastoral Theology

Pastoral theology is a separate field from practical theology and should be reserved as strictly relating to the role and function of the clergy. However, the vagueness of terminology often causes inconsistent labeling.[74] As a formal academic field, pastoral theology came into being in the nineteenth century, though its ambiguous identity regarding practical theology, as well as a lack of investment by the academic community, has led some to wonder if pastoral theology (also sometimes known as pastoral studies) should be abandoned as a formal area of study.[75] It is unlikely for such a thing to occur, as the practical applications of research in this field, as well as the current needs of many churches and denominations, require theological engagement with the pastoral role.

C. W. Brister described pastoral theology as follows:

> The branch of "practical theology" that studies human development in spiritual, moral, and behavioral perspective, reflects upon the church's caring functions in light of the Christian faith, enhances pastoral caregiving tasks, and in the process, contributes to the larger body of Christian knowledge.[76]

As a subset of Christian theology, pastoral theology articulates the role and function of a pastor.[77] This pastoral theology not only dictates the ecclesiological structure and governance of the local church, but also provides a concrete cultural ethos in which future pastors and members can be socialized.[78]

If American Quakerism lacked an articulated pastoral theology, one of the most damaging consequences would be a lack of common understanding regarding pastoral leadership and authority. According to Ryan LaMothe,

> Because of the necessity and importance of leadership, pastoral theological reflection must include a systematic examination of the type(s) of leadership necessary to address various individual, family, communal, and social maladies.[79]

Pastoral theology helps facilitate cooperation between clergy and congregation by articulating the understanding and expectations of the pastoral role.

Why Pastoral Theology?

The Friends church is facing a problem that appears to be the opposite of other denominations. In many denominations, the role of the clergy is clearly articulated, and the position is imbued with tradition. The relevant issue for these denominations is the unclear expectations of the congregation (or laity). A passive church experience, coupled with a lack of community, could be cited as a reason for declining church attendance. In response, denominations have scrambled to find ways to bring the laity into active participation and belonging with their church (Vatican II is an example of a major overhaul in this direction). While the pastors in these denominations are well-trained and educated and possess a clear understanding of their role, the people in the pews don't necessarily have any of these things. Their social connection to the church is in competition with other affiliations.

The Friends church has the opposite problem. Since its inception, the culture of the Friends movement has been one of the "priesthood of all believers." Each member is empowered to follow the leading of the Holy Spirit (which is confirmed by scripture and the community of faith) and minister wherever they may be. This egalitarian mindset allowed for formerly secular jobs to be imbued with a sacred vocation. What the Friends church didn't have, when they began hiring pastors, was a clear understanding of the pastoral role. Thus, a Quaker pastoral theology is needed to guide the actions and attitudes of Friends pastors so that they can serve effectively.

Ecclesiology

Ecclesiology derives its name from *ekklesia*, the common term used to describe the church in the New Testament and early Christian literature (this term will be explored further in chapter 9). For "church," the simplest definition is provided by Michael Jenkins, who writes, "Whatever it means when we say 'church,' it has meant at least in part *those who have been called out throughout history by God to worship God.*"[80] At its most basic, ecclesiology refers to the study of the church (i.e., what the church is, what the church does). It is an exploration of the calling, gathering, worshiping, and sending community that we have labeled "church." Ecclesiology not only explores the theological conceptualizations of the church, but also the concrete models of actual church practice, as well as the interplay between the two.[81] As a subset of the larger theological endeavor, ecclesiology has not been an explicit or primary focus of theological research until the modern era.[82]

Ecclesiologies are often denominationally contextual, or if written broadly, placed within a specific stream of theology and Christianity.[83] The danger of this is that, through the continuing articulation of differentiation and uniqueness between the various movements of Christianity, there is a drift away from ecumenism and cooperation, and into parochialism. Ola Tjørhom offers a blistering critique of this drift:

> A major reason why ecclesiology has wandered astray into the realm of separation and strife is that we have turned this discipline into *disparate institutional theories of parochial churches.* Instead of stressing unity as an indispensable ecclesial mark, the doctrine of the church has become a demarcation zone where we engage busily in digging trenches and ignore opportunities for building bridges.[84]

The hesitancy to apply an ecclesiological framework to Quakerism may stem from the view of the movement as not simply an organization, but a "spiritual organism."[85] But if the Friends church is to thrive in its God-given mission, there must be a proper understanding of the theological reason for its existence.

Leadership Terms

Leadership

While leadership is a topic of great importance, there is a paucity of understanding.[86] The following definitions are not exhaustive, but they provide examples of how different scholars (and different fields) view leadership. A review of these definitions can help reveal the conceptual scope as well as common themes:

> Leadership is the "art of inspiring others in a team to contribute their best towards a goal."[87]

> "Leadership means getting things done through and with the help of other people . . . getting others to follow your lead."[88]

> "*Leadership* is the creation of structures that permit people to participate effectively in the achievement in worthwhile goals."[89]

> "People change when they are taught by other people whom they find relatable and inspiring. The people who do the teaching, the relating, and the inspiring we call leaders."[90]

> "Leadership is not about popularity. It is about gaining people's trust and moving them forward."[91]

> "Throughout history and in cultures everywhere, the leader in any human group has been the one to whom others look for assurance and

clarity when facing uncertainty or threat, or when there's a job to be done."[92]

"Leadership encourages action by people and organizations to achieve positive outcomes of what is desired and helps them foster positive attitudes and behaviors in themselves and others."[93]

"The development of a clear and complete system of expectations in order to identify, evoke, and use the strengths of all resources in the organization—the most important of which is *people*."[94]

What is Leadership?

At its core, leadership is influence, which is one of the only common themes found among these and other definitions.[95] The dividing line between effective and ineffective leadership is that "good leaders influence people."[96] Now, influence appears to be morally neutral, used equally by both good and bad leaders, and the outcomes of the leadership often dictate the understanding of the influence (i.e., role model vs. propaganda). Also, we must remember that many people have influence who may not deserve it and who may use it for nefarious reasons. For the purposes of this book, leadership will be understood as influence utilized for positive ends for the leader, the follower, and the organization. The elevation of influence removes the necessity for external symbols of leadership and allows every person to engage in leadership regardless of context.[97]

This new understanding frees the concept of leadership from the historical shackles of positional authority—leadership as the divine right of bosses. Because of the free flow of information and dismantling of social hierarchies occurring in contemporary society, leadership cannot be viewed as merely positional power gained through the command and control of knowledge.[98] Rather, there must be a move from "exerting power *over* people to generating waves *through* them."[99] Concordantly, regarding the church, any reference to leadership in this book should be understood as the power of influence, rather than any inherent authority derived from a position, education, wealth, or other status symbol.

Management

Pastoral ministry involves the daily activities of running the church. Although leadership is often conflated with management, the two are different concepts, with different scopes and outcomes. Management is a narrower field than leadership, and it deals with the achievement of organizational goals.[100] Leadership, in contrast, is the influencing of behavior of individuals and organizations.[101] According to Herminia Ibarra, "Management entails doing today's work as efficiently and competently as possible within established goals, procedures, and organizational structures. Leadership, in contrast, is aimed at creating change in what we do and how we do it, which is why leadership requires working outside of established goals, procedures, and structures and explaining to others why it's important to change."[102] Management involves reviewing and improving organizational processes and empowering members of the organization to maximize those improvements. While the detail-oriented efforts required of effective management are often perceived as inferior to the big picture efforts of the leader, organizational success is dependent upon effective management.

Organization

Organization might be defined as a group of people connected and interdependent through combined effort to achieve a common goal.[103] It is helpful to think of organizations as either informal or formal.[104] An informal organization is any gathering of people working cooperatively for a period of time, often organically or spontaneously (this could also be called simply a group).[105] A formal organization, by contrast, evokes the typical image of an organization, but is defined as "a rational structure of interrelated activities, processes, and technologies within which human efforts are coordinated to achieve specific objectives."[106]

Chapter Two
History of Friends and the Adoption of the Pastoral System

Brief History of the Friends Movement

Arguably, one of the reasons for the lack of a unifying culture among Friends churches is that the history of Friends, from which we should draw our cultural cues, is not very well known by many pastors or members. What is necessary is a history lesson on the Quaker principles and practices that distinguish the movement from other denominations. The difficulty arises in the revelation that, although the Friends movement was numerically small, its impact on the world was nothing short of astounding. To capture the length and breadth of Quaker history would require numerous volumes.

Recognizing these limits, this chapter is a basic historical narrative of the Friends movement that should aid any pastor or person who has recently joined the Quaker church and may be unfamiliar with our historical roots. It may also be beneficial as a refresher for those more familiar with Quakerism.

History

The Religious Society of Friends (Quakers) began through the spiritual experience of George Fox, an Englishman born in 1624, who at the age of nineteen, experienced a spiritual crisis.[107] Dissatisfied with the pastoral care of both the Puritan and Anglican clergy, Fox wandered restlessly until he had a supernatural vision—a realization that truth and salvation could be attained through the direct experience of God, without the mediation of a priest or other artifice of the religious establishment.[108] Emboldened by this revelation Fox set out to share this truth by preaching in various villages and gaining converts to his message.[109]

The content and style of his preaching was confrontational, and he was imprisoned many times for various charges.[110] However, despite Fox's criminal record, his preaching and teaching attracted many figures to the movement, people who later became influential, not only to the movement itself, but in the course of history as well. Such figures as Margaret Fell, Robert Barclay, and William Penn (founder of Pennsylvania) helped propel the movement from a radical fringe sect to an association that was structured both organizationally and theologically.[111]

The ethos of the Religious Society of Friends revolved around some core principles. Quakers believed in the direct deliverance of divine truth and salvation, a mystical encounter without sacerdotal mediation.[112] Thus, the church existed as a fellowship meant to express and develop the divine-human connection within the context of community.[113] Quakers also disposed of sacramental elements (e.g., baptism and the Eucharist), preferring a spiritual expression in place of symbolic experience.[114] The universal equality of humanity also included an understanding of the universal priesthood of all believers.[115] Quakers refused social mores (e.g., use of titles, or bowing and doffing one's hat) that emphasized social distinction, counter to the understood notions of universal equality.[116] Plain speaking—full of sincerity and without guile, and for the edification of others—was one of the pillars of early Quakerism.[117] Simplicity, originally known as plainness, mirrored the testimony of plain speech by promoting simple dress (which was quite a statement in the age of seventeenth-century English aristocracy which valued fine clothes, powdered wigs, and ceremonial swords).[118] These distinctives reflect the flattening of the social stratification, causing a radical effect on the formation of both Quaker worship and organizational leadership.

For this book, the universal ministry is the most relevant pillar of early Quakerism, as it pointed in the direction of future Quaker ecclesiology. This universal ministry drew its inspiration from 1 Peter 2:5, which speaks of the "priesthood of all believers."[119] Fox believed that England's forced tithe system, along with the stringent educational requirements for ordained ministry, had created a professionalized priesthood devoid of the Spirit, which enriched itself off the taxation of the masses.[120] In response, Quakers enacted an ecclesiology that recognized "that of God" in everyone—the ability for God to speak truth through any person, regardless of gender, race, or social class. Thus, "lay ministry" (common parlance in contemporary times but anathema to the values of early Friends) was understood as primary to the work and worship of Quakers.[121] One could argue that the theological implications of this universal priesthood gave birth to other aspects of Quaker testimony, such as the removal of social distinctions among its members.

As a consequence of this theology and ecclesiology, Quaker worship differed remarkably from the common Catholic or Protestant services of the time. Worshipers would sit in silence for an extended time (sometimes up to eight hours) punctuated only by vocal testimony given by those compelled by God to share.[122] While sermons were given, they were not the center of worship but, especially at the beginning of the movement, a way for leading figures to bring a concern. Silence, aided occasionally by vocal ministry, comprised the entirety of Quaker worship services.

The governance of meetings also reflected the rejection of hierarchy, with an egalitarian leadership model where power and authority were diffused throughout the congregation. In the local gatherings, the meetings for business were understood as meetings for worship, to collectively seek the will of God, in unity, through silence.[123] Decisions were made only through unity.[124] A clerk, whose main goal was to gain the sense of the meeting—and accurately record the consensus decision in the meeting minutes—led the meetings.[125] Women had their own parallel meetings, which was considered revolutionary for the time.[126] The meetings and positions combined to create a paradigm of leadership and authority that was egalitarian and poly-participatory.

In addition to these leadership elements, the role of minister also developed. During Quaker worship, some were recognized as consistently contributing vocal ministry and of having the gift of preaching. In recognition of these gifts, the ministers were recorded (recording merely recognizes, in writing, the already present gifting of God); while technically still a function of the denomination, this should not be confused with any priestly consecration.[127] These ministers would preach regularly in home meetings, as well as be released to travel and engage in missionary activity. Because of this understanding of leadership, it was possible to have many ministers in the same meeting. Elders, recognized for their spiritual maturity, offered pastoral care to the members of the congregation and provided accountability for the ministers.

This ecclesiology was maintained basically without adaptation until the late nineteenth century. At that point, revivalism swept through America, drawing thousands of converts to the various denominations, including Friends.[128] Unfortunately, the established Quaker ecclesiological system was not equipped to handle the wave of new Christians, and it struggled, through the use of elders and ministers, to pastorally care for these new converts and indoctrinate them into the nuances of Quaker worship and life. To solve this problem, meetings began to hire and financially support pastors—church leaders who would preach to and care for members. This shift was progressively, albeit slowly, adopted by many yearly meetings. A dramatic shift also occurred in the shape of Quaker worship, with a traditional sermon taking the place of extemporaneous preaching.

The adoption of the pastoral system points to the possibility of ambiguities regarding the understanding of the role of pastor in a Quaker church. A paradox has arisen: many Quakers recognize the need for pastors but also espouse a universal ministry.[129] These ambiguities, paradoxes, and discrepancies (from monthly meeting to monthly meeting, and from yearly meeting to yearly meeting) are a potential source for the lack of uniformity regarding a Friends pastoral theology.

The Adoption of the Pastoral System

Even though the pre-pastoral system was entrenched in the ethos of Quakerism through its theological beliefs, as well as centuries of tradition, it was ultimately superseded by the pastoral system in yearly meetings in the Midwest. The pastoral system was adopted by the yearly meetings over a relatively short period of time (thirty to forty years) because of unique circumstances never before faced by Quakerism.

The adoption of the pastoral system was necessitated by the extreme growth of the Friends movement occurring in the second half of the nineteenth century. This growth was the result of the revival efforts of traveling evangelists. These evangelists, though Quaker, were adherents to the holiness movement that arose during the last half of the nineteenth century.[130] Thomas Hamm described it further:

> Inspired by the largely Wesleyan Holiness movement that was extremely influential in the second half of the nineteenth century, they argued that sanctification was a second, instantaneous experience, achieved, like salvation, through faith in the efficacy of the Blood of Christ.[131]

It was often spoken of in mystical terms, as seen in writings from minister J. Y. Hoover:

> I was buried by baptism into Christ and raised a new man in Christ Jesus. When I met my beloved wife at Hesper, I found she too had passed over at Kadesh and we sat together in the vineyard of Eshcol and feasted on the old corn of the land. This experience prepared us for work we never could have borne, a life we never could have

lived, in a justified experience only. Some of the early Friends speak of two conditions or states of justification, but with J. J. Gurney, we prefer to call it sanctification according to Scripture.[132]

This mystical experience not only breathed new life into those who experienced it, but it also either ignited or rejuvenated their ministry.[133] Henry Harold, in a remembrance of evangelist and pastor Amos T. Kenworthy, wrote of Kenworthy's sanctifying experience: "He was then and there baptized with the Holy Ghost and with fire, and at the close of his long life he bore testimony that he had never since that day failed to perform a known duty."[134]

The effect of the sanctification movement on these evangelists was seen almost immediately. Besides pursuing with great zeal the missionary endeavors of their traveling ministry, they also introduced several new elements into Quaker services, including singing, an anxious bench for potential converts at the front of the meeting, and open and loud vocal prayers.[135] These innovations, though resisted by the elders, were embraced by young Quakers.[136]

Manifestations of the Spirit were also expected, including sobbing, wailing, and responding to altar calls, which were foreign to most traditional Quaker meetings. Despite the unfamiliarity, most traveling preachers continued to implement these innovations in the church with great effect.

The revivals, like many others, brought many new believers into the fold, according to Hamm:

> After 1875, the movement became evangelistic, as the revivalists tried to reach out to the unchurched generally. The result was a steady growth of membership and expansion into new

areas, especially in the Midwest. Indiana Yearly Meeting, for example, had by 1890 established two quarterly Meetings with over a thousand members in areas where less than a dozen Friends had lived in 1875.[137]

It has been claimed that this time was "Quakerism's greatest ingathering of souls since the days of George Fox."[138] The result of this explosive growth was that the ecclesiological systems were overwhelmed. The volunteer pastoral care provided by the elders was not enough to handle the wave of new converts, some of whom had never experienced Quaker worship with its corresponding spiritual and social ideals.[139] The cadre of recorded ministers was not sufficient to reach all the places of need, and the yearly meeting was unsure of how to respond. Eventually, necessity required the local congregations to pay a pastor who might shepherd the congregation full-time.

The speed with which the congregations grew in certain areas required a restructuring of local meetings, with a professionalized clergyperson instated to lead these new converts, and who often had no prior experience in the ways of Quakerism. However expedient this move was at the time, the rapid adoption of the pastoral system provides the possibility that the obstacles present in early Quakerism may still be present today.

Despite the barriers hindering the pastoral system (which are explored in the next chapter), the various yearly meetings gradually adopted this ecclesiology. By the end of the nineteenth century, the pastoral system had spread.[140] In the journal of Nathan and Esther Frame, the following examples are found of pastors serving during their travels, along with their corresponding dates of encounter:

> We met Amos Sanders here who was pastor of a Friends' Church lately organized at Noblesville [1891].
>
> Luramall Terrell, pastor of Friends' meeting at Albia [1897].
>
> Here we met Jesse McPherson, who had been pastor of this meeting [1897].[141]

In addition to this general adoption of pastors, there seemed to be a general acceptance of the pastoral system by the Quaker population. Lorton Heusel notes in his research, "John Wilhelm Rowntree in a paper entitled 'Pentecost' startled his readers by revealing that at the turn of the century sixty-two percent of all Quakerdom had abandoned the idea of an entirely unsupported ministry."[142] Regardless of the normalization of the pastoral system throughout the various yearly meetings, it was and still is a polarizing issue among Quakers.

Conclusion

On one hand, there are those who feel that a professionalized clergy is entirely incompatible with the ethos of historic Quakerism. On the other hand, there are some who believe that the pastoral system saved American Quakerism, and without it many of the current churches or yearly meetings would not exist.[143] To move forward with the articulation of a pastoral theology, the issue of whether the pastoral system is compatible with the Friends movement must be addressed. This question is the focus of the next chapter.

Chapter Three
Compatibility and Issues

Are Quakerism and the Pastoral System Compatible?

Many of the obstacles to the adoption of the pastoral system emerged from the beliefs and teachings of early Quakerism. These beliefs regarding pastoral ministry continued, with slight modification, until the late nineteenth century. The move to protect tradition and the "Quaker way" led to severe conflict regarding the professionalization of American Quaker clergy. Some viewed said professionalization as an imposition of authority figures into the established ecclesiology—a conflict that existed even to the late twentieth century.[144]

The historical and theological foundation of Quakerism appeared to be founded upon an intense anti-clerical strain. Further exploration of the literature reveals that these obstacles, though formidable, are not insurmountable. That's because these obstacles are outcomes of the sociocultural and religious climate that birthed and nurtured the Quaker movement. Understood in their proper context, they are refutations of excess seen in the religious institutions of seventeenth-century England. They do not negate the possibility of a pastoral system true to the roots of Quakerism. In fact, they can be helpful in providing historical guidance to the shaping of the pastoral role.

An exploration of early Quakerism shows that these obstacles require an intentional effort at transitioning the pastoral system into the movement as well as articulating the pastoral role in the Friends church—efforts that did not occur except in minor instances (perhaps the only major initiative to analyze the integration of the pastoral system into the yearly meeting was one by Indiana in the 1890s). Challenges to the adoption and evolution of the pastoral role include a professionalized clergy, changes in worship style, elder leadership, and financial support.

Professionalized Clergy

One of the biggest obstacles to the adoption of the pastoral system was the bias against a professionalized clergy. Early Friends felt that perceived differences between clergy and laity were artificial and unbiblical. Any move toward a professionalization of a clergy class would face tough challenges as it had to overcome the dominant egalitarian ethos of the Friends movement.

It should be noted that those opposed to the pastoral system were fully aware of the challenges facing the Friends church in America. However, even a clear vision of the needs of the membership was not enough, for some, to overrule centuries of tradition.

According to Seth Hinshaw:

> Although Friends at this time were struggling with the problem of inadequate ministry in

> many local situations, they were not altogether ready to accept workers who would be called pastors. Many Friends felt that to do so would be a lamentable departure from time-honored customs. The need for more adequate spoken ministry and shepherding care in countless local situations was critical, but Friends were not clear as to the right solution.[145]

Hinshaw's summary presents the philosophical conflict among Quakers as a very evenhanded debate, when in fact it was quite contentious. It is through the gauntlet of this fierce denunciation that the early proponents of the pastoral system traveled.

Not only were there denunciations by people within the Friends movement, but from the organization itself. The official faith documents of the yearly meetings are another place to explore the bias against the pastoral system. One of the cornerstones of early yearly meeting disciplines, regarding pastoral ministry, is the prohibition against a paid clergy, or "hireling ministry"; this is also seen in the minutes of the yearly meeting sessions.[146] These prohibitions are often lengthy. However, they are similar enough across the yearly meetings that the following example from the 1854 Indiana Yearly Meeting Discipline is sufficient to communicate the essence of the prohibition.

> Let us keep in remembrance this fundamental principle of our profession, that it is under the immediate teaching and influence of the Holy Spirit, that all acceptable worship is performed, and all Gospel Ministry supplied; that this pure and powerful influence, in vessels sanctified and

prepared by the Divine hand, is the essential qualification to that work. The gift, therefore, being divine, the service is freely and faithfully to be discharged, without any view to reward from man, agreeably to the express command of Christ, our head and high-priest, "Freely ye have received, freely give." (Matt. X. 8).

And where any of our members are so regardless of this testimony, as to contribute to the support of an Hireling Ministry, and vindicate such conduct, they ought to be tenderly labored with, to convince them of their error; but if this prove ineffectual, and they persist in their unfaithfulness, the Monthly meetings to which they belong, should proceed to declare our disunity with them—such conduct being opposed to our testimony for the Free Ministry of the Gospel, which is "without ministry and without price."[147]

Not only was supporting a paid clergy against the commands of Jesus, but it was also grounds for dismissal and disownment (excommunication) from the local congregation. The yearly meeting's position was unequivocal (at least at first). To support a professionalized clergy, even if it was the most expedient and effective course of action, would be tantamount to abandoning the very thing that made one a Quaker. This barrier was one of the most insurmountable for those wishing to see a pastoral system adopted.

Response to Professionalized Clergy Objection

One objection to the pastoral system is the early Quaker stance against a professionalized clergy. But it can be argued that abuses of power by the Anglican clergy were the intended target of the early Quaker rhetoric, not the pastoral system.

Misunderstood Anti-Intellectualism

The critique, by the early Quakers, of a professionalized clergy class was not against a professionalized clergy, in principle, but in the qualifications required and the social stratification that professionalization caused. While educational standards for ministers were critiqued and ultimately abandoned, it was not education itself that was opposed, but the social inequalities created by such academic rigor. Any move toward a standardized clergy within the Friends movement would have to explicitly ascertain the social and organizational impact of such a move, and then alleviate or mitigate that impact.

What vaulted a person into the specialized ranks of Anglican clergy was education. It was the education of an Anglican vicar that was a point of contention between Quakers and the Anglican Church. In fact, one of George Fox's first openings, or divine revelations, was that "being bred at Oxford or Cambridge, was not enough to fit and qualify men to be ministers of Christ."[148] Fox and other Quakers saw negative outcomes associated with a rigid and defined educational path toward pastoral ministry.

But the evidence against education of the minister may not be as straightforward as it appears. When one views the apparent anti-intellectualism of early Quakers in light of their social and religious context, it becomes clear that the early Quakers were not intent on abolishing education and intellect among their ministers. Rather, the Friends movement opposed a strict and stratified educational path as the sole way to become authorized for pastoral ministry.

Quakers railed against the system of pastoral education of the time, partly because, according to Frank Peake, "It was generally assumed in the United Kingdom, prior to the late nineteenth century, that to be a lawyer, doctor, or priest was, primarily, to be a scholar and a gentleman."[149] English culture had imbued pastoral ministry with a gravitas reserved for nobles, the wealthy, or the intelligentsia. This social ladder was climbed through education: "The universities were organized to provide a programme of undergraduate studies leading to the M.A., and graduate studies leading to doctorates in divinity, law, and medicine. Of these three, the doctorate and career path of divinity studies were the most prestigious."[150] A minister without an education could not, in the system of the time, be considered a minister at all.

The efforts spent on this education, both in money and time, were considerable. This became an issue in the actions and attitudes of the clergy, according to Robert Barclay:

> But to be plain, I believe he intended not that it was from the gift or grace of God they were to preach, but from their acquired arts and studies, which have cost them much labour and also some money at the university; and therefore, as he that puts his stock into the public bank, expects interest again; so these scholars, having spent some money in learning the art of

> preaching, think they may boldly say, they have it not freely; for it hath cost them both money and pains, and there they expect both money and ease again.[151]

Thus, the ministerial career was connected with the need for a salary commensurate with the time, energy, and money invested in preparing for ministry. While this may seem logical, it was inexcusable to the early Quakers. Such people, in the words of Fox, were "shepherds that fed themselves, and clothed themselves with the world, and sought after the fleece and so made a prey upon us, and upon the people."[152]

Another concern regarding clergy education was the lack of spiritual growth among the ministers during and after their educational journey. In Barclay's theological *magnum opus*, he addressed a forward to the clergy, noting that their

> great learning, so accounted of—to wit, your school divinity, which taketh up almost a man's whole life-time to learn, brings not a whit nearer to God, neither makes any man less wicked or more righteous than he was.[153]

Fox also addressed the inconsistency between theological education and knowledge, and spiritual life and vitality, rebuking the clergy: "And to all you the word of the Lord, that hath learned the letter of the scripture, your Hebrew, Greek, and Latin, [but] who hate the light within . . . so ye are clouds without water, and all your knowledge, Hebrew, Greek, and Latin is natural; and the natural man knoweth not the things of God."[154] According to Fox's writings, studying biblical languages was considered natural compared to the supernatural teachings of the Holy Spirit.

Theological education and training doesn't make someone a minister. Something else is required. H. Larry Ingle summarized Fox's position:

> If a professed minister did not exemplify this new birth then he could not be a true minister. Thus neither education nor approval and ordination by a classic invested a minister with authority: only the divine action of God's grace could accomplish that end. His revelation cut the ground from under the established ministry and substituted for it the infinitely broader principle that God could and did—had not Fox himself heard the divine word?—speak to anyone willing to listen.[155]

In fact, some of the writings were so strongly opposed to education as to border on the absurd. Barclay wrote of the classical education of both the clergy and the upper classes:

> The second part of their literature is logic and philosophy, an art so little needful to a true minister, that if one that comes to be a true minister hath had it, it is safest for him to forget and lose it for it is the root and ground of all contention and debate, and the way to make a thing a great deal darker than clearer.[156]

In this statement, Barclay is referencing the classical rhetoric and logic received in divinity school, which were utilized in the sermons and writings of the ministers of the day. According to early Quaker leader James Nayler, "The ministers of the world receive their learning at Oxford and Cambridge . . . and speak a divination of their own brain, which is conjuring; and bewitch the people with those things which are carnal."[157]

Regarding the polemics against ministerial education, the socio-religious context matters. For example, even though George Fox did not have a formal education, his knowledge of the Bible was unparalleled. Penn described Fox as having an "extraordinary gift in opening the scriptures. He would go to the marrow of things, and show the mind, harmony, and fulfilling of them, with much plainness, and to great comfort and edification."[158] Though uneducated, Fox was not unintellectual. In addition to the legacy of the Friends movement, there is also record of more than 3,000 epistles that Fox wrote, along with other written works, which speak of his contributions to the religious world. [159]

The same can be said of other early Friends preachers. The apparent disconnect between the lack of education and the eloquence and depth of their message was noticeable. Penn wrote of some audience reactions to the preaching of Friends ministers:

> The accomplishments, with which this principle fitted even some of the meanest of this people for their work and service, furnishing some of them with an extraordinary understanding in divine things, and an admirable fluency, and taking-way of expression, gave occasion to some to wonder, saying of them, as of their Master, "Is not this such a mechanic's son, how came he by this learning?"[160]

In fact, it was inconceivable to some that these ministers of humble origins had these abilities, causing them to "suspect and insinuate they were Jesuits in disguise, who had the reputation of learned men for an age past."[161] The novelty of uneducated men speaking words of theological depth with authority is reminiscent of the disciples of the early church, recorded in Acts.

It is those stories, recorded in Acts, that provided the foundation for how the early Friends understood their ministerial education. Like the followers of Jesus who were gifted with the Holy Spirit, so Quakers gifted with the same Holy Spirit were given the words of God to speak. Penn wrote, "They went not forth, or preached, in their own time or will, but in the will of God; and spoke not their own studied matters, but as they were opened and moved of his Spirit, with which they were well acquainted in their own conversion."[162] It was the will of the Holy Spirit that guided the minister into the appropriate place of ministry, and also provided the content of the message.

One of the most telling pieces of evidence against an outright rejection of education by the Quakers is the major benefit reaped by the movement from its most educated members. Robert Barclay's *Apology*, a defense of Quaker beliefs, has been celebrated as a major work of theological literature by both the masses and by major thinkers of the era, including Voltaire.[163] Elton Trueblood articulated Barclay's value:

> No spoken message, however vivid, can endure unless it is provided with a written and intelligible form. . . . The potent leader needs the intellectual follower to turn his vivid and aphoristic expressions into something which is logically defensible. It was this need which was met by Robert Barclay when the infant Quaker Movement was only about twenty-five years old.

> Without Fox, Barclay would have had very little to say, but without Barclay, what Fox said would have been forgotten.[164]

What makes this statement so complex is that Barclay was highly educated, in both England and Paris.[165] The veracity of his *Apology* stems not only from its logical coherence, but also from its readability. While Barclay is quoted above as treating education with suspicion, there is reason to infer that perhaps this critique is not aimed solely at education.

The evidence points to a possibility of not an outright rejection of ministerial education, but of the socio-religious context in which the education was based. The idea of a fixed educational path that determined one's eligibility for ministry was anathema to Friends. Disregarding such a path, as Friends did, made one ineligible for the priesthood and thus required a new understanding of what made a minister. Had theological education been separated from the path to ordination in the Anglican Church, perhaps the conversation regarding education would have been different. As it stands, one should view the opposition to theological and classical education as more of a populist opposition to a stratified clergy class than to the educational system itself.

A pastoral system is not necessarily in opposition to the early Quaker ethos. One might even argue that an educated clergy is not detrimental. What matters most is God's calling and obedience to God's will. The point is that a critique of an educated clergy is not a critique of education, but of the social and spiritual ills that were present among clergy of the day. Therefore, an educated clergy, deeply rooted in the spiritual and egalitarian ethos of the Friends movement, would fit within early Friends theology and ecclesiology. However, any move toward a standardized clergy within the Friends movement would have to explicitly ascertain the social and organizational impact of such a move, and then alleviate or mitigate that impact.

Worship Style

The pastoral system, which is the focus of this research, emerged from the programmed styles of worship in the Friends Church, which was a divergence from the historical Friends practice of unprogrammed worship. Any transition from an unprogrammed worship style to a programmed service would require a dramatic ecclesiological change and ethotic transition. While not insurmountable, this shift would require extensive theological and ecclesiological integration into the extant ethos and praxis.

Unprogrammed Worship

Evidence that the early Quakers rejected any form of pastoral ministry outright is the typical Friends worship service. But in order to understand the marked departure in style and substance of a Quaker meeting, one must understand a typical service of an Anglican church, officiated by an Anglican priest. In addition to facilitating the Eucharist, the clergy preached a sermon or homily, which became one of the focal points of the service, especially since the Reformation.[166] One might also compare the established religious practices of the Puritans, and other separatist groups, as their worship mirrors the structure of the Anglican Church.

The worship in the manner of Friends was dramatically different in both its style and its focus. In the churches of the day, the sermon, or expounding of scriptures by a minister, was the focal point of the service, along with the dispensing of the sacraments. According to Douglas Gwyn, "Instead of singing or reading Scripture or administering sacraments, the faithful would sit, sometimes for nearly three hours, in silence, until someone presumed to speak under the inspiration of the spirit."[167] M. H. Plugh described a typical unprogrammed worship service in detail. In a typically unassuming structure, Quakers gathered and sat in seats "arranged to form a perimeter around an empty center."[168] Music and a sermon, typical in most Protestant churches, are conspicuously absent in Friends unprogrammed worship. The worship service begins, and "for the duration of the meeting members sit, co-present in silence, only breaking for vocal ministry."[169] This vocal ministry is assumed to be a revelation from God.[170] The theological underpinning to this vocal ministry by anyone in the meeting is the notion of the inward light of Christ that dwells in every believer and the notion of the priesthood of all believers. Also separating worship in the manner of Friends from other denominations was that it was highly participatory, even poly-participatory, as it represented a tradition of universal distribution of charismata to all members of the congregation.[171] By stripping the church of its sacramental symbols and imbuing it with an egalitarian ethos, the Quaker worship became, in the words of Jane Yolen, "a third form of Christianity, a religious democracy."[172] What was assumed is that this religious democracy has no place for a professionalized clergy.

Vocal Ministry

However important silence was to Quaker worship, vocal ministry was equally important, in order to exhort, evangelize, teach, and discipline. Even though one of the pillars of Friends' worship was silence, and the critique of the established, professionalized clergy assumed a critique of a sermon-centered worship service, preaching (also known as vocal ministry) was a very important aspect of Quaker worship. Radically, this vocal worship was open to all, regardless of age or gender.[173] According to Rufus Jones, "The meeting for worship is, however, not all silence . . . the silence is preparation."[174] Pink Dandelion articulates the tension between silence and vocal ministry:

> Given the power of silence, speaking was a risky business and could only be validated as authentic by how it had "reached" people after the fact. At the same time, hesitation to speak was also a shortcoming, betraying a lack of passivity and obedience.[175]

According to Douglas Gwyn:

> The function of vocal ministry within the Quaker meeting for worship is to *gather* the worshiping fellowship into a common understanding of the gospel and of Christ's will for that group. Thus, Quaker ministry serves twin purposes of teaching and exhortation.[176]

Vocal ministry arose from the silence through various people in order to communicate the truths of God to the larger congregation. The expectation of a prepared sermon seemed to contradict these notions of waiting on the Lord.[177] The emphasis on multifold expressions of vocal ministry, on the surface, appears to preclude a pastor-centric, sermon-focused worship style.

Shift to Programmed Worship

But is this a fair conclusion? Concerning programmed worship, "The focus of a programmed meeting is the pastor's sermon."[178] Michael Graves explained the differences between local churches that has created the spectrum of understanding and practice concerning lay vocal ministry and preaching.[179] One should imagine a completely unprogrammed meeting at one end of the spectrum, then, at the other end of the spectrum, "The college- and seminary-educated pastor preaches the sermon and virtually no one in the congregation expects to be allowed, let alone encouraged, to stand and deliver an immediately inspired message, however brief."[180] At this extreme, the vocal ministry reminiscent of earlier Friends is not emphasized or enacted. Because of this lack of emphasis on lay vocal ministry, there are differing expectations concerning the pastor's role in worship. This would also affect the overall expectations, by the congregation, of the pastor's authority and leadership.

In the middle of the spectrum, there exists a paradigm where preaching is still central, but open worship and lay vocal ministry are also emphasized. According to Graves, this paradigm exists "among some Evangelical Friends in smaller meetings or churches, a vestigial version of the silent meeting may take place at a 'programmed' service."[181] This period of silence lasts around five to ten minutes and has been called

"Friends Communion."[182] During this time, there are opportunities for congregants to publicly speak, but there is still an expectation that the pastor will deliver a prepared sermon.[183]

Pink Dandelion also highlighted the remnant of open worship found within programmed meetings.[184] He noted that "in many Evangelical Quaker Meetings, there is still a period of 'open worship' or 'communion after the manner of Friends' towards which all other programming points."[185] Instead of being merely a vestigial remnant or an afterthought to the service, it is the focal point around which the meeting is planned. "Some pastors see the music, readings, and message as aids to help 'centre' the worshipping community."[186] Dandelion offered the disclaimer that only some of the pastors and/or churches maintain this view—a warranted caveat, for in America, these open worship-centric congregations appear to be rare.

On the surface, there appears to be a substantive difference between unprogrammed worship and programmed worship, but they are not as different as they appear. It has been argued that the differences between programmed and unprogrammed worship are superficial, as the principles underlying both are the same (this was emphasized in writings seeking to quell the discord between both current programmed and unprogrammed meetings, as well as between the historical unprogrammed Quaker tradition and the contemporary pastoral reality).[187] The core components of each are the corporate gathering for worship and the public proclamation of the truths of God. Therefore, with some intentionality, a programmed service can exist within the theology and ethos of earlier Friends.

Elder Leadership

One major source of ambiguity regarding the leadership and authority of a Quaker pastor is the presence and power of the elders in relation to the pastor. The position of elder in the Quaker meeting existed to provide leadership, both to the congregation and to the cadre of ministers who attended and spoke during worship. In this role, elders were also protectors of faith and practice for the meetings in which they served, including the faith and practice of the ministers.[188] This role of guardian makes sense. In the process of guarding the traditions of Quakerism, however, the elders can stifle innovation. As Michael Birkel noted, "It is a difficult balancing act to be the conservators of tradition, especially when that tradition itself has a new commitment to be open to the revelation of new truth."[189] Often, elders overreacted to new events in the church, leading to discipline of the offenders.

Now, even though the term "offender" is used to describe someone who violates the explicit and implicit rules of a Quaker meeting, it perhaps overplays the nature of the actual offense. For example, J. Y. Hoover related an incident earlier in his life when one of his friends was corrected by the leadership of the church:

> The aged minister turned to my young companion and said: "I believe thee said a few words in meeting this morning. I want to tell thee that I have no faith in a gospel that comes through hair." (The young man wore a short beard on the under part of his face).[190]

The fact that facial hair was grounds for discipline highlights the level of social rigidity found in these faith communities in the early nineteenth century. Hoover shares another example, where his appearance merited church discipline:

> The elders were all dressed in the fashion of Friends of a hundred years ago. After a time of silent deliberation one of them who seemed to take Peter's place as spokesman turned to me and said that they had felt a concern to talk with me about my dress (which was all very plain, except my overcoat which was a double breasted and had a turn down collar).[191]

The authority to speak into even the minutiae of the lives of the meeting allowed for strict discipline regarding faith and practice. According to Birkel,

> At times, as a body, elders became stodgy and stuffy, holding to the letter more than the Spirit who gives life. As a result, to be "eldered" at times meant simply to be harshly criticized, to be upbraided for not adhering to the decorum of the Quaker culture. At one time the elders' tendency for conservation clashed with the ministers' bent for innovation, and this played a sad role in the schisms of the nineteenth century.[192]

Any innovation attempted in the church would have to meet the approval of the elders, or else be popular enough to override their wishes.

It is no surprise, then, that the elders of certain monthly meetings would be opposed to the innovation of the pastoral ministry. Not only was it an ecclesiological change that ran contrary to faith and practice of early Friends, but it also brought with it some more troubling elements. Because many of the preachers who advocated for a pastoral system emerged from the Wesleyan Holiness movement, which itself found new life in the revivals of the day, the ministers brought with them an expectation of worship that was not common among Quakers. Nathan and Esther Frame, traveling evangelists and later pastors, made this notation in their journal concerning the innovations brought into the Friends church:

> There have been marvelous changes in Friends meetings since we first became members among them. Singing, vocal prayer, testimony, exhortation, reading the Scriptures, preaching, revival, or protracted meetings, the custom of inviting persons to rise in the public congregations or come to a certain place for prayer have now become very common in most of the Friends meetings in this land, whereas they were the exception twenty years ago, and singing was unknown in a Friends meeting.[193]

Not even the stern rebuke of the elders could stop the wave of revival and its corresponding flood of new converts from dramatically changing the ecclesiological landscape of American Quakerism. The adoption of a church pastor merely added the position into the extant retinue of leadership positions. Without a clearly communicated balance of power between the pastor and the elders, there was confusion and also conflict regarding the bounds of a pastor's leadership and authority.

Response to Elder Leadership Objection

Misinterpretation of Early Quaker Anti-Clericalism

Early Quakers were concerned with the level of authority the local pastor held in a congregation. It has been assumed that one of the pillars of the Friends movement was a complete and total rejection of any form of pastoralized or hierarchical ecclesiology; this is incorrect.[194] Rather, the situation was more nuanced. George Fox and other Friends protested against social inequalities, injustices, and abuses of which the clergy system of the Anglican Church happened to be a part.[195] Also, in presenting a radically different vision of spirituality and ecclesiology, Quakers offered both implicit and explicit critique of the Anglican Church. The early Friends movement sought to reform the structure and praxis of a true, primitive Christian community of faith.[196]

To understand this "primitive Christianity," one must understand the social dynamics of the Church of England within village and city life. The Anglican vicar held a lot of clout within his community, for often the "parson might be the only educated man in a small village, the one to whom parishioners would turn for advice on more than spiritual matters."[197] This influence, along with the nature of the profession, elevated the pastor above the common citizen. Raymond Chapman writes of clergy who "were pluralist incumbents of rich livings . . . some of them younger sons of the aristocracy who enjoyed large incomes and virtually unlimited leisure."[198] Robert Barclay offered another picture of the path of some of the religious leaders:

> And others, come to age, upon the same account betake them to the same trade, and having these

> natural and acquired parts that are judged the necessary qualifications of a minister, are thereby admitted, and so are bred up in idleness and pleasure, thinking it a disgrace for them to work with their hands; and so just study a little out of their books, to make a discourse one or twice a week during the running of an hourglass; whereas the gift, grace, and Spirit of God, to call and qualify for the ministry, is neglected and overlooked.[199]

To the common people, this clergy could seem quite distant and unfamiliar with their needs and struggles, especially if the clergyman was a pluralist (holding more than one ministry post in order to secure the land and stipend) and rarely present.

Another area of authority and control was, as mentioned above, the pulpit and facilitation of the worship service. According to H. Larry Ingle:

> Power over the pulpit, a major instrument of social control where the model of deference to one's betters was regularly enacted through the submission of the parishioners to their "superior," their minister, was thus taken from secular and religious leaders and bestowed, via the ineffable promptings of God's spirit, on any George-come-lately.[200]

Thus, the Anglican clergy had a structure of social control and stratification in which they limited access through the requirements of education, ordination, and licensure.

In response to this limited-access ecclesiastical system, the Quakers provided a path for anyone who felt the calling of

God on their lives to serve that calling in ministry. However, this ministry was significantly different in tone from what was common. According to Fox, those "whom Jesus Christ made ministers, he made them not masters."[201] They were not to lord over others (through the exploitive tithe system) nor of themselves (in choosing the choicest ministerial positions), but rather in complete obedience to the will of God. According to Barclay,

> Every true minister of the gospel is ordained, prepared and supplied in the work of the ministry: and by the leading, moving, and drawing hereof, ought every evangelist and Christian pastor to be led and ordered in his labour and work of the gospel, both as to the place where, as the to the persons whom, and as to the time when he is to minister.[202]

Through this radical obedience to God, the pastor became not the master of the congregation, but a servant to the congregation.

One must be careful not to overstate the critique of a specialized ministerial class as if it were an outright rejection. For example, Pink Dandelion wrote,

> Quakers were also particularly critical of the separated ministry. First, the clergy preached an anachronistic way that held the people back from the new experience now available to them. Second, they were paid for the word of God that was free. Thirdly, they themselves were unnecessary, a symbol of apostasy and stratification.[203]

The suspected corruption of the Anglican clergy caste led to many points of divergence between the Quakers and the Church of England; but the notion that pastoral ministry was rejected is incorrect. Early Quakers conceptualized and implemented an organized ecclesiology that included ministers and religious authorities.

Even though Quaker theology and ecclesiology recognized the universal priesthood of believers, certain members are recognized for their gifts in ministry and leadership, and thus called upon to exercise these gifts. One of the main points of departure regarded the notion of ordination and credentialing. According to Barclay,

> Moreover, those who have this authority may and ought to preach the gospel, though without human commission or literature; as on the other hand, those who want the authority of this divine gift, however learned or authorized by the commissions of men and churches, are to be esteemed but as deceivers, and not true ministers of the gospel.[204]

Rather than an extended process of ordination and licensure for its ministers, the Quaker movement recognizes that such processes may not truly discern who has been called and gifted for ministry. In response, those who feel called show their calling through obedience in faithfully ministering, as well as by the effects of such ministry, as recognized by the congregation. God is the ultimate ecclesiastical authority. Barclay explained:

> So this is that which gives a true substantial call and title to a minister, whereby he is a real

> successor of the virtue, life and power that was in the apostles, and not of the bare name: and to such ministers we think the outward ceremony of ordination or laying on of hands not necessary, neither can we see the use of it, seeing our adversaries who use it acknowledge that the virtue and power of communicating the Holy Ghost by it is ceased among them.[205]

Authority is given to the ministers by God, but that authority is not unlimited, nor is it to be used for personal gain. Rather it is to be used a sacrificial gift for the good of the body of believers and the good of the kingdom of God.

At no place was the notion of a pastoral system completely ruled out. While the current system may be beyond repair, the basic ecclesiology underpinning it (i.e., the pastoral system) is not. The question is: had a pastoral system existed that exhibited the ethos and praxis of authority and leadership outlined above, would the early Friends have embraced it or rejected it? It seems clear that they might have embraced it as the answer to their critiques of the Anglican Church.

Financial Support

It cannot be overstated how difficult it was for some Friends to adapt to the notion of paying a minister for service.[206] The traveling evangelist, and later pastor, J. Y. Hoover spoke of this philosophical barrier to the financial support of pastors and ministers. During one ministry trip, he noted, "Two Friends objected to the Michigan Friends paying the expenses, which they had offered to do, fearing it might be supporting a hireling ministry."²⁰⁷ For years, paying a pastor was equated with sin worthy of excommunication, so it is understandable that this barrier would be difficult to overcome.

Even when this philosophical barrier was overcome, other obstacles remained. Financial support, when given by Friends congregations, seems from some reports to be somewhat stingy. Nathan and Esther Frame write of financial support from a certain meeting, "Of course we were not promised any remuneration in any way except the rent of the little house for a few months. This was considered great *liberality.*"²⁰⁸ Not only were Quakers not used to giving ministers a living wage, but also many churches simply did not have the resources to do so. This hampered the adoption of the pastoral system until the notion of a circuit ministry, taken from the Methodists, was adopted as well.

Response to Financial Support Objection

The objection to financial support of a professionalized clergy is better understood in the context of the forced tithe system in seventeenth-century England. Quakers didn't reject any form of pastoral support. Rather, major point of conflict between the early Quakers and the religious establishment was the issue of forced tithes, or the mandatory maintenance of the Church of England.²⁰⁹ According to Laura Brace, the tithe system in England was a mandatory tax on the production of the population in order to support the ministry and clergy of the Church of England.²¹⁰ Brace described the tithe system as such:

> For collection tithes were divided into three main categories: predial tithes came from things

grown in the ground, or the natural increase of the livestock; personal tithes were taken from the profits on commodities gained through art, science or labour; and mixed tithes came from goods which combined nature and labour such as milk, cheese and wool. These were further divided into great tithes paid to the rector from corn, hay and wood and small tithes paid to the vicar on other types of goods.[211]

There was seemingly no part of the labor and production of the people that was not subjected to the tithe. This caused much resentment among the populace, but with little recourse.[212] According to Brace, tithes were "an indiscriminate tax which did not provide universal benefits. They were levied on everybody, regardless of religious allegiance, but they provided a maintenance specifically for the Anglican clergy."[213] While it can be assumed that many did not favor the tithing system, any active resistance was met with swift punishments. Those who did not pay could find "their goods distrained for three times the value of the original tithes, and themselves imprisoned for non-payment."[214] Any resistance based on religious principles involved considerable risk to one's property and freedom.

The early Friends were vocal in their opposition to the tithe system. George Fox found the idea of forced maintenance to be unsubstantiated by scripture. According to Fox:

> And for taking tithes, in the old time Levi was to receive tithes, and the strangers, the fatherless and widows were to come and eat, and be filled within his gate; but this was according to the law; and here you see the priests of the world do

not act according to the law, in which were types and figures of Christ; and when Christ came, those he sent forth were not to have a bag, nor a stick to defend them, nor two coats, nor brass, nor silver; but freely ye have received, freely give, the workman is worthy of his meat. So they neither walk according to the law, nor the gospel.[215]

In Fox's understanding, the tithe system found in the Torah was but a shadow of what would be fulfilled in Jesus Christ. According to Fox, Christ's direction to his disciples to enter an itinerant ministry with no established support and very few personal belongings stands as the norm for contemporary pastoral ministry.

Fox is even stronger in his critique of the tithe system in some of his other epistles, "*Tythes* have been set up among the (called) *Christians* by force and Command, since the Apostles days, and Christ in the Flesh, from whom there is no Example for *Tythes*,"[216] and soon after writes even more forcefully, "So they that take *Tythes*, and they that give *Tythes*, are Antichristian, and do deny Christ come in the Flesh."[217] This condemnation was based on the Quaker interpretation of Jesus' command in Matthew 10:8, "Freely you have received, freely give."[218] The tithe system was not only direct disobedience to Christ's command for ministers, but caused the Anglican priests to take on the role of oppressor of God's people. Fox says of the clergy of the day,

> Pharaoh thou oppressor, Pharaoh thou task master, Pharaoh thou proud one, which layest heavy burthens upon the innocent and righteous seed, and oppresses the just, plagues and woe is thy portion, as was Pharaoh's, who taxes, and

> oppresses, and causest the just and righteous seed to labour under thee.[219]

Those who were called to serve the people and lead them to freedom have become, in Fox's eyes, those who bring people into bondage. Such a situation was unconscionable for early Quakerism.

In addition, Friends were also tapping into the populist resentment against forced tithes. What is interesting is that, even though the policy of forced maintenance itself could be characterized as unjust, the only social implications the early Friends focused were the negative effects on the actions and attitudes of the clergy. The attitude that the early Friends railed against was dependence on and love of money caused, in their minds, by forced maintenance. Douglas Gwyn wrote of Fox's attitude toward the Anglican clergy, regarding them as "merchandizers of the gospel, in contrast to Christ's free teaching."[220] H. Larry Ingle summarized the ethos of opposition against the system, writing that early Quakers believed that the "minister 'is a hireling . . . who does nothing but for filthy lucre, preaching only for tithes, pigs, geese, and capons,' whereas Quakers freely received and freely gave. Walking in rags, 'they railed at riches.'"[221] The most scathing reference to the attitudes of those clergy supported by the tithe system comes from Robert Barclay:

> They become hereby so glued to the love of money, that there is none like them in malice, rage, and cruelty. If they be denied their hire, they rage like drunken men, fret, fume, and as it were go mad. A man may sooner satisfy the severest creditor than them; the general voice of the poor doth confirm this. For indeed they are

far more exact in taking up the tithes of sheep, geese, swine, and eggs, &c., and look more narrowly to it than to the members of their flock: they will not miss the least mite; and the poorest widow cannot escape their avaricious hands."[222]

Barclay also noted the actions of the clergy against those who refuse or defer their tithe obligations, writing, "And some of the priests have been so enraged, that goods thus ravished could not satisfy them, but they must also satisfy their fury by beating, knocking, and wounding with their hands innocent men and women, for refusing, for conscience' sake, to put into their mouths."[223] The treatment of those who did not pay as criminals stems from the systemic nature of the tithe, which was a "tax underpinned by the coercive mechanisms of the state. They were a part of the juridical apparatus . . . a power exercised by the magistrate."[224] Thus, the clergy persecuted the very ones they were called to shepherd.

However, it must be noted that the critique was against the negative effects of forced maintenance, and also of those clergy who, in the act of supporting such measures, denied the teachings of Jesus and oppressed the people they were called to serve. Barclay wrote that "the only way then soundly to reform and remove all these abuses, and take away the ground and occasion of them, is to take away all stinted and forced maintenance and stipends."[225] The solution is not an abolishment of pastoral ministry, but to have a ministry that exemplifies the teachings of Jesus: "And as they freely received what they had to say from the Lord, so they freely administered it to others."[226]

Once forced maintenance is removed, pastoral support becomes almost a non-issue, with Quaker practices mirroring those of other free church ecclesiologies. Voluntary support of ministers, especially itinerant ministers, was encouraged during the early periods of Quakerism, with Barclay writing,

> If God hath called any from their employments, or trades, by which they acquire their livelihood, it may be lawful for such, according to the liberty which they feel given to them by the Lord, to receive such temporals—to wit, what may be needful to them for meat and clothing—as are freely given by those to whom they have communicated spirituals.[227]

If the attitude of the Quaker ministers is that of one who willingly ministers without expectation of reward or support, then it is perfectly acceptable, even encouraged, to support that minister in his or her ministry. It is when expectation or coercion appears in the attitudes or teachings of the minister regarding material support that a problem emerges. Therefore, a financially supported pastoral system is not excluded from early Friends ethos, but rather needs to express itself as sacrificial and voluntarily supported.

Problems Not Practically Overcome

Even though the previous section showed how the common objections to pastoral ministry in the Friends movement have been overcome philosophically and theologically, this does not mean that they were dealt with practically. The previous section merely proves that there are no theoretical objections that discredit the pastoral system; it was still a jarring transformation for many Friends churches. Because of the unfamiliarity with the pastoral system, and the strenuous objection to it by a sizeable portion of yearly meeting members, a shift this momentous required an intentional period of discourse, forethought, strategic planning, and thorough conceptualization of the expectations of the pastoral role in American Quakerism. But this did not occur. Rather, the adoption of the pastoral system took place piecemeal, with little or no understanding of its far-reaching consequences.

Of course, the biggest failure (and the reason for this book) was that there was not a concerted effort by the yearly meetings to articulate the expectations of the pastoral role. The one exception would be Indiana Yearly Meeting, which in 1893, commissioned a committee to explore this issue. While I appreciate their efforts and subsequent support, I am troubled that this report, once given, was neither acted upon by the yearly meeting nor further discussed (the committee disbanded soon after). The conceptualization and articulation never left the level of committee, nor were its conclusions officially acted upon.

Besides a lack of general understanding of the role and place of the pastor, other practical considerations also were given short shrift by the yearly meetings. These provide additional evidence that there were deficiencies regarding the effort required to integrate the pastoral system into the ethos of American Quakerism. The practical considerations explored here are the uneven adoption of the pastoral system, the shift in worship, and insufficient financial support. When necessary, Kansas Yearly Meeting is used as an example to illustrate the events occurring in other yearly meetings.

Uneven Adoption of the Pastoral System

The impetus for the pastoral system emerging in many yearly meetings was the evangelical influence of neighboring churches and denominations, as well as the spread of revivalism. Responses to these unexpected changes was often disjointed. In North Carolina, for example, the adoption of the pastoral system was neither pre-planned nor strategic, but rather a gradual movement as individual churches hired pastors.[228] The different yearly meetings often experienced radically varying rates of adoption. Iowa Yearly Meeting underwent a swift adoption, for after only three years of the pastoral system, it had fifty-one pastors, with forty-seven receiving some form of financial support.[229] On the other end of the spectrum, Springfield Monthly Meeting, in North Carolina Yearly Meeting, did not adopt the pastoral system until 1914.[230] California Yearly Meeting came into existence as a pastoral yearly meeting, with the pastoral system as an assumed starting point.[231] This inconsistency highlights division regarding professionalized clergy between members and churches in the yearly meetings, and it reveals a lack of unity regarding the pastoral role.

Example of Kansas Yearly Meeting

To highlight this uneven adoption, one only has to look at the records regarding pastoral hires in Kansas Yearly Meeting. Over the course of the 1890s, the adoption of the pastoral system seemed to move slowly, with definite resistance in terms of pastoral compensation.[232] Possibly as a response to this, definitive action was taken to provide each monthly meeting with the services of a pastor. In 1897, Kansas Yearly

Meeting announced that "each Meeting, when practical, shall constitute a pastoral charge . . . other Meetings to be so grouped as to form pastorates of sufficient strength to be self-supporting."[233] The yearly meeting also demanded that each meeting adopt "systematic efforts of financial support" in order to raise the necessary funds to support a pastor.[234] This demand, issued by the authority of the yearly meeting, should have ended the division between the pastoral and non-pastoral meetings, creating a uniform organizational expectation of a paid, professionalized clergy.

However, the percentage of non-pastoral meetings within Kansas Yearly Meeting from 1899 to 1910 never falls below 10 percent (with the average being 15 percent). This means that, even after the top-down organizational shift toward the pastoral system by the yearly meeting in 1897, nearly one out of ten churches did not hire a pastor during that decade.

Shift in Worship

The centrality of the pulpit marked a definite shift from traditional Quaker unprogrammed worship. To some, this centrality smacks of idolatry, for they note the word "pulpit" is derived from the Latin word for "stage"—a fitting description of both its placement and the expectation of performance from it.[235] While I do not agree with such statements, they highlight the issues in shifting from a decentralized, unstructured worship to a structured worship with new elements (such as music) and that is centered on the act of solo preaching (this is illustrated in figure 1). Such a shift not only requires concerted effort to overcome resistance to these changes, but also to situate the working relationship of pastor and congregation.

Unfortunately, this did not occur. The transition toward programmed meetings led to discord and resistance. Unfortunately, while there are some comments made in yearly meeting sessions about the benefit of programmed, musical worship (especially evangelistically), there does not appear to be any strategic planning or efforts to embrace programmed worship as a definitive denominational shift. The lack of a unified shift often led to the individual meetings choosing the timing and level of adoption. While some local meetings transitioned quickly, others held out for much longer (for example, it was not until 1905 that Liberty Monthly Meeting allowed an organ to be used in worship).[236] Others, who planned to never adopt these elements, broke away to form the Conservative branch of Quakerism. In any case, the issues regarding programmed worship and its place among Friends was not adequately discussed by the yearly meetings.

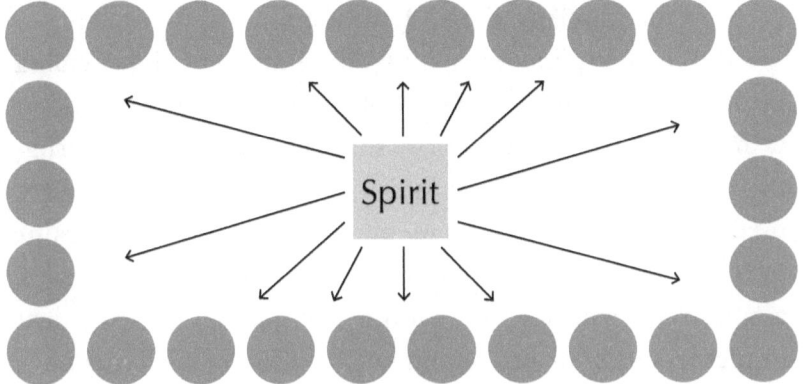

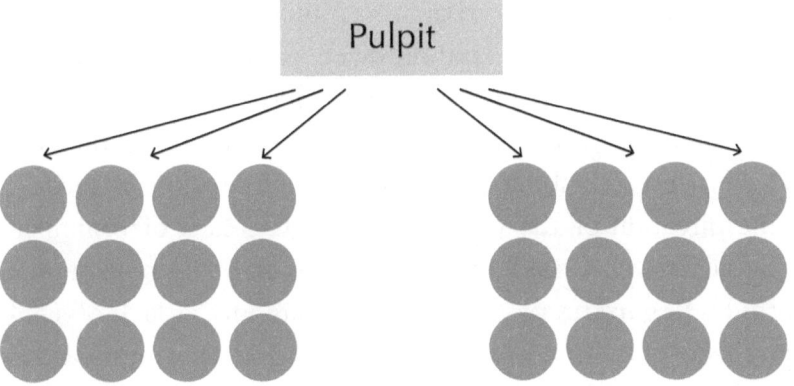

Figure 1: Shift in Worship

Insufficient Financial Support

The disagreements over clergy financial support, both practically and philosophically, have been crippling to the pastoral movement in American Quakerism.

While yearly meetings and superintendents have called for increased financial support of ministers, these calls often went unheeded.[237] Even worse, some yearly meetings, during the early periods of the pastoral adoption, refused or were unable to make a unified statement regarding financial support.[238] This lack of an authoritative, binding statement of a minimum standard of support for pastors (or practical implementation of any statements) led to the local meetings dictating the level of support, often to the detriment of the pastors.

Example of Kansas Yearly Meeting

The failure of the forced organizational shift, along with the complete absence of standardized compensation requirements (in spite of relentless calls for increases in clergy financial support), revealed the possibility that the yearly meeting leadership lacked the authority to enact decisions regarding the direction of the yearly meeting. This lack of organizational power would hinder any top-down organizational shifts. Regarding pastoral financial support, a lack of centralized authority would be evidenced by a continual call for increased financial support, and would also explain why those calls went unheeded.

An alternative explanation could be that the yearly meeting minutes simply used the wrong rhetorical strategy for communicating the financial needs of pastors. In the case of

Kansas Yearly meeting, contextual analysis revealed several different rhetorical strategies. This analysis does not assume an explicit strategy or conscious choice behind the differing tones of the comments, but it does reveal a difference in content, logic, and emotion. Whatever the rhetorical strategy, however, yearly meeting members remained unresponsive.

Exhortation

These comments calling for increased financial support mention the responsibility of the church to provide financial resources for pastors to do the work of the Lord, free from the burdens of self-supporting one's ministry.[239] The tone is generally pleasant and framed as exhortation, encouraging the congregation to partner with God in the work of the Kingdom.[240]

Cost-Benefit Analysis

During the second decade of the pastoral system, the dominant tone found in the comments reflected a form of "cost-benefit analysis." Churches should increase the funding of their pastor so that they may benefit from a completely liberated pastor. An example, though coded under the theme "benefit," displays the strategy of cost-benefit analysis by reporting that "the meetings that have best supported their pastors, so that they could do definite work, are our strongest and most hopeful meetings, and the various gifts are being best developed."[241] It was a worthy investment to support the pastor, for it will lead to an overall improvement in church health.[242]

Bait and Switch

There were several instances of the comments beginning with a positive affirmation regarding some aspect of the financial situation but ending with a castigation and a call for increased financial support. Comments of this nature often paint an initially positive picture of the situation before pointing out the reality of some financial deficiencies.[243] For example, it was noted that "there has been a small increase in pastoral support. . . . However, the average pastoral salary . . . is only $200.00. . . . This item must have our best consideration."[244] These minor celebrations are short-lived, as they are quickly subsumed by the call to increase giving to support pastors.[245]

Human Interest

Another strategy was to highlight the deprivations experienced by the pastor, in order to motivate through sympathy.[246] An example of this from 1925 relates that "many of [their] pastors must necessarily spend fifty to seventy-five per cent of their time in secular work that their families may be clothed and fed; all because of the lack of support."[247] Another example illustrated the pastor as being neglected in favor of paying down church debt.[248] By portraying the pastor as a model of pity, perhaps members would be moved by emotion to increase their donations.

Pleading/Scolding

The strongest evidence of the organizational impotence of the yearly meeting leadership is found in this category, where the tone of the comments seems to alternate between damning shouts and shrill pleadings. Examples of scolding include comments where it was hypothesized that stinginess and deliberate delinquency, rather than any external economic factors, were to blame for the deficient giving.[249] However, it could quickly escalate, as it did in 1921, when the lack of pastoral support was deemed embarrassing. Pleading comments seem to throw caution to the wind, grasping at anything that may elicit a response.[250] The following example is from the 1978 minutes:

> Along this line is also the consideration of salary and benefits. A little less than half of the reports indicated there was not a salary increase to offset inflation. Bear in mind that no increase is a decrease. I am well aware of the financial pinch all of us are in, but encourage you to not only review an increase, but consider the base salary in light of costs of living in your area today. If your meeting is unable to meet such a salary, please release your pastor to seek additional employment to supplement his salary.[251]

This quote encapsulates the seemingly helpless response of the yearly meeting leadership to the financial struggles of the pastors. While the leadership fully recognizes the deteriorating financial condition of the clergy, its only recourse is to continuously communicate these needs, often with no response.[252]

Absence of Denominational Authority

The analysis of the comments regarding clergy financial support revealed that no matter the tone or content of the comment, the response, over the majority of the existence of Kansas Yearly Meeting, was apathetic and/or deficient. This finding reveals two things: It provides an explanation as to why a standardized compensation plan was never implemented. The yearly meeting lacked the central authority to implement standards and could not overcome the possible obstacles, such as an entrenched minority of anti-pastoral members who utilized the consensus model of decision-making to stall implementation, or (more likely) a disinterested majority that historically was apathetic to increased financial recompense for clergy.

It also reveals that the failure to implement this single element of ecclesiology points to the fact that larger ecclesiological elements, such as an articulated pastoral theology, were beyond the grasp of even the most motivated yearly meeting leadership.

Overall Unwillingness to Financially Support Clergy

Despite the failures of yearly meeting leadership to properly conceptualize, articulate, and communicate the pastoral role, along with congruent financial necessities, the failure to financially support the yearly meeting pastors ultimately lies with the yearly meeting members themselves. The lack of denominational leadership regarding clergy financial support would perhaps be irrelevant if the membership increased its overall giving. Then local meetings, flush with donations, might increase the pastor's salary.

Some contemporary yearly meetings have set minimum standards of financial support for pastors, creating a culture of expected practices for the local churches. Regardless, the longitudinal findings point to a history of miserliness, which, when coupled with relatively powerless yearly meeting leadership, led to inadequately supported clergy—a condition that is still observed in many Friends churches today.

Chapter Four
Necessity of Quaker Pastoral Theology

Stewart Newman is correct in noting that "the problem of maintaining in practice what is professed in principle is real."[253] The struggle in the Friends movement is to maintain the ideals of early Quakerism in local practice, while also maintaining pastoral leadership. An articulated pastoral theology can help both pastors and congregations build up and maintain the transcendent culture of Christ-centered Quakerism against the constant pressure of cultural erosion. Yet still some may wonder at the necessity of Quaker pastoral theology, whether such specificity may be detrimental to a more ecumenical trajectory for American Christianity.

This reticence, though, may not be a theological response but a cultural one. Mats Alvesson, writing of shifts in modern organizational culture, notes that earlier generations, influenced heavily by the Protestant work ethic, embraced high standards of morality, having authority figures, and a willingness to sacrifice at work and at home.[254] Now, however, "the modernization of traditional morality, partly driven by the development of hedonistic mass consumption, means the cultural reproduction of corporate life no longer goes on automatically."[255]

In American Christianity in the late twentieth century, this embrace of cultural pluralism was spurred by a latent frustration with "particularism," or the differentiation between denominations based upon small details.[256] This may have contributed to the rise of non-denominational churches, fueled by a diminishment of any esoteric tradition or cultural elements that may hinder church attendance. While this approach may have been effective in previous decades, the pendulum now seems to be swinging the other way. More people are now being drawn away from mainstream evangelicalism and into denominations with richer heritage, liturgy, and culture, increasingly attracted to forms of piety and Christian tradition that were heretofore unknown to them. As such, the Friends movement has an opportunity to spread the gospel to a new generation through the richness of our heritage and the unique ways God has equipped us to make disciples. A clear pastoral theology can help facilitate this.

Just as other denominations have articulated pastoral theologies, which guide the training, hiring, and expectations of pastors serving within the denomination, the Friends church can likewise benefit and better achieve its missional aims.[257] Four key considerations in creating a Quaker pastoral theology stand out: the future of the Friends movement, church growth and effectiveness, strengthened pastoral ministry, and preserved Christian orthodoxy.

The Future of Friends

Some view the current divergent trajectories of the evangelical and liberal Friends movements as unsustainable on both sides, requiring a dramatic change of course or repentance.²⁵⁸ Though that sentiment may be extreme, it seems clear that the present rate of fracturing and lack of any attempts to articulate cohesive identities may put the future of the Friends movement at risk. In a world with myriad options, churches and denominations must "find a way to differentiate [themselves] from the competition in an enduring fashion."²⁵⁹ Penny Becker, writing in reference to the United Methodist Church, examines this issue:

> A vital question for denominational leaders, then, is how to communicate effectively their tradition's most important or central ideas to local congregations, which are also influenced by many other sources in forming their own local sense of identity ("who we are") and mission ("how we do things here").²⁶⁰

An established practical/pastoral theology allows a denomination or movement to maintain its core convictions in the face of a changing culture. It also protects against unwanted and unwarranted changes in ministry brought about because of cultural change. Since practical/pastoral theology functions in the realm of the experiences and lives of people, it is also the most susceptible to cultural influence (and so are the pastors). Without a strong, articulated pastoral theology, it is often up to the individual pastors and churches to decide a response to the issues facing them. Historically, we have seen divergent responses to issues lead to conflict and division even between churches in the same yearly meeting.

Also, practical and pastoral theologies of denominations are informed by their social and historical context and tradition, resulting in a nuanced practical theology tailored to each denomination's needs.[261] Unfortunately, these denominational cultures seldom garner reflection until moments of crisis or change, when it's already too late for alteration.[262] For example, it has been proposed that, during the revivals of the 1800s, the differentiating principles of Quakerism were lost as Friends were forced to use a more common vocabulary with new converts.[263] This loss was largely unrecognized until recently, when the decline of Friends churches in America raised the issue.

Thankfully, the answer to a revitalized Friends movement in America is quite simple: the restoration of the values and ethos of early Quakerism—values that led to rapid growth in spite of heavy resistance and persecution. Not only does a renewal of Quaker values restore the vitality of the key testimonies of the Christian experience, but it also offers people a previously unfamiliar way to experience the grace of God and express their devotion to Christ in daily life. To promote Christ-centered Quakerism is to promote the legacy of our spiritual forebears and provide a path for Quakerism to speak to future generations.

Church Growth and Effectiveness

It is evident that humanity is predisposed toward groups and, further along, organizations.[264] We are social creatures, and involvement in groups is nearly unavoidable.[265] Thus, organization should be viewed positively, for it "allows groups of people to leverage assets more efficiently and scale in ways that aren't possible for individuals."[266] It is important for the peace, harmony, and efficiency of these various groups that members recognize the benefits and detriments of how their groups are organized. Failing to do so not only courts organizational disaster (such as the failure of churches and yearly meetings), but also invites individual harm (as opposed to involvement in supportive groups that help maintain psychological health).[267]

For an organization or movement (such as a church) to adapt to a rapidly changing future, it is necessary to self-evaluate to recognize what is truly important to the movement, and what is unnecessary or perhaps even harmful to the future of the movement. Many believe that the greatest obstacle to the spread of Christianity is the church itself.[268] By responding to this reality through clear-sighted housecleaning, one can identify the detrimental aspects of American, Christ-centered Quakerism, and allow opportunities for creativity and vision to inform how Friends will share the gospel with the world.[269] The hope is that this conceptualization of a Quaker pastoral theology will begin the conversation that can be finished at the yearly meeting and local church levels—what does a Christ-centered, American Quaker pastoral theology look like?

Current and Future Pastors

When the expectations and boundaries for the leadership of the pastor are articulated, favorable conditions are created for the pastor to "do" leadership. The more a leader engages in leadership actions, the more they are recognized as a leader by others, which creates a virtuous cycle through which a person begins to internalize their identity as a leader.[270] The cycle continues, building a leadership capacity that benefits both the leader and the organization.[271] However, many in the Friends movement have failed to credit these expectations (or a culture of encouragement and support by the local churches), as seen in a statement by Hubert Mardock in the 1950s:

> Young men and women preparing to become Friends pastors have sensed a certain lack of dignity and significance in this vocation and a decided coolness on the part of many Friends towards pastoral service.[272]

A stronger, unified culture would not only improve the conditions of current pastors, but also enrich the soil from which future pastors may be called by God.

Another benefit of an articulated pastoral theology is that it narrows the divide between belief and action. Unfortunately, there has been a separation of "theology" from "practical theology," which began in Christian colleges and seminaries.[273] The consequence of that separation is that theology is more easily viewed as an abstract, conceptual exercise, while practical theology is forced to fit a results-oriented, organizational growth mindset. In terms of pastoral training and education, this separation has the potential to matriculate pastors who are either theologically astute or managerially prepared, but not both. By grounding pastoral theology in the soil of scripture and building on that foundation the positive principles of organizational excellence, the Friends Church can begin to "sustain pastoral leadership that is truly practical and truly theological."[274]

Orthodoxy

Throughout Friends history, drifts from orthodox Christianity (more than differences on minor theological points) have been both devastating and unnecessary. A coherent Quaker ethos, rooted in orthodox Christian theology, lived out through Quaker testimonies, and preserved and passed on through an articulated pastoral theology and ecclesiology, ensures that essential Christian doctrines are not neglected or abandoned by rogue churches. If such a trespass were to occur, then the centrality of the gospel provides clear evidence for proper restorative action on the part of the yearly meeting. The hope is that, regardless of minor differences in theological beliefs and practices, that the central, essential doctrines of Christianity would be maintained across Christ-centered Quakerism in America.

Solution: Transcendent Culture

Considering the pressing needs of Christ-centered Quakerism, one can see that these issues relate to the necessity of an overarching culture that would guide the movement and its members. The articulation of a pastoral theology and additional theological elements help facilitate the creation and maintenance of such a culture. Some may wonder, given the perceived personal nature of Christianity, whether exploring the Friends movement through the lens of organizational culture is necessary or beneficial. However, research shows that "institutions exert a certain influence upon their surroundings and, in turn, are affected by their surroundings."[275] To be a Quaker is to be influenced both by one's local church and the broader cultural heritage of the Friends movement, however strong or weak it may be at the time. While conceptual models of organizational culture, such as the one of American pastoral Quakerism, may appear to oversimplify a complex mix of elements and issues, they do help provide a manageable framework from which to help understand the past, solve current problems, and explore the potential future of the movement.[276]

Organizational Culture

Culture can be broadly defined as "everything with which an individual is concerned and involved in society."[277] It is these innumerable aspects of life that combine to form culture, which then, in turn, informs future people and traditions.[278] In the same way, organizational culture should be understood as containing such elements as "shared values, beliefs, assumptions, patterns of relationships, and behaviors."[279] These elements are often supported and reinforced through actions, symbols, and rituals, as well as other less formal components (language, jokes, etc.).[280] Typically, these elements are represented as explicit or implicit traditions, passed down generationally through individual interactions (as from parent to child) or corporate culture (in defining what makes Baptists "Baptist").[281] These social norms are "sometimes explicit, sometimes implicit, largely internalized, and often deeply held."[282] Whatever their form in the church, they shape the way both clergy and congregation view worship, fellowship, polity, and mission.

Can Culture Be Changed?

While traditional organizational thought imagined culture as a rigid structure that contains and connects values, behaviors, and artifacts, new perspectives emphasize the dynamic, fluid process of cultural creation, adaptation, and change.[283] These new perspectives better fit with the common perception of the world around us, which seems to be in a continuous state of flux, easily exemplified by the fleeting nature of tastes in fashion and entertainment. Since "institutions exert a certain influence upon their surroundings and, in turn, are affected by their surroundings,"[284] one must not think in terms of something concrete and unmovable, but rather a shifting and responsive process, shaped by the surrounding culture and the choices of the members.

This understanding provides an important opportunity for those within evangelical Quakerism. David Hurst, writing of organizational renewal, notes that it is possible for a mature organization to experience a revival of the "values, feelings, excitement, and emotional commitment often experienced only in the beginning of an organization's life."[285] Within Quakerism, there is the opportunity for a double revival: a spiritual revival and a revival of our organizational mission. Not only can we have the freedom to embrace the historic testimonies of Quakerism without fear of drifting into universalism, but we can also embrace Christ-centered orthodoxy without fear of drifting into away from our uniquely Quaker identity. If culture is fluid, then these elements, recently in opposition, can be merged into a culture that prophetically puts into practice the commands of Jesus. This new culture, in short, is our greatest testimony—that God has chosen to speak, not just through other denominations, but through Quakerism, and that God still has a purpose for us.

Cultural Creation in the Friends Movement

Knowing the importance of organizational culture and identity for the continued and future success of Christ-centered Quakerism, how shall we go about creating an identity and ethos that reflects both our heritage and our future? First, it is important to see ways historical Friends shaped their identity and culture. Mary Hatch uses the example of cultural artifacts as an interesting lens through which to view this process. According to Hatch, cultural artifacts can challenge the values and assumptions previously held by an organization or movement.[286] An organization, when faced with such a challenge, has two possible responses:

> The artifacts are ignored or physically ejected (e.g., destroyed or removed) by members of the organization, or they are accepted and incorporated alongside culturally produced artifacts to reflect back on the values. If absorbed into the culture, such artifacts work retroactively to realign values as the culture adjusts to their presence.[287]

This framework provides a way to understand the cultural changes that have occurred, and continue to occur in the Friends movement. For much of Quaker history, the movement dealt with perceived challenges to the cultural norms both swiftly and definitively. During the Quietist period, meetings disowned members for a variety of reasons, though with the purpose of repentance, corrections, and reconciliation of the disowned member.[288] Regardless of the offense, the underlying reason for sanction was to protect the culture against influences that ran contrary to the ethos of the movement. This method was, in a sense, counterproductive and unsustainable as it shrank the movement while at the same time hindering future growth through isolation. Yet it is consistent with the understanding provided anything that did not fit within the Quaker label was disowned, and the movement's culture shared deep transcendent testimonies.

As in the Quietist period, Christ-centered Quaker churches (especially in the evangelical Friends church) still practice an intense protection of the movement. However, in almost complete reversal of the Quietist period, it appears that many seek to protect the movement from the testimonies of Quakerism itself. The culture of American pastoral Quakerism has changed so much that the very testimonies by which God spoke through the movement historically are treated as foreign entities to be isolated and destroyed. Far from being an exaggeration, it seems clear that many of the testimonies that previously defined the movement are now treated with distrust (as an extension of liberalism) or ignorance (lacking a recognition of heritage). A transcendent culture that emphasizes both Christian orthodoxy and Quaker distinctives will help prevent extremism from flourishing.

Cultural Unity vs. Diversity

One of the key issues regarding any articulation of a Quaker ecclesiology or pastoral theology is the paradox of a religious movement predicated on individual experience yet functioning with governing bodies meant to impose order and exercise discipline over members.[289] The question arises as to whether a uniform culture is truly possible in contemporary American Quakerism, or whether such a culture would smother the freedom inherent in the DNA of the historical Friends movement.

Researching the role of organizational culture and corresponding ethical behavior among its members, Amanda Sinclair describes two distinct paths by which organizational culture may be utilized to change norms, beliefs, and behaviors. One avenue is for an organization to seek after a strong, unified organizational culture through which "the presence of organisational values and norms . . . are shared by all."[290] This culture is articulated through various means, and seeks conformity often through "subtle socialisation of organisation culture."[291] The second path recognizes that "organisations are nothing more than shifting coalitions of subcultures. . . . Diversity and debate is construed as potentially a better safeguard for ethical behaviour."[292]

I propose that both elements can and should be understood and utilized for the creation of sustainable cultural change in the Friends movement.

It must also be noted that, though often the terms "centralization" and "decentralization" are used in regard to organizational decision-making, the concept is much broader. The terms have also been used to describe organizational structure, indicating a decentralized organization with self-contained and self-sustaining elements, as in the structure of yearly meetings.[293] However, just because the yearly meetings are separate organizational entities does not mean that they must have separate cultural entities.

Cultural Unity

If a coherent pastoral theology is to be understood and applied in a beneficial way within American Quakerism, then there must be a semblance of unity in terms of cultural values and norms regarding the pastoral role. This unity is achieved through the adoption of a unified, articulated ethos regarding the expectations of pastors in Christ-centered Friends churches with the goal of shifting the norms in the local churches and yearly meetings regarding the pastoral role.

This should not be seen as a proposal of a centralization of dogmatic authority, power, and control in the yearly meeting. One only has to look at the Quietist movement to see the detrimental effects of over-centralization of authority, combined with an oppressive cultural ethos. One can also see, in the twentieth century, the strengthening of the yearly meeting officers through the centralization of power away from the quarterly meetings. The danger of any centralization of power, regardless of intention, is the possibility of tyranny.

Decentralized Diversity

The antidote to any possibility of tyranny lies in the paradox of both decentralized diversity and cultural hegemony. Diversity, or freedom, is often perceived as the hallmark of George Fox's movement, so any supposed attack on that individual or congregational sovereignty is viewed as anti-Quaker, and is often resisted at all costs.

Yet it is in the example of historic Quakerism that one sees the damage wrought by unfettered freedom within the movement. The Nayler incident sparked an existential reflection regarding freedom and authority within the emerging Quaker movement, leading to measures of accountability to prevent future incidents from occurring. Those who propose an absolute freedom should recognize that, while the Friends movement does emphasize an individual relationship with Christ Jesus, this autonomy is understood through the context of faith community.

Both-And

The solution to ecclesiastical tyranny is not unfettered freedom, and tyranny is not the appropriate response to anarchy. Yet it is in that tension that decentralized diversity holds cultural hegemony in check (and vice versa), providing the Friends movement with the answer to the perennial problem of local meeting autonomy and yearly meeting unity. Recent reorganizations highlight this seemingly ubiquitous conflict between the yearly meeting and the local congregations.

A potential solution to this renewed struggle lies in the top-down authority of the yearly meeting found not in the structure's organization, but in the unified culture. This culture is stewarded and passed down by those serving in the yearly meeting to the local churches.

Proposed Paradigm

This book attempts to provide a coherent explanation of the cultural norms necessary for a biblical and sustainable Quaker pastoral theology. The proposed themes should be understood in this "unity-diversity" paradigm, as they provide a theological and cultural framework to provide unity across the yearly meetings, while allowing for diversity in local expression. The paradoxical outcome to the equal emphasis on unity and diversity is that, when implemented correctly, one will promote the other. The local congregations, possessing freedom in local expression, will nonetheless be guided by a strong, unifying culture that guides their decision-making and connects them to the necessary fellowship of other churches—the yearly meeting—to which they serve and submit, as the yearly meeting serves and submits to them. Thus, freedom and unity coexist, providing for a strengthened yearly meeting and strong, Christ-centered Quakerism.

Christ-centered Quakers and Cultural Maintenance

One should not view this pastoral theology as the endpoint regarding organization, culture, and identity amongst Christ-centered Quakers. For no matter how well pastoral theology is articulated or established as the norm for yearly meetings and local churches, the process is not finished. A form of cultural maintenance must occur, by which members re-enact this culture in their daily individual and corporate decisions.[294] No articulated praxis, no matter how well-conceived, will be perfectly relevant for all time. Christ-centered Quakerism must be constantly engaged in rigorous self-reflection, attempting to discern the state of its fidelity to orthodox Christianity expressed through Quaker principles, as well as reviewing the meaning and effectiveness of its worship rituals and ministry efforts. In this way, Christ-centered Quakerism can always be improving, seeking to be the most faithful light of God to the world.

A Word of Caution

There is always a chance that organizational culture could be so strong in over-specifying pastoral expectations and behaviors that it could limit the diversity of aspiring pastors.[295] However, the benefits of a transcendent culture outweigh potential dangers. While only the first step, a Christ-centered Quaker pastoral theology can begin the conversation of cultural creation. This is not a strengthening of the Friends movement for its own sake, but for the spreading of Christ's kingdom and the glory of God.

Chapter Five
Current Pastoral Expectations

Before creating a pastoral theology, it is important to understand the explicit expectations of the yearly meetings. This was done by analyzing the Faith and Practice/discipline of the American pastoral yearly meetings. The yearly meetings explored in this chapter are Northwest Yearly Meeting of Friends Church, Alaska Yearly Meeting of Friends, Evangelical Friends Church—Southwest, Evangelical Friends Church—Mid America Yearly Meeting, Rocky Mountain Yearly Meeting of the Friends Church, Evangelical Friends Church—Eastern Region, Wilmington Yearly Meeting of Friends, Iowa Yearly Meeting of Friends, Indiana Yearly Meeting of Friends, Western Yearly Meeting of Friends, and North Carolina Yearly Meeting of Friends.

Northwest Yearly Meeting of Friends

Northwest Yearly Meeting of Friends is comprised of "churches in Idaho, Oregon, and Washington." The yearly meeting has its origins in the migration of Quakers to Oregon in the early and mid-nineteenth century.[296] This migration increased after 1870, and "Oregon Yearly Meeting was established in 1893."[297] In 1902, the Oregon Yearly Meeting, along with ten other yearly meetings, established the Five Years Meeting, an organization consisting of "a uniform discipline and a permanent organization of delegated powers"[298] It later renamed itself Northwest Yearly Meeting of Friends and joined the Evangelical Friends Church International at its inception.

Alaska Yearly Meeting of Friends

Quakers began missions work in Douglas, Alaska, in 1887, with the founding of a school by missionaries from Kansas.[299] The Quaker presence and ministry in Alaska waxed and waned for many years and included Friends churches in Kotzebue birthed out of a missionary endeavor by California Yearly Meeting (which would become Southwest Yearly Meeting).[300] Kotzebue then became the seat of a new yearly meeting. According to the discipline,

> The Kotzebue Sound Mission was opened by missionaries from California Yearly Meeting having been sent here in 1897. Since that time a force of workers has been continued on the field and funds furnished to develop the work, until the forming of an independent Yearly Meeting, Alaska Yearly Meeting, in 1970.[301]

The yearly meeting is currently made up of twelve churches in Alaska.

Evangelical Friends Church—Southwest

Evangelical Friends Church—Southwest began as California Yearly Meeting in 1895, as "an outgrowth of Iowa Yearly Meeting."[302] Though originally a part of the Friends United Meeting, Southwest Yearly Meeting withdrew in 1993.[303] Southwest Yearly Meeting then joined Evangelical Friends Church International. The yearly meeting contains more than forty churches in California, Arizona, Nevada, and Utah.

Evangelical Friends Church—Mid America Yearly Meeting

Quakers first came to Kansas to minister to the Shawnee and opened a mission in 1836.[304] Kansas Yearly Meeting came into existence in 1872.[305] In 1978, Kansas Yearly Meeting changed its name to Mid-America Yearly Meeting[306] and joined Evangelical Friends Church International at its inception.[307] In 2000, it changed its name again to Evangelical Friends Church—Mid America Yearly Meeting.[308] The yearly meeting has over sixty churches in Kansas, Oklahoma, Colorado, Texas, and Missouri.

Rocky Mountain Yearly Meeting of the Friends Church

Rocky Mountain Yearly Meeting began as a series of churches planted under the auspices of Nebraska Yearly Meeting.[309] Due to theological differences, Nebraska Yearly Meeting left the Five Years Meeting (now Friends United Meeting).[310]

Because of this separation, it reorganized in 1957 to become its own independent yearly meeting and renamed itself Rocky Mountain Yearly Meeting.[311] It currently contains fourteen churches in Colorado, Nebraska, and Arizona.

Evangelical Friends Church—Eastern Region

Evangelical Friends Church—Eastern Region began as the Ohio Yearly Meeting—specifically, as the Gurneyite side that emerged from the splitting of the Ohio Yearly Meeting in the nineteenth-century.[312] The yearly meeting joined the Association of Evangelical Friends in 1965, and also Evangelical Friends Church International at its inception.[313] The meeting contains ninety-three churches in the United States and Canada, "including Michigan, Ohio, Pennsylvania, New York, New Jersey, Illinois, Virginia, North Carolina, and Florida."

Wilmington Yearly Meeting of Friends

In 1870, Miami, Center, and Fairfield Quarterly Meetings founded Wilmington College in Ohio "as a school to educate their Quaker youth and the community young people."[314] Out of this institution, Wilmington Yearly Meeting was formed in 1892 as an offshoot of Indiana Yearly Meeting.[315] Later, meetings in Tennessee transferred from North Carolina Yearly Meeting to Wilmington Yearly Meeting.[316] It was almost entirely a pastoral yearly meeting, having been formed after the revival periods of the late nineteenth century, and is affiliated with Friends United Meeting.[317] Currently, there are seventeen churches in the yearly meeting in Ohio and Tennessee.

Iowa Yearly Meeting of Friends

Quakers settled in Iowa in 1835 on land purchased from Native American tribes by the American government.[318] A yearly meeting was formed in 1863 as an offshoot of Indiana Yearly Meeting.[319] It was claimed that the pastoral system appeared even before the period of revivalism that prompted its adoption in other yearly meetings, though it was slow to catch on in some areas.[320] Later, out of Iowa Yearly Meeting, Oregon and California Yearly Meetings were planted.[321] Presently, there are thirty-three churches in the yearly meeting.[322]

Western Yearly Meeting of Friends

In 1854, a request was made by three quarterly meetings, located in western Indiana, to form an independent yearly meeting out of Indiana Yearly Meeting.[323] After committees and deliberation, Western Yearly Meeting formed in 1858.[324] Later, it was one of the founding yearly meetings of the Five Years Meeting, which became Friends United Meeting, in 1902.[325] There are presently thirty-eight churches in the yearly meeting.[326]

Indiana Yearly Meeting of Friends

The first Quakers arrived in Indiana in 1799, and the community grew, through many forms, until a yearly meeting formally met in 1821.[327] Three future yearly meetings were the progeny of Indiana Yearly Meeting: "Western Yearly Meeting in 1858, Iowa Yearly Meeting in 1863, Kansas in 1872, [and] Wilmington in 1892."[328] Affiliated with Friends

United Meeting, there are currently forty-seven churches in the yearly meeting.[329]

Friends Church of North Carolina

The first Quakers arrived in the Carolinas in 1665, with enough growth to organize a yearly meeting in 1698.[330] The outbreak of the Civil War caused many Friends to migrate west, jump-starting a surge in the westward expansion of Quakerism.[331] Affiliated with Friends United Meeting, it presently contains thirty-one churches.

Themes

Concepts of pastoral expectation found in at least half of the Faith and Practice or discipline documents of each yearly meeting were considered themes. These themes are as follows: alignment with the Faith and Practice, pastoral authority and "domination," sharing responsibility, lay participation in worship, pastoral care, preaching, and committees.

Alignment with Faith and Practice/Discipline

One major expectation that emerged is that a pastor's ministry and leadership align with the guidelines of the denominational document, the Faith and Practice. In Rocky Mountain Yearly Meeting, the "pastor must carry on their labor in harmony with the principles of the *Faith and Practice.*"[332] Similarly, Mid America Yearly Meeting states that "pastors must carry on their labor in harmony with the principles of the denomination and agreeable to the provisions of this book of *Faith and Practice.*"[333] The Northwest Yearly Meeting calls on pastors to "affirm through public ministry the *Faith and Practice* of the Yearly Meeting."[334] Southwest Yearly Meeting states that "Friends pastors are expected to teach and preach in harmony with our theology as expressed in *Faith and Practice*."[335]

In Iowa Yearly Meeting, the necessity of pastoral alignment with the discipline is mentioned regarding pastors transferring from other denominations, and as a requirement for recording candidates to have studied the document.[336] Western Yearly Meeting obliquely mentions alignment, but specifically only in relation to the "standards of daily living set forth in the Queries" of the Faith and Practice; the same is true in North Carolina.[337] Indiana is more explicit regarding this requirement, with an expectation of a commitment to its principles, and that pastors "without reservation, support and declare these truths."[338] In these ways, the Faith and Practice/discipline acts as a theological and practical boundary for pastors in these yearly meetings.

Variance

Eastern Region Yearly Meeting does not mention alignment with the Faith and Practice as a requirement for its pastors. However, this variance is mitigated by their statement that "The Senior Pastor is encouraged to keep before the people the doctrines, testimonies, and history of the Friends Church."[339] Since the Faith and Practice or discipline is typically the repository for Friends theology, praxis, and history, it can be reasonably assumed that the Faith and Practice would be a resource and guideline for this.

By contrast, neither Wilmington nor Alaska Yearly Meeting makes any mention of alignment with the Faith and

Practice at all. The absence of such an explicit statement does not negate an implicit assumption that pastors in these yearly meetings are expected to be in concordance with the Faith and Practice. However, the complete lack of such a statement (a unique variance among the sample) does raise the question as to why it was not included.

Pastoral Authority and "Domination"

One word that emerged in relation to pastoral authority and pastoral ministry in the church is "dominate." The Faith and Practice of the Mid America Yearly Meeting states that "pastors should not in any sense dominate the work of the church, but should strive to bring every officer and committee to full activity and efficiency."[340] Alaska Yearly Meeting asserts that "pastors must recognize that they are not to dominate the business of the Meeting and that they are to serve under the direction of the Ministry and Counsel."[341] The Northwest Yearly Meeting Faith and Practice states, "The pastor should in no sense dominate the church but should serve it."[342]

Other yearly meetings, while not using the term "dominate," are clear in their expected limitations of pastoral authority. According to Wilmington Yearly Meeting, "Pastors are considered as co-workers with the members of the Meeting," diminishing any sense of hierarchical authority accompanying the office of pastor.[343] This statement was also found in Western and Indiana Yearly Meetings.[344] North Carolina also has the same statement above, but it further notes that the pastor should possess "the skills of a competent leader without being 'priestly' or losing the spirit and status of the servant."[345] The overall message is that any form of hierarchical, positional authority should be avoided and resisted.

Variance

Rocky Mountain, Eastern Region, and Iowa are unique in that they do not mention pastoral authority at all. On the other end of the spectrum, Southwest Yearly Meeting devotes a paragraph to articulating the authority of the pastor. This paragraph is prefaced by a sentence explaining that pastors in the yearly meeting, though some are paid and some are volunteer, "all hold the office and authority of the pastor." This is expounded upon in the next paragraph:

> God gives the pastor spiritual authority through gifted ministry, persuasion, character and the power of the Holy Spirit. Through faithfulness, integrity and longevity the pastor gains influence which adds personal authority. Through Recording or Commissioning as a Friends Minister the church recognizes the pastor's God-given authority to lead and influence. All of these, and more, combine to give the pastor significant authority in the church.[346]

The presence of this paragraph outlining pastoral authority does not automatically put it in contradistinction with the yearly meetings that denounce pastoral domination, but their unique perspective is telling in the sense that it indicates a differing view of the role of pastor. However, in addition to the paragraph outlining the authority of the pastor, there is a paragraph titled "Limits on Authority," which speaks of the unity needed between the pastor and the elders. This unity is described as such:

> God only has one will. When a pastor and the elders do not agree, someone is confused, and obviously it is not God. The pastor and the elders need to take time to seek the unity that the Holy Spirit brings in making decisions.[347]

Within this unity there is still a demarcation of authority. For while "their office and role in the church should give pastors a special hearing in all meetings, . . . a wise leader will understand that the united voice of the elders takes precedence."[348] While authority is given to the pastor in the Southwest Yearly Meeting, it is bounded by the authority of the church elders.

Alaska Yearly Meeting, while possessing the elements of the majority theme, also contains an interesting variance regarding pastoral authority. According to Alaska Yearly Meeting, not only is the pastor not to dominate the meeting, but he or she is to "be at all times in subjection to the advice and counsel of the Ministry and Counsel."[349] It also states that "the Pastor should at all times be in submission to the Meeting."[350] This notion of submission elevates the prohibition against pastoral dominance to an expectation that the pastor is ultimately the servant of the congregation.

Sharing Responsibility

Directly related to the concept of domination and pastoral authority is the theme of sharing responsibility. Specifically, it is the notion that a pastor does not possess sole responsibility for the spiritual health or the shepherding of the congregation. Instead, that responsibility is shared with multiple persons or a committee. In the Rocky Mountain Yearly

Meeting, "The pastor and the Spiritual Life Ministries Committee share the responsibility for the spiritual care of the congregation."[351] In Mid America Yearly Meeting, "The pastor and the Elders Board share the responsibility for the spiritual care of the flock."[352] In Northwest Yearly Meeting, "The pastor and elders share responsibility for the spiritual care of the church."[353] Alaska Yearly Meeting states, "It is the duty of the pastor with the Ministry and Counsel to have general oversight of the shepherding of the flock."[354]

Indiana Yearly Meeting notes that the pastor and the Ministry and Oversight Committee should "share equal responsibility with each member for decisions and implementations," as well as that both pastor and committee "shall cooperate in developing the spiritual life of the Monthly Meeting."[355] In North Carolina, the pastor and Ministry and Counsel Committee must have a "clear understanding of the work to be done cooperatively. . . . When this is done, the pastor may expect the full support of the Meeting on Ministry and Counsel in prayer, counsel, and cooperative efforts."[356] Similarly, Iowa Ministry and Counsel Committees should "give prayerful support to their pastor and work cooperatively in mutual counsel."[357] Finally, Wilmington and Western Meetings include the exhortation that "ministers, elders, and pastors can accomplish their work with greater efficiency through close cooperation and frequent consultation."[358]

Variance

Eastern Region Yearly Meeting makes no mention of shared responsibility of spiritual care and shepherding, but the variance presented by Southwest Yearly Meeting is much more nuanced. While the document does not explicitly state that responsibilities are shared, it obliquely references the theme through its exposition of cooperation between the pastor and Elders/Ministry and Counsel. According to the Faith and Practice, "The pastor and the elders need to take time to seek the unity that the Holy Spirit brings in making decisions." Also, "Pastoral leadership gains more credibility and influence through the advice and counsel of the members of the Elders/Ministry and Counsel. This is not to be a competitive exchange but rather a cooperative seeking of the mind of Christ, desiring to know and to do his will."[359]

Lay Participation in Worship

Connected to the notion of the priesthood of all believers is the idea of pastors creating the space for members to worship or exercise their gifts during the time set aside for worship. Northwest Yearly Meeting describes this expectation: "The pastor should take care that in meetings for worship the members of the congregation are afforded the opportunity for their exercise of ministry, as the Lord may lead."[360] Mid America Yearly Meeting echoes this, stating that pastors must take "care that opportunity be afforded in all meetings for worship for the free exercise by members of the congregation of any gifts for service which the Lord may have conferred."[361] Rocky Mountain Yearly Meeting's statement is the same as Mid America's. Alaska Yearly Meeting expects that pastors will give "opportunity for quiet worship and for expression by other members of the congregation."[362]

Indiana Yearly Meeting notes that the pastor should "recognize the privilege and responsibility of others to participate vocally in the meeting for worship" (a statement which also appears in North Carolina), as well as endeavoring to "bring all members of the Monthly Meeting to a sense of their responsibility for ministry."[363] Western Yearly Meeting and Wilmington note, for the pastor, the "need of preserving in every meeting that freedom of expression which is vital to the membership in group worship."[364]

This theme seems to point to the idea that pastoral leadership, in these yearly meetings, involves helping create and shape both the structure and ethos of the worship service so that members have the opportunity to develop and use their spiritual gifts for the glory of God and the edification of the congregation. This creates a participatory culture where the worshipers feel the freedom to express themselves as the Lord leads. This culture mirrors the ethos of the early Friends worship services.[365]

Variance

Southwest, Eastern Region, and Indiana do not have any mention of this theme.

Pastoral Care

Another key theme in these yearly meeting documents is the expectation of pastoral care. How pastors shepherd their congregations will often shape their ministerial legacies. Southwest Yearly Meeting articulates this well by stating,

"Long after people have forgotten the sermons and the programs, they will recall the time the pastor stood by them in crisis or conflict."[366] A majority of the Faith and Practices contain references to expectations of pastoral care of the congregation. These expectations are often explicit and detailed, creating, in some, a checklist of requirements to fulfill or opportunities for the pastor to minister.

Eastern Region Yearly Meeting outlines the expectations for the pastor as involving "close personal contact with the people, which will involve counseling at home in hospitals and homes in order to know the needs of people and how to serve them effectively. . . . Time should be set aside for weekly visitation."[367] Mid America Yearly Meeting calls on pastors to fulfill their duties by creating "a program of systematic calling in the homes of members and other attenders, by individual counseling, by giving attention to the sick and bereaved, and by helping the needy in the name of the church."[368] Rocky Mountain Yearly Meeting mirrors this last statement, creating a bulleted list that includes items such as "systematically call in the homes of members and attendees; . . . be available for counseling, or refer people to appropriate counselors; . . . visit the sick and bereaved; . . . help those in need."[369] Southwest Yearly Meeting describes this expectation similarly: "Visiting the sick, comforting the bereaved, counseling the troubled, encouraging the discouraged, helping the weak, setting captives free from spiritual bondage, and standing by those in crisis are much-appreciated functions of the pastor."[370]

Variance

There is a minor variance with the Rocky Mountain Yearly Meeting's Faith and Practice concerning the expectations of pastoral care. While there is mention of pastoral care, it deals primarily with guidance toward membership than any elements mentioned by the other yearly meetings.

In Alaska Yearly Meeting, it is the duty of the pastor (along with the Ministry and Counsel) to

> have general oversight of the shepherding of the flock, to be watchful of the interests of absent members, to visit the families of the attenders of meetings, to extend a special care to these attenders who are not members and to invite them to join in membership when they are prepared to do so. They shall extend watchful care over Associate members, and encourage them to become Active members as soon as they are prepared to do so.[371]

Indiana Yearly Meeting, Western, Wilmington, and North Carolina only mention the welfare of the congregation and community, but do not go into any further specifics.[372] Iowa Yearly Meeting has no specific mentions regarding pastoral care.

Preaching

Preaching also emerged as a majority expectation in the Faith and Practices. According to Southwest Yearly Meeting,

> Preaching and teaching are highly valued in Scripture, worthy of double honor. (1 Timothy

> 5:17) Pastors are to preach and teach God's word, communicating it effectively and applying it to their hearers' lives. Preaching the word of God and teaching the scriptures are God-given means of building up the church. (1 Timothy 4:1–2; Hebrews 4:12–13) Pastors must take sufficient time for study and preparation for preaching and teaching, so they can feed the flock with the best from God's word and apply it to daily life. Friends pastors are expected to teach and preach in harmony with our theology as expressed in *Faith and Practice*. Pastor's ability to communicate with individuals and groups throughout the church greatly affects their fruitfulness.[373]

This not only grounds the importance of preaching in scripture, but labels it as a means of growing and strengthening the church. It also highlights the expectation that pastors are to spend adequate time preparing the message, making sure it is applicable to and aligns with Friends theology.

Eastern Region Yearly Meeting also provides a lengthy articulation of the expectation of preaching from the pastor:

> The preaching of the Word must grow out of a well-trained understanding of the Word, reception to its authority, understanding of the principles of interpretation, and faithful and disciplined reading and study of the Scriptures. This is a matter of gift and inspiration and of disciplined study. No pastor can function without both. In preaching, the pastor must not only be

> faithful to the meaning of Scripture but also relevant to the needs of the congregation. Preaching, whether evangelistic or teaching in character, must always be aimed at a verdict: acceptance of salvation, obedience in discipleship, or taking steps toward maturity in Christlikeness.[374]

This emphasizes both study and faithfulness to meeting the spiritual needs of the congregation, much like the Faith and Practice of Southwest Yearly Meeting. It also emphasizes the expectation that preaching be geared toward the goal of conversion or greater discipleship in the listeners.

Comparatively, Alaska Yearly Meeting provides scant elaboration concerning the expectation of preaching. It merely notes that the "pastor must give careful attention to preparation for preaching, for teaching,"[375] along with guiding the worship service. The only other mention of preaching in the section involves replacement preachers for when the pastor is absent. It notes, "The pastors should always endeavor to work in harmony with the Ministry and Counsel when inviting anyone to supply the pulpit."[376]

Mid America Yearly Meeting and Rocky Mountain Yearly Meeting mention preaching, though both in passing. Rocky Mountain Yearly Meeting provides a bulleted list of pastoral expectations but prefaces the list with "in addition to the preaching ministry."[377] Mid America Yearly Meeting also provides a quasi-list of pastoral expectations, prefacing it with "in addition to pulpit ministry."[378] Similarly, Northwest Yearly Meeting provides half a sentence, listing one of the responsibilities of the pastor as to "preach for the edification of the church, as led of the Lord."[379]

Iowa Yearly Meeting briefly states that "pastors [should] present well-prepared Gospel messages."[380] With a much longer statement involving preparation, Indiana and North Carolina expect that pastors

> should prepare themselves by careful, prayerful study to expound the Scriptures, to awaken the consciences of those who hear, to inspire a longing for Christ and to guide all the congregation, particularly young people and children, in the search for God and the Christian way of life.[381]

Western and Wilmington contain a line regarding preaching, but that connection is revealed only through its context, stating that pastors "are expected to serve the meeting in the field of the public ministry."[382]

While preaching is a unanimous theme among the yearly meetings, the amount of space given to articulating the theme varies dramatically. On the surface, it appears that some yearly meetings emphasize the importance of preaching more than others. However, this cannot be proven from the data alone, as there are other factors at play. For example, it must not be automatically assumed that the Alaska Yearly Meeting does not emphasize preaching simply because their statement is short. Rather, it seems possible that this is a product of the small size of the Faith and Practice (twenty pages), rather than a variance concerning the expectation of preaching. This and other factors limit explanation of differences, at this point, leaving only the observation of the varying amounts of texts given to highlighting the theme of preaching.

Committees

The expectation of the pastor as member of, advisor to, and attender of committees stands out as another dominant theme found in the documents. The Southwest Yearly Meeting articulates several different expectations concerning the pastor's involvement with various committees. First, "The pastor is one of the elders, a member of Ministry and Counsel. In as far as is possible, the pastor should be present at all meetings of the Elders/Ministry and Counsel."[383] Second, "The pastor is also a vital member of the Nominating Committee, and this group must not meet without the pastor being present."[384] Finally, the Faith and Practice elaborates the pastor's responsibilities concerning the remaining committees:

> A pastor is to keep cooperative relationships with all church committees. The pastor is a member of all committees and will attend most of the major committee and ministry meetings. Because of time limitations, a pastor may determine which ones require personal attendance and which to delegate to pastoral staff members or to other elders.[385]

Eastern Region Yearly Meeting envisions the pastor as "an ex-officio member of all Commissions and committees," in which the pastor is "expected to be a leader and administrator."[386] Rocky Mountain Yearly Meeting expects the pastor to "encourage the ministries of the meeting and may attend committee functions in an advisory role if he or she chooses or is needed."[387] Northwest Yearly Meeting lists this expectation in their numbered list of pastoral responsibilities, stating that the pastor should "serve as an advisory member of the church committees and departments, giving counsel to organizations such as the Sunday school and Friends Youth, reinforcing their concerns through public ministry."[388] Alaska Yearly Meeting writes that the "pastor should attend meetings of important committees of the church and attempt to keep all groups working together in harmony and love."[389] Mid America Yearly Meeting articulates this theme as such:

> The pastor is an advisory member of all committees appointed by the church and exercises necessary supervision over their activities, lending incentive and encouragement when needed and giving advice and instruction for the proper functioning of these agencies. The pastor may assist them further by presenting special messages (or giving way for an invited speaker to do so) on the special phases of their work.[390]

Indiana Yearly Meeting expects that its "pastors should maintain a cooperative relationship with all the committees of the Monthly Meeting, assisting in their programs and policies."[391] Iowa and Western pastors are to "serve as an ex officio member of all committees."[392] North Carolina leaves the expectation of committee to the discretion of the local church, while Wilmington pastors must "sustain a cooperative relationship with all committees of the Meeting, assisting in their programs and policies when called upon."[393]

Variance

Minor differences between yearly meetings revolve around the expectations of attendance of the pastor at committee meetings, ranging from the pastor to be present at as many meetings as possible to not even mentioning attendance as an explicit expectation.

Synthesis

Considering the previous yearly meetings' majority themes and pastoral expectations, it seems possible to capture the spirit of the various ideals in a unified statement:

> A pastor is expected to work with the leadership of the church to shepherd and care for the congregation. A pastor's leadership and authority is never to be used to dominate the church, but rather used to serve the church in cooperation with the church leadership. This pastoral care involves visitation, counseling, and general help to those in need. There should also be concerted effort to create a space and climate for members to develop and express their gifts and ministry. A pastor should also preach biblically-sound messages which are informed by diligent study and prayer. This preaching and teaching should align with doctrine and praxis outlined in the *Faith and Practice*. A pastor is also expected to be involved with the work of the various committees in their church, advising them and attending the meetings when necessary.

Conclusion

This survey shows that there have been attempts at clarifying the pastoral role within Friends ecclesiology, which allows us to build on previous work and helps point to pastoral topics of importance to Friends churches in the last 150 years. However, this work has been irregular, leaving room for an attempt to provide a uniform, complete articulation of pastoral theology, finishing the journey for conceptualization.

Chapter Six
Methodology

Now that a case has been made for the necessity and benefits of Christ-centered Quaker pastoral theology, the next step is to begin its conceptualization and articulation. To hopefully allay suspicions and overcome objections, this pastoral theology will be supported by three separate paradigms of evidence: Bible/theology, historic Friends, and leadership.

In addition, the presentation of the three together also addresses some concerns held by various stakeholders in the Friends movement. There are those who worry that adherence to the historic values and testimonies of Quakerism will compromise or contradict the tenets of orthodox Christianity. There are also those who fear that the suppression of Quaker distinctives will lead (or has led) to a bland evangelicalism, devoid of the unique ways that God has chosen to speak through Quakerism. Another recent, though vocal, movement has also emerged, calling for an abandonment of historic Friends' ecclesiology and decision-making processes, citing their perceived lack of effectiveness and their hindrance to church growth. The hope is that the cooperation of the three forms of evidence will show these three contingents that a Christ-centered Quaker movement need not be hindered in the ways they fear.

Below is a foundational review of each of these paradigms (within which are themes and topics related to the paradigm), along with the practical ways each section will support the conceptualization of a Christ-centered pastoral theology explored in the next several chapters.

Three Components of a Quaker Pastoral Theology

Bible and Theology

A discussion of a Christ-centered Quaker pastoral theology must have its foundation in both the Bible and theology. As Bernard Prusak succinctly explains, "There would be no Church without Jesus."[394] Pamela and Michael Cooper-White state definitively: "As Christian practitioners, we minister with practices that are grounded in Scripture and informed by the work of centuries of theologians who came before us."[395]

Bible

Quaker scholar Michael Birkel has claimed that "early Friends used biblical language to describe their inward experience."[396] However, though biblical language was the foundation of Quaker preaching, correspondence, and communication, it must be stressed that the Bible was not simply the lens by which they interpreted their experiences. Nor, as implied by others, was it simply an accident that Quakerism emerged in a Christian context. The use of biblical language emerged from the simple fact that Quakerism was a

Christian sect. Thus, Christ-centered Quakerism holds to the truthfulness and authority of scripture.[397]

Two extreme viewpoints regarding scripture show the potential dangers. There are those who disregard the role of the Holy Spirit and other modes of revelation, viewing scripture as the sole source of God's communication to mankind—a form of bibliolatry. There are also those who disregard scripture as irrelevant, seeking only a spiritual connection with God, unmediated by any sacred text and, at its worst, unmoored from any orthodoxy. While maintaining the importance of scripture, Christ-centered Quakerism recognizes that biblical knowledge itself is insufficient without a connection to God and obedience to the leading of the Holy Spirit.[398] In fact, one could say that Christ-centered Quakerism recognizes the authority of scripture as a record of true religious experience—an encounter with the Living God—which early Quakers sought to experience themselves.[399]

Christian practical theology relies on scripture, for it is a "citadel of authority in religion."[400] One only has to look at the process of hermeneutics (biblical interpretation) to see its similarity to practical theology.[401] Just as a student of the Bible explores the truths of scripture and seeks application in their context, so does practical theology seek to explore the truths of God and their application in specific ministry contexts.[402] And just like hermeneutics, practical theology holds scripture as a source of spiritual truth, illumined by the Holy Spirit. It is worthy of our study and application.

Like our Quaker forebears, who recognized the dangers of over-individualism regarding religious experience, Christ-centered Quakerism emphasizes the interpretation of scripture in the context of community. This simply means that understanding scripture regarding both basic and complex issues is facilitated through conversation, listening, and Spirit-led unity. There are many benefits to communal interpretation. First, it allows the full expression of diverse gifts in the congregation, and for those who have faithfully studied the Bible and its context (both academically or personally) to share and edify the congregation. Second, communal interpretation avoids immature hermeneutics predicated on the individualistic fallacy that "the Bible must be taken to mean what it means to me."[403] Finally, it is undeniable that we are shaped by our context—that "social and ecological context influence the mind-set that churches bring to the Christian message"—including our reading of scripture.[404] By seeking diversity in our churches (in every way), communal interpretation brings numerous and diverse perspectives on scripture, enriching the church's understanding of God's leading. Above all, communal interpretation removes the tyranny of a pastor-dictated hermeneutic and recognizes the dignity of all believers in expressing the impact of scripture on their lives, for the benefit of the body.

Even though there are those in the Friends movement who pay lip-service to the authority of scripture, the reality of its role in many monthly meetings is suspect.[405] The proof of biblical fidelity, for Friends churches, is the way that it shapes the actions and attitudes of its members. A neglect or marginalization of scripture cannot but manifest itself in the congregation and individual members in negative ways.

Theology

Theology emerges from a composite Greek word *theos* (God) and *logos* (word/reason/study/language), which was Latinized into *theologia* (an intellectual discourse about God).[406] Historically, it has been understood and referred to as the science of studying God and the relationship of God to humanity and the created order.[407] Many define it now as any form of thinking, discourse, and articulation about God.[408] As a pursuit, theology should "seek to understand God's creation, particularly man and his condition, and God's redemptive working in relation to mankind."[409] The organization of these pursuits into a coherent system is then called "systematic theology" or "constructive theology."[410]

The Protestant emphasis on scriptural authority and infallibility, though helpful in distinguishing the Protestant movement from the Catholic church, has left a distorted legacy where deep theological thinking and reflection about scripture (giving God's truth utmost respect) are supplanted by a shallow reading of the text. This shallow reading, disengaged from the testimony of scripture and from the illumination of the Holy Spirit, becomes a disrespectful disengagement of both mind and spirit. Theology is not the realm of intellectuals, clergy, or those who simply want to know about Jesus. Theology occurs when anyone approaches God and seeks to understand God's leading at the crossroads of reality, society, and the existential questions of life. Every Christian who thinks about their faith is a theologian of sorts.[411] Thus, theology, as an intellectual and spiritual pursuit, has a place in Christianity, the church, and the daily life of a Christian.

Also, proper theological understanding, discourse, and teaching are important (and have been throughout

Christian history) because there will always be people and movements who, either unintentionally or maliciously, distort the Gospel.[412] Clark Pinnock writes that "in theology, mind and heart—study and prayer—are both important."[413] Conversely, wrong theology not only corrupts one's intellectual views of faith, but also has the potential to distort one's life away from the restored *imago Dei* that Christ provides. When creating a Christ-centered pastoral theology, one must properly interpret scripture, utilizing the communion of saints and cloud of witnesses provided through the collected Christian theology of church history, an, most importantly, the discernment of the Holy Spirit.

Bible and Theology Component in Practice

With the assumption that scripture is truthful and authoritative, the Bible can be utilized as a lens to view the conceptualization of each pastoral domain. The goal is to have direct scriptural support for each proposed domain, revealing that the approach is biblical. In addition to scriptural evidence, examples from theology and church history will be used to support positions presented here. The same pitfalls exist in both tasks: selectively choosing only examples that support the arguments. However, since one of the purposes of this book is to show that a Christ-centered pastoral theology is not heretical or unbiblical, and not to prove that a Quaker pastoral theology is prescriptive for all Christians, the danger of twisting theological positions and historical situations is significantly lower. When offering examples from theology or church history, concerted efforts will be made to provide sufficient evidence of correct understanding and use.

Friends History

See chapter 2 particularly for a full review of the history of Quakerism.

Friends History Component in Practice

In order to create a pastoral theology that aligns with the historic principles of Quakerism, elements from Friends history will be utilized to corroborate the choices made. While emphasis will be given to early Friends history, examples from throughout the existence of Quakerism will also be utilized. As with biblical prooftexting, the danger is that only examples that support the propositions in this book will be used, and for every example provided, there is always a possibility of another that is contradictory. In addressing this reality, the utmost effort has been put into capturing the overall spirit of Quakerism through these choices.

Leadership

Pastoral theology supports, guides, directs, and informs pastoral ministry. Ontologically, the two are so intertwined as to constitute a union of theology and practice. Because pastoral theology and pastoral ministry are mutually informative, any pastoral theology must not only be grounded in scripture and theology, but also in the daily details of pastoral ministry. One of the foundations for a Christ-centered pastoral theology must be the leadership a pastor must implement in the course of their congregational work. To understand the role of leadership in pastoral ministry and pastoral theology, it is important to recognize the inter-relationality of human existence and the role of leaders in facilitating human betterment. Although leadership studies has often been self-categorized by self-contained leadership theories, this book will avoid espousing any specific leadership paradigm, but draw from common and beneficial elements.

As social creatures, our most basic interactions (a greeting or simple question) exist solely because of our inherent willingness and ability to engage in communication, participation, and cooperation with others.[414] In fact, society itself could be viewed as an "organic creature—a complex growth of living relationships."[415] Leaders seek to understand and influence these complex social interactions in order to achieve goals, and a leader's power is derived from this ability.[416] In our context, one must understand the role of the pastor as a personal, group, and organizational leader.

As a personal leader, a pastor must embody the integrity and principles that cause them to influence those around them.[417] This impact comes not just from charisma, but from a purpose and passion for the movement to which the leader is affiliated. For a pastor, personal leadership means living a Christ-like life, and letting that life speak in every interaction throughout the day. It also means possessing the empathy and relational abilities to connect with people in order to guide them.[418]

Group leadership involves the leading of informal groups of people. In leadership and organizational literature, organizations are either understood as informal or formal.[419] For example, a weekly gathering of people who love comic books would be considered an informal organization, while a start-up business that sells comic books would be a formal organization. For the sake of simplicity, informal organizations will be referred to as "groups," while formal organizations will retain the title "organization."

Group leadership's importance derives from the common understanding that "there can be no leadership where there is no team."[420] Any group requires leadership to achieve its goals. However, a leader in this situation usually does not have the established structures and processes for which an organizational leader benefits. Instead, leadership remains much more informal, with the goal being not only to inspire self-betterment in the individual, but to aim individual transformation and collaboration with others to achieve the mission of the group.[421]

An organizational leader is one who leads a formal organization by casting a vision and creating strategic aims, and by using organizational structures and processes to help implement that vision and achieve those aims. An organizational leader is at the same time a visionary and a manager, using discernment and understanding to steer toward goals. Organizational leadership is sometimes tricky, especially when one realizes that formal organizations, such as churches, often start as informal organizations (like weekly Bible studies) and transition to formal organizations. When one looks at the beginnings of the Friends movement, one sees an example of this transition from an informal organization (those following George Fox and preaching a similar message) into a formal organization (with monthly meetings and systems of accountability).

While local churches and yearly meetings are definitely formal organizations, the issue of Christ-centered Quaker churches in different yearly meetings and denominations is a little fuzzy. It cannot be said that the affiliation of these churches are a formal organization simply through their theological orientation, for there are no definitive purposes or processes to guide or connect them. But even though this broad affiliation can only be considered an informal organization, these churches can still unify under a shared testimony and culture that can strengthen both the churches and the overarching message of Christ-centered Quakerism.

Potential Pitfalls of Leadership Studies

While some claim that the church has failed to adopt business and organizational principles into its practice, the reality is that many pastors, denominational leaders, and authors advocate the integration of modern leadership practices into the life of the church.[422] This reflects a growing trend in leadership and organizational literature. In addition to leadership and organizational theory, there are also contemporary works on leadership, business, productivity, and strategy. The growth of this subgenre stems from the increasing entrepreneurial culture emerging in America, which has led to a demand for learning that was once reserved for those in business school. Interestingly, many of these texts stray from typical business/organizational offerings (e.g., accounting) and focus more on personal development and organizational innovation (e.g., creativity, communication, leadership, ethics, etc.). Many pastors read these books in hopes of improving their leadership in the local church. The danger is a temptation to abandon both biblical and historic Friends' understanding of leadership to copy the "latest and greatest."

Also, even though the modern American evangelical church has sought guidance in contemporary leadership theory and practice, the business world has not reciprocated in kind. Very little leadership literature has been written utilizing the church as a model. That which does is often written by those connected to some degree with the church or religious movement in question.[423] The reason for this could be attributed not only to the poor organizational functions of most churches, but to the church's theological underpinnings, which may conflict with leadership theories rooted in self-interest.[424] In fact, it has been posited that humanist pragmatism, rather than Christian morality, is the foundation of effective leadership in the twenty-first century[425] raising the issue of potentially humanist theoretical foundations for understanding Christian leadership.[426]

Another danger is the unthinking use of business tactics in the church. We have inherited an American religious tradition that has drawn a sharp distinction between the sacred and the secular, making such talk of the business of the church sound worldly. The outcome of this is that formal exploration of organizational analysis through a theological lens has been limited.

Finally, the simplest fear is the most troubling: perhaps the tenets found in leadership literature are bogus.[427]

However, the refusal to integrate organizational and leadership theory into theological discussions of the church did not remove such thinking from pastoral leadership. Instead, especially through the 1980s and '90s, pastors merely read business and leadership books, applying their findings (sometimes recklessly) to their ministries. If it appeared that any specific method was moderately successful, it was often then retrofitted with scripture and theological evidence to support it, a pragmatic approach to ecclesiology that has not been beneficial to sustained American church growth. Any theological exploration of the church that utilizes leadership and organizational theory/practice (including this one) must take care to avoid this trap.

Rationale for Utilizing Leadership

Exploring a Quaker pastoral theology through the lenses of organizational and leadership theory differentiates this work from previous efforts, which typically utilized only historical and theological methods to analyze the trajectory of the Friends movement. Applying leadership theory and organizational analysis to the American Friends ecclesiology provides two major avenues through which to extend the academic dialogue. First, using organizational theory within a pastoral theology provides a legitimate avenue for discussing the nature of the church as an institution/organization and the pastor as a leader.

Though the potential pitfalls of using contemporary leadership and organizational literature have been outlined, the reason for the negative outcomes associated with the use of such resources needs to be understood before disregarding the entire field. The breakdown between business and practical theology occurs because the underlying assumptions of each discipline often differ greatly. In many business and leadership books (especially those written for a popular audience), the assumption is often to use one's talents for self-promotion and promotional advancement. Even positive moral qualities are seen only for their beneficial ends.[428]

A serious integration of leadership theory with theology could create an effective, mission focused, biblical, and Christ-like leadership paradigm, achieving the sometimes disparate aims of organizational leadership and ministry, without having to sacrifice aims from either. Unfortunately, such an integration is outside the scope of this book. Instead, organizational and leadership theory are implemented in the conceptualization process of the pastoral domains, allowing research and conclusions from this academic discipline to speak into what has typically been only a theological and historical approach.

Additionally, the application of leadership theory allows for a clear affirmation of Quaker pastoral theology as a differentiated and beneficial model, sufficient for both American pastoral Quakerism and pastoral leadership in general. Because many of the first pastors hired by Friends meetings were from other denominations, they brought their ecclesiological and pastoral expectations into their new roles. The subsequent failure of the yearly meetings to create a coherent pastoral theology allowed these norms to be adopted by local meetings and reinforced by later Friends' affiliation with the Wesley-Holiness movement. Churches, yearly meetings, and pastors—inheritors of this cultural confusion—have responded by seeking the pastoral norms of other movements to guide the discussion.

Leadership Component in Practice

A wide range of modern leadership texts have been explored, which represent the popular expressions of what works in modern businesses and organizations. Throughout the various domains of the pastoral theology, they will be cited as part of the leadership component of the analysis. The goal is to show that Christ-centered Quaker leadership is in no way contradictory to the modern themes of leadership (unless such a contradiction is justified), but is actually supported by contemporary leadership literature.

Chapter Seven
Gender

The issue of gender in pastoral ministry is a point of contention for many Christians. Views regarding women clergy are often fairly cemented, separating denominations and movements that would otherwise be fairly aligned in theology and practice.

Bible and Theology

Looking at the gospels and the early church, Jesus crosses existing social barriers (John 4; 8:1–11; Mark 5:24–34). One of the most vivid examples is the story of Mary and Martha, where Mary sits and learns under Jesus and is praised for doing so (Luke 10:38–42). Writing of this passage, Carol Gallagher notes, "How revolutionary! A man inviting a woman to sit as a disciple, as a student at the Rabbi's feet, an equal in a very unequal world."[429] Not only that, but women are commissioned, in Matthew 28:1–10, to "take the message of Jesus' resurrection, and bear witness faithfully."[430]

Regarding Acts and the New Testament letters, we see clear evidence that women played a vital role in the leadership of the church. For example, Acts 18 shows Priscilla and Aquila taking a leadership and teaching role over Apollos, with no apparent approbation or consequence.[431] At the end of Romans, Junia is mentioned as an apostle, again with no comment (in spite of later efforts to masculinize the name and remove the feminine presence from early church leadership).[432] There is undeniable evidence that women were a part of public ministry and leadership in the early church.

However, there is still a scriptural issue that must be addressed. This obstacle, placed in front of women seeking to engage in public ministry, is the apparently direct prohibition of such by Paul, found in 1 Corinthians 14:34 and 1 Timothy 2:12. Because both passages are very similar, only the Corinthian passage will be referenced. There have been many challenges to this interpretation of Paul's injunction.[433] The overall evidence points to specific, contextual issues being addressed, rather than a universal and timeless declaration.[434] Also, it must be noted that Paul, if he is prohibiting women preaching, is not consistent. As Quaker Margaret Fell noted, in 1 Corinthians 11:3–4, Paul's admonition for women to have their heads covered when praying or prophesying presupposes that women did pray and prophesy.[435]

When one takes a broad view, a paradoxical cycle has occurred, through which the dominant cultural attitudes affected the way these passages were understood, which then informed the cultural norms regarding women, which then further entrenched the hermeneutic stance regarding these passages, and so on. In fact, more often than not, it is due to the nostalgic norms of patriarchy rather than the testimony of scripture that a marginalized gender class in the church feels normal in the first place.

Key to any hermeneutic is that it must be "sustainable"—it must have consistency and utility when used throughout scripture. When taken at face value, the modern implementation of a gender-restricted clergy is based on an inconsistent, unsustainable hermeneutic. Linda Belleville reveals this hypocrisy clearly:

> A woman can teach astrophysics at a Christian university, but she cannot teach an adult Sunday school class on the biblical doctrine of creation. She can work as a certified public accountant for a Christian company, but she cannot keep the church's books. A woman can be a trustee of a liberal arts college, but she cannot serve on the church deacon board. She can be a chief administrator at a Christian hospital, but she cannot serve on the church council or board of elders. A woman can lead children's worship, but she cannot conduct congregational worship. She can preach the children's sermon, but she cannot preach the congregational sermon.[436]

The singular exception of pastoral ministry as precluding women is not only hermeneutically indefensible but also doesn't make much sense when placed in context. A gender-restricted clergy is not only unsupported by scripture, but shown through experience, wisdom, and common sense (all valid forms of God's revelation), to be untrue.

A gender-restricted clergy is an obstacle to evangelism, missional activity, and the life of the church. The only evangelistically pragmatic thing for churches to do now is to remove gender restriction for clergy. There is no practical obstacle to opening pastoral roles to women.

Historic Friends

One of the central elements of Quakerism in seventeenth-century England was the inclusion of women as full members, participants, and ministers within the movement. This was in marked contrast to the standard religious views of gender at the time.[437] Early Quakers also fearlessly challenged the political system when it contravened God's law or promoted injustice.[438]

This was done primarily through letters and other literature, such as Mary Dyer's prison letters to the Massachusetts General Court, though there were instances of Quaker women appearing naked both in church and in public to communicate the "spiritual nakedness" before God to those who would persecute Quakerism.[439] These brave ministries were not without consequence, as many Quaker women faced arrest, imprisonment, corporal punishment, and, in the case of Mary Dyer, execution.[440]

Margaret Fell, another luminary in early Quakerism, not only participated in ministry of Friends, but also helped support the nascent movement logistically, politically, and theologically, both in her home at Swarthmore Hall and her extensive correspondence. Robynne Healey wrote of Fell: "Her own activity and the work of her daughters and other women she led had a significant impact on crystallizing the belief in spiritual equality at a strategic time early in the life of the sect."[441] Promoting the equality of women in ministry, Fell wrote a biblical defense of women's ministry in the short pamphlet with a long title: *Women's Speaking Justified, Proved, and Allowed of by the Scriptures, All Such as Speak by the Spirit and Power of the Lord Jesus. And How Women Were the First*

That Preached the Tidings of the Resurrection of Jesus, and were Sent by Christ's Own Command, Before He Ascended to the Father, John 20.17. In this pamphlet, Fell interprets scripture, refuting the popular objections to women preachers.⁴⁴² For example, Fell utilizes the perceived "weakness" of women to show that women are perfectly positioned to be used by God to preach the gospel. She writes, beginning with Genesis 5:2:

> Here God joyns them together in his own Image, and makes no such distinctions and differences as men do; for though they be weak, he is strong; and as he said to the Apostle, *His Grace is sufficient,* and his *strength is made manifest in weakness,* 2 Cor. 12.9. And such hath the Lord chosen, even *the weak things of the world, to confound the things which are mighty; and things which are despised, hath God chosen, to bring to nought things that are,* 1 Cor. 1.⁴⁴³

While the equality Fell wrote of has not always materialized ecclesiologically,⁴⁴⁴ the overall action and intent of the movement has been to recognize the God-given place of women as ministers in the church.

Leadership

It can be easy to view the church as archaic, especially when compared to the perspectives of modern society, however, this may not be entirely accurate. While some important strides have been made in leveling the playing field between men and women, those strides have been made in relatively recent history, and there are still extant inequalities.

One of the largest areas of gender inequality in America is the workforce. One of the most persistent features of the labor market in America is "occupational segregation," by which certain career positions are perceived as off-limits to certain demographics, including gender.[445] As such, ministry is not the only profession with a profound gender imbalance.

Even where gender ratios approach equality, women in the workplace still face challenges like compensation inequality.

Pastoral Paradigm

Christ-centered Quakerism believes in God's universal call to ministry for every believer. This extends into pastoral ministry, where women and men are recognized as equal recipients of a divine pastoral calling. Christ-centered Quakerism recognizes and supports a gender non-restricted clergy—a humble obedience to the will of God in calling whomever God may choose, and a fidelity to God's Word, which proclaims that all possess the image of God.

The reality is that this prophetic testimony of equality remains a testimony because there not only remains general gender inequality, but also a specific resistance to women clergy in many parts of Christendom. Christ-centered Quaker churches must be more intentional about discerning, encouraging, and fostering a woman's call to pastoral ministry.

There must also be an intense self-reflection and transparency on the part of churches during the hiring process, so that women are not marginalized. While marginalization may go unrecognized by the search committee, it is still unacceptable. Until there is a cultural shift and the legitimacy of women pastors is firmly held by all Friends churches, there must be an overemphasis, on the part of churches and yearly meetings, on hiring women, creating congregational cultures that embrace women clergy.

Some may question the effect this emphasis would have on discerning whom God has called to that specific church. One must recognize that if a church has refused or neglected to interview or hire women pastors, then it is almost certain that the church has shut the door on a God-led candidate and acted in disobedience by waiting for an acceptable male candidate to appear.

Chapter Eight
Proclaim

Preaching

Preaching, in the Western Protestant tradition, encompasses a majority of the seen duties of the pastor in front of the congregation. Preaching, as an act, is understood as the proclamation of the revelation of God to hearers.[446] In fact, it has been called "one of the most sacrosanct church practices of all."[447] At its base, it is the verbal communication of a theological message, that elucidates the truths of scripture for an audience, not only during regular worship services, but also at special events.[448] While there are many different forms of preaching, most involve the explanation of a passage of scripture and its relevance and application to the lives of the audience.[449] It is also a form of teaching that enlightens the congregation to the truths of scripture. Preaching also involves the preparation, research, and crafting of the sermon before its public performance, as well as the attempt to shape the message in order to reach the culture and context of the audience.[450]

Theologically, preaching is understood as a sacramental mediation of scripture within a covenantal community.[451] It is also a vital part of the both historical and contemporary worship. Conceptually, preaching is an art form born of natural talent, disciplined study, and rhetorical composition.[452] The benefit of effective preaching is a communication of God's truth to an audience, which results in theological education and spiritual formation of the audience.[453] Also, preaching allows for the vision of the pastor, doctrinal essentials, and a church's ethos to be communicated in a corporate setting.[454]

Pastoral Paradigm

Scripture and Story

Without falling into the trap of being overly prescriptive in outlining the form and structure of preaching, it is worth highlighting two key elements necessary for effective homiletics: scripture and story (narrative).

Scripture

The core of Christian preaching must be the correct interpretation, explanation, and proclamation of scripture. A sermon is distinct from a self-help message (though a sermon should help people), an inspirational speech (though a sermon should inspire), nor a lecture (though a sermon should teach and instruct), a political address (though a sermon should address the various areas of a believer's life), or a morality tale (though a sermon should instill godly, moral living). A sermon should be a message of God's truth, illumined by the Holy Spirit, through an exploration and explanation of scripture. Out of that foundation can emerge all the elements that make a sermon edifying, informative, and entertaining.

Though some may object to that description, strong preaching has the potential and the obligation to be an engaging, entertaining, life-transforming encounter, proclaimed in Spirit and in truth. There should be complete freedom to explore the myriad ways to effectively communicate the truths of God to people.

Ronald Byars provides an exhortation and warning for those undertaking the act of preaching:

> Through human speech and personality, Christ the Word becomes present to the people of God. But this sacramental action is short-circuited when preaching becomes another kind of public speech—propaganda, or therapy, or setting out a political program, or promoting a good cause or a denominational project, or adult education, or even Bible study. When preaching becomes lecture or book review or scolding or desperate to be "useful" in any way, it falls short of what it's meant to be.[455]

Story

Pastors, though drawing their sermons from scripture, utilize any number of styles, rhetorical strategies, and other elements to help facilitate effective communication. However, because of both its general (non-contextual) and specific (current cultural) relevance, as well as its perceived under-utilization, the homiletical use of story or narrative will be emphasized.

A stereotype of twentieth-century preaching is the "three-point sermon," by which the text is expounded and proclaimed, utilizing three major points (with sub-points, illustrations, and applications throughout). This systematic, rational approach to preaching may be difficult for those more receptive to a narrative/story format for learning the truths of God.

While this is not a call to do away with the sermon structured around points/ideas/movements, it is a recognition of the creative and missiological possibilities in narrative or storytelling preaching.[456] Such preaching can reduce the distance between the text and the audience, holistically engaging the listener through emotion, conflict, and resolution, and move away from an overreliance on rational argument as the sole tool of the preacher.[457] Regardless of the shape of narrative or storytelling preaching, the goal is to engage the audience with the truths of God, revealed in scripture, in a way that moves beyond mere rationality, and into the realms of life and will. This occurs through the use of evocative language to connect the listener to memories, emotions, and life experiences.[458] In summation, Calvin Miller describes narrative as a "force that postmodern preachers must use and listeners must reckon with. . . . Narrative handcuffs intrigue to the biblical text; . . . the homily gains relational force when the sermon is passionate enough to be visceral and story-driven enough to be visual."[459]

Relating to both passion and story, the pastor, when preaching, should also seek to draw the hearer into the grander narrative of God, a narrative that engages a believer's personal faith journey within the context of the redemptive work of Christ.[460] Christians' faith is not merely their own—they belong to a work much bigger than they are, a work that requires a life of obedience and sacrifice.

Unfortunately, modern preaching often obscures any form of larger struggle in which the church is engaged, minimizing perceived obstacles to a Christian life. It is possible, however, that a message calling for sacrifice may be received better than a message of easy faith if that call is linked to something worthwhile, meaningful, and impactful. Modern preaching, guilty of diminishing this struggle, inadvertently diminishes the impact of a Christ-centered life.

As Christians, our faith is grounded in a compelling narrative (the Gospel) through which we view the world in a whole new way. This narrative of God was communicated by the early church in such a way as to cause a minor sect in the backwaters of the Roman Empire to have an outsized influence, spreading throughout the known Roman world in a few generations. One could argue that if churches were to regain the ability to communicate the power of this narrative, then perhaps the church would again spread with the same speed and power as in the first hundred years of Christianity. A pastor's task, then, is to both communicate the life- and world-changing power of the Gospel, and to shepherd Christians to communicate it (with both words and actions).

Participation

Quaker pastors should seek to honor the place of preaching, while recognizing the unique perspective the Friends tradition brings to the process of preaching. This perspective anchors the pastor by reminding them that preaching is not the sole possession of an elevated clergy, but is a work of the Spirit that could be gifted upon anyone. While the pastor may have a recognized and recorded aptitude for preaching, may have engaged in educational endeavors to prepare for ministry, and may be financially released for full-time ministry, these things do not grant the pastor the authority of sole communicator of God's truth. Instead, pastors should seek to foster a collaborative environment regarding the sermon, during its creation, at proclamation, and during the week.

A pastor should hold loosely to the pulpit, allowing others, both inside and outside the local congregation, the opportunity to preach. This achieves a triple benefit of communicating the universal ministry of believers, providing practical opportunities for members to practice their gifting or potential calling, and providing the pastor the occasional respite. When a pastor is preaching, they should recognize that of Christ in others, along with the unique insights and perspectives of church members, and seek their input during the sermon creation process. Lest anyone mistake this as an advocation for "sermon by committee," the principle here is to avoid the danger of narrow-mindedness and self-importance present when one avoids or ignores outside input.

By instituting these values in local churches, there comes an increased level of participation and engagement. "While the sermon remains a single-party communication event, it is embedded with and represents an actual interactive, multi-party communication process in which a group of ordinary people are discerning, articulating, and practicing."[461] Rather than a mere didactic process aimed at a passive audience for the purpose of giving information and entertainment, preaching can become an active collaboration through which the preacher and the congregation explore scripture and allow it to shape and mold their lives as well as the mission of the church.

Bible and Theology

Scripture

The centrality of scripture in preaching is well-evidenced, though using the term "scripture" may be occasionally anachronistic. Throughout biblical history, the act of preaching has been seen as the explication of God's truth (which later became codified in writings). Deuteronomy exists as a prime example of public proclamation to the people of God. The book itself is structured around multiple sermons (most likely three sermons and two poems) of Moses to the Israelite people, prior to entering the Promised Land.[462] Its value, as an example, stems from the fact that it contains exposition (of the Mosaic covenant), instruction, and exhortation.

Further examples of Old Testament preaching are found in the prophetic books. Though one often thinks of prophesying as telling the future or foretelling, the majority of the prophecies spoken against the nations were not foretelling but forth-telling.[463] They were proclamations of the way things were (idolatry and covenantal unfaithfulness) versus the way things ought to be (seeking after God).[464] This persuasive proclamation, designed to elicit a response from the hearer, utilized many different rhetorical and poetic forms, and often included theatrical actions and props.[465]

In the New Testament, the gospels present Jesus as engaged in preaching, with the preeminent example being the Sermon on the Mount (Matthew 5–7). While the homiletical practice of explicating scripture appears redundant for the incarnate God, the Sermon on the Mount reveals Jesus interacting with both the Old Testament scriptures and oral tradition, even while he subsumes or intensifies them to the level of a new covenant—a homiletical fulfillment of the Law (Matthew 5:17), and an ethical/spiritual guide for believers. Earlier in his ministry, Jesus engaged in scriptural proclamation in his hometown synagogue, publicly reading a passage of Isaiah. From the initial reaction of the audience ("all eyes were fastened on him"), one can deduce that this was typical practice during synagogue worship. These examples and others show a Christological model of preaching that emphasizes the explanation, interaction, and proclamation of scripture.

It is in the rest of the New Testament that one sees preaching reach its ascendancy. One of the core missions of the early church was the *kerygma*, the "public proclamation of the Gospel,"[466] also known as "the ministry of the Word" (Acts 6:12). While apostolic preaching first explicated Hebrew scriptures to show the validity of the crucified and resurrected Messiah, later faith communities began using, in their preaching, some of the apostolic epistles, as well as the newly-recorded gospels. This pointed to a recognition of their value as potentially sacred and inspired.

This homiletical emphasis on scripture has led to the rise of the expository method, where passages of scripture are consecutively preached (often verse-by-verse). While this method does have its benefits, and its intent is admirable, it has spawned a near fanatical fan base. This has led to claims that expository preaching is the superior homiletic method (if not the only true method), and that its use will result in evangelistic gains.[467] This narrowing of acceptable homiletical methods is both unnecessary and can ultimately be harmful to preaching and evangelistic efforts. As long as the message of a sermon is derived from and faithful to scripture, then the form and structure of the message is of secondary concern. Also, the systematic and logical explication of verse-by-verse preaching (with its emphasis on historical context and grammatical parsing) may cloud the beauty and richness of narrative found in scripture.

Story

Given American Christianity's inheritance of the Western philosophical tradition, it is not surprising that early American homiletical structure, promulgated by clergy trained in the classical tradition, followed, for the most part, a logical structure. The example of Jesus, however, points to the use of narrative and story to communicate the truths of God.[468] While it is recorded that the parabolic structure of Jesus' preaching did confuse and confound many (Matthew 13:10–12), it should also be noted that the use of stories did help people remember his teachings. Today, in fact, it is a safe bet that even those unfamiliar with the Bible could rattle off the title of one of Jesus' parables. For the original audience, Jesus' use of story structures brought them "into a narrative world where there are development, plot *and* resolution."[469] Taking this idea of plot and resolution to an even broader scale is the apostle Paul whose preaching and writing were grounded in narratives pointing to a meta-narrative of God's ultimate redemption of creation[470] and played a major role in early Christian preaching.

Participation

During most of Christian history, the sermon, while important, was secondary to Eucharist as the center and purpose of worship.[471] In Catholic theology and ecclesiology, it is necessary for the priest to facilitate Eucharist.[472] Subsequently, there is a perceived divide between the clergy and laity. While the Reformation attempted to mitigate this division by emphasizing *sola fide* and *sola scriptura*, the subsequent changes maintained the divide, but under different pretenses. The Reformation shifted the pulpit to the center of the worship space and worship service, making it the primary source of teaching, through scripture, about God.[473] Subsequently, those who were ordained to ascend the pulpit held a place higher than the common layperson, "[elevating] the clergy to a position of prominence."[474] This, in turn, has minimized historical examples of participatory homiletics.

However, the resurgence of narrative and story as a mode of preaching can help shatter the false elevation of the pulpiteer, by reminding Christians that they "can confess [their] faith wherever [they are] . . . just by telling a story or a series of stories."[475] Concordantly, a participatory homiletic may actually mirror the worship services of the apostolic church, in which there was the possibility of multiple speakers and messages, as well as audience engagement and dialogue (1 Corinthians 11–14).[476] The sermon does not have to be a method of domination and hierarchy, but an act of humility and service by the pastor to a congregation, who in turn engage the truths of God as they dive deeper into scripture.

Historic Friends

There are two main arguments against the common Protestant practice of the sermon as the focal point of the service. First, there are claims that any preaching that is not extemporaneous runs afoul of the Quaker way of openness to the Holy Spirit, and thus should be distrusted (as a human creation rather than a message from God). The second argument is that the notion of positional preaching (where the pastor does most of the preaching in a church) seems contradictory to the poly-participatory nature of Quakerism.

At the heart of the objection regarding the pastoral system in worship is the role of the pastor as preacher. The issue becomes whether there are any specific people called or expected to speak these truths beyond what is expected of a normal worshiper in a Friends meeting. If not, then a pastor, regularly sharing a message, would be somewhat out of place in Friends ecclesiology. However, evidence points to certain individuals within the movement who were recognized as having the calling and gifting for preaching. These ministers spoke regularly at meetings, even to the point of issue. George Fox wrote to those ministers, pleading with them to, in a sense, wait their turn, and to not be the first among many ministers to speak in the meeting.[477] This, and other evidence, points to the notion of people within the movement essentially separated from the rest of their congregation because of their gifting. Out of this separation came an abundance of preaching.[478]

Scripture

But what was the content and style of these ministers' preaching? Can their message even be considered sermons, and their efforts preaching? Differences regarding preaching are evident between the Quakers and other religious groups of the day. Douglas Gwyn compared preaching styles, commenting that "Puritans preached and lectured by expounding the texts of scripture, while Quakers preached Christ, the living Word within them, speaking through them (see 1 Cor. 13:3)."[479] However, this may be an overreach, as scripture saturated the messages, sermons, and epistles of the early Friends. As Charles Evans notes:

> The early Friends were remarkable for their diligent reading of the Holy Scriptures, as their memoirs or journals show, and their belief was firm that they would never be found contradicting the revelations of the Holy Spirit to the soul.[480]

A better comparison is made by Jackson Cope, who looks at the rhetorical styles of the common preacher of the day alongside the Quaker.[481] Cope noted that the Quaker "'plain' style manifestly supplanted the highly-ornate, rhetorical tradition of English prose which had burgeoned in the extravagances of Arcadian rhetoric and Euphuism to flower in the early seventeenth century's 'Senecan amble.'"[482] The plain style was exacerbated by the fact that "early Quakers claimed to preach *impromptu*, that is, without prior, contextually situated, intentional preparation."[483] However, there is no evidence that any critics, either historical or modern, doubted that what these Quaker ministers were doing was preaching, whatever the content.

The evidence points to a worship service that included specified members regularly speaking what can reasonably be called sermons. In both preaching and written correspondence, George Fox and other Quaker ministers utilized scripture and biblical terminology heavily.[484] In a sense, there were preachers regularly contributing God's truth to the public consciousness of the congregation; this is similar to what was occurring in most Anglican and Puritan worship services. Although Quaker services differed in style, preaching occurred in both. Ministers were necessary to faithfully and regularly deliver the word of God, and a pastoral system, which provided this regular preaching, could possibly have been acceptable in the early Quaker paradigm.

Story/Narrative

Early Quakers' ministry was shaped by a meta-narrative grounded in scripture and ignited within their hearts and minds. This narrative was apocalyptic, in which Quakers helped bring about a "new order of Church government radically at the disposal of Christ's leadership . . . [and Quakers] were confident that this power should overthrow the established church structures which stood in opposition to Christ's immediate reign."[485] This apocalypticism was not limited to ecclesiology, but to the entire apostate world, against which Friends would prophetically testify.[486] The early Friends movement created an eschatology, out of which one experienced the second coming of Christ as a personal, contemporary experience, while, at the same time, looking forward to a future second coming.[487]

Today, one cannot help but see the wide spectrum of narratives within the Friends movement, each one dictating a different faith and practice. However, even within a movement that was perceived as valuing individuality above all else, there are broader narratives of individual congregations, yearly meetings, and Quakers. However, the Christian origins and foundation of Quakerism demand the meta-narrative of scripture act as the narrative exemplar for contemporary Christ-centered Quakerism.

Participation

It cannot be denied that the early Friends movement rejected most elements common in worship, specifically the sacraments and music.[488] This did not mean that there were no avenues of participation for the congregation, as the entire service was participatory, and the ability and opportunity for vocal ministry were not limited to a specialized class of clergy. All who were led by the Spirit could stand and speak/preach; this worship was not dependent on education or level of articulation, but on "spiritual sensitivity"[489] and obedience to the leading of God.

This freedom, however, was neither unlimited nor unaccountable. The elders and overseers of each meeting were on guard for vocal ministry that contravened the standards of orthodox Christian theology or propriety.[490] Any transgressions would have been countered with a contradicting message afterward, as well as visitation with the transgressor by the elders of the meeting. While, at first blush, these measures seem oppressive, they did allow for freedom of participation by anyone in the meeting, while at the same time protecting the tenets of Christianity. Past transgressions, such as the messianic ride of James Nayler, pointed out the dangers of unbounded freedom—dangers perhaps even greater than the oppression of the Anglican Church. The freedom to participate, balanced by communal accountability, led to a participatory, yet discerning worship service.

Leadership

Story/Narrative

One of the marks of an effective leader is the ability to communicate informatively and persuasively. While it may appear that the most effective and charismatic speakers are born with the gift of communication, most reach a level of proficiency through practice, rhetorical study, and a recognition of what will best reach an audience. While this should give hope to many—that intentional practice can improve a person's communication skills—there is still the issue of audience understanding. The standards of effective persuasion have changed, and continue to change, over time. For example, political speeches in the 1850s contained college-level vocabulary and rhetoric, while similar addresses during the 1940s were delivered at a sixth-grade level.[491] This does not necessarily mean that society has gotten less sophisticated, but may simply reflect the democratization of politics and the desire to reach a wider audience.[492] Regardless, shifting audience expectations mean that the wrong rhetorical strategy can result in a disconnect with one's audience.

Narratives, though long relegated to the realm of childhood, are now recognized as "[providing] a quick and easy way for people to acquire lots of knowledge in a vivid and engaging way."[493] Stories are also creative emotional moments that can change people's viewpoints and perspectives, allowing them to find meaning in their own stories from this larger narrative.[494] The power of narrative is best seen in communicating the goal, vision, and culture of an organization to both its members and the public. The organizations that communicate a compelling narrative are often the ones that gain a devoted following and have an oversized influence (sometimes in spite of their small size).

Teaching

The role of teaching in a church should be understood as distinct from the act of preaching, though they appear similar in many ways. In many churches, the act of teaching falls under the purview of a Christian education department. Though often diminished to the wrangling of volunteers for various Sunday school classes, the Christian education department (and Christian education itself) should be understood as having a much deeper and more meaningful purpose that is necessary for the edification of the saints and the fulfillment of the church's mission.

According to Don Browning, "Christian religious education should be understood as a process of practical theology aimed at creating individuals capable of entering into a community of practical theological reflection and participating in the action that would follow from it."[495] Teaching, in the context of the church, should seek not only to educate, but to instill members with the theological and cultural knowledge necessary to help facilitate participation and growth within the community. In addition to biblical knowledge, church educational programs should focus on "theological ethics,"[496] intrinsically connecting the ministry of preaching and teaching, for, according to Browning, "Our proclamations of grace and forgiveness must be closely related to discernments of the practical obligations of the Christian life."[497] Throughout, the pastor should be present and active, and seek to teach scripture in order to "equip the people of God for the work of ministry and for the mission of God."[498]

While the typical educational paradigm, Sunday schools,[499] have declined in many churches throughout America, this does not mean that the ministry of teaching has or should diminish. Rather, it is often that the impetus has shifted unknowingly within the church, with Bible studies and small groups (either at the church or at home) taking on the burden of biblical education.[500] The problem is that many small groups and Bible studies may not have the training or understanding to create an educational event, replacing teaching with devotional and fellowship aims. With some preparation and training, Bible studies and small groups can still have an atmosphere of fellowship and devotion, but also regain a telos of equipping the saints for work in the Kingdom.

Pastoral Paradigm

Proclamation of scripture does not begin nor end in the pulpit, but should saturate communities of faith. Currently, this is done through Bible studies, Sunday schools, and small groups. However, there are two issues with the current expressions of corporate Bible study. One major issue is that the teaching ministries are often haphazard in terms of their connection with the pulpit message and/or needs of the community. Usually, the curriculum is dictated by whims of the group leader or the theme of the purchased curriculum.

The decline in Sunday school and Bible study attendance points to the reality that there may be a need for a more unified, strategic approach.

Second, the dominant form of Bible study tends to lack a meaningful, enriching dialogue. Historically, group studies were taught by a leader, with the rest of the group in a passive, receptive role as in a classroom. In the last few decades, this has shifted to a more egalitarian, discussion-based model. However, this model is incomplete, for it does not account for the potential pitfalls that can occur in these settings. Such issues include the temptation to show off biblical knowledge, to argue over fine points of theology, and to strong-arm every lesson to one's soapbox issue, resulting in ineffective studies, fractured groups, and unsustainable fellowship.

Instead, these teaching ministries should be facilitated by leaders who model themselves after the example of a Christ-centered Quaker pastor: a person who has the knowledge necessary to expound and communicate scripture, but who does not allow that knowledge to lead to superiority or an autocratic atmosphere. Rather, the leader should use their knowledge and training to bring out the richness of the text, all the while continually pointing the scripture's message back to the specific context of those present. After engaging all participants and encouraging all voices to be heard, any teaching ministry session should close with a practical call for the message of the particular passage to be lived out by the participants. Additionally, teachers should provide space for what is most lacking in many people's lives, times for reflection, "safe, quiet spaces—rich soil where growth occurs."[501]

Regardless of context (either formal church classes or small groups/Bible studies), Michael Birkel provides a contemporary Quaker perspective on the group study of scripture, proposing that the key is to approach the study with a spirit of humility and generosity, both to the scriptures and to fellow participants.[502] The goal is that teaching ministries become not just a place of education, but one of discipleship, community, and a purposeful application of scripture in the individual and corporate life of the church.

Bible and Theology

In the Old Testament, the concept of teaching appeared most often related to a family's obligation to pass on the covenant to the next generation (Deuteronomy 6:7; 11:19). During the pre-exilic period, the parents had the main responsibility for educating their children in the commands of the Torah, especially in memorization and recitation,[503] a responsibility that continues to be felt even in modern Judaism. This emphasis on the religious education of children highlights that "the future of Israel [was] dependent on the transmission of the experience of God's mighty acts in history, and his demands, to each successive generation."[504]

This covenant education also occurred when Jerusalem was rebuilt and repopulated after the exile. During a sacred assembly, Ezra stood and publicly read the Torah, while the people listened and worshiped (Nehemiah 8:5–8). As he was reading, the Levites, apparently scattered throughout the crowd, were also reading from the Book of the Law and "instructed the people in the Law . . . making it clear and giving the meaning so that the people understood what was being read" (Nehemiah 8:7–8 NIV). It was through this didactic event that the people were reintroduced to the Mosaic covenant and how their lives should reflect that covenantal status and blessing. Even now, the reading and explanation of scripture provide a theological and historical precedent for contemporary efforts of personal and corporate study of scripture.

One of the most relevant New Testament passages relating to teaching is the Great Commission (Matthew 28:16–20). While the Great Commission is one of the better-known texts in American Christianity, there is a word that seems to be largely overlooked in terms of crafting the church's priorities: "Therefore go and make disciples of all nations, baptizing them in the name of the Father and of the Son and of the Holy Spirit, and *teaching* them to obey everything I have commanded you" (vv. 19–20). The early church embraced these teachings of the apostles, the "body of material considered authoritative because it was the message about Jesus of Nazareth proclaimed by accredited apostles."[505] Despite the importance placed on teaching by the apostles of the early church,[506] however, it appears, anecdotally, that the American church puts its emphasis on "make disciples" (which it often doesn't do) and preaching (which is not found in the Great Commission), but not "teaching." Teaching does not seem to have the weight one would expect from its presence in the Great Commission.[507] Yet the original audience would have understood the task of teaching as involving "instruction no less serious than Jewish sages customarily provided their students."[508]

Further on, the church fathers not only wrote about theology and doctrine for pedagogical purposes, but also wrote about the ministry of teaching itself. Augustine wrote tips and strategies for the effective education of catechumen, including the use of humor and having the students sit.[509]

The common method of any education during these first centuries after Christ was a catechetical method, by which a student would learn through question and answer.[510] This was based on the traditional Greco-Roman process of education extant in that period,[511] and it allowed for both teaching and discipleship.

Even though teaching, as a distinct ministry, may seem like a modern ecclesiological innovation, its roots go back to colonial America. Each Congregationalist church had two clergymen: a pastor and a teacher.[512] While the preacher provided sermons that addressed the spiritual lives of the congregation, the teacher offered lectures on doctrinal issues.[513] These two positions were alike in authority, deference, and respect, and pointed to the Puritan proclivity for theology and doctrine.[514] It is unclear why the pastor-teacher system did not continue in American Christianity, as many other Puritan elements did. A possibility may be found in the documents of the Westminster Assembly of 1643–1653, which allowed that, if a congregation only had one minister, the sole minister was to perform both duties.[515] Perhaps this allowance, and financial/logistical concerns, led to the permanent melding of the two positions. Whatever the cause, the ministry of teaching appears to have been subsumed under the ministry of preaching in American Christianity.

Historic Friends

Friends' religious education differed from other Christian movements, though some similarities were apparent. Like the catechistic culture of the early church, early Quaker leaders, such as Robert Barclay and Isaac Penington, developed catechisms that outlined the proper understanding of faith, a practice that continued into the twentieth century.[516] However, these catechisms don't appear to have been as widely used as other informal educational methods. In addition to the informal enculturation through implicit communal pressure, the yearly and monthly meetings also utilized open-ended queries, advices, and a discipline.

The queries were a set of questions that were originally used by London Yearly Meeting to gather statistical data as well as to ascertain the moral and religious "state of the church."[517] These questions did not have a codified answer (though the answer was often apparent from the question) but were meant to lead to personal reflection toward the implicit answer. They were meant for personal and corporate reflection and focus to open oneself (and the meeting) up to the truths of God revealed through the Holy Spirit.

The advices were statements of guidance and practice that helped maintain some uniformity of behavior among Quakers.[518] The published advices covered a wide variety of topics, including behavior, marriage, parenting, children, self-examination, and worship.[519] These advices, along with the queries, served as an unofficial manual to guide individuals in living out the commands of scripture through the paradigm of Quakerism.

A yearly meeting's discipline (later called a Faith and Practice by some yearly meetings) was a further explication of ecclesiological rules and standards, often with the queries and advices included. The discipline was meant to be the common wisdom of the members of the yearly meeting, and the standard of faith and practice. Problematically, many of the behaviors and standards of the early Friends movement were implicitly shared rather than explicitly codified.

Today, the main problem appears to be that many in the movement are either unaware of the contents of their Faith and Practice or disregard it as unauthoritative for faith and practice.[520] Also, in many pastoral meetings, the use of queries and advices has been disregarded. The vehicles for teaching and enculturating distinctively Quaker theology and practice have been minimized, weakening the Quaker influence in Christ-centered Quakerism.

Though even Bible study and scripture reading had fallen out of favor by the Quietist era, they did experience a resurgence during the early 1800s. According to David Le Shana, "This return to Scripture reading and study had an important part in preparing the way for revival."[521] The problem was that while family and group Bible study was in resurgence, there still was not a formal, standardized system to enculturate members in the community of the Friends. When the revivals occurred in the late 1800s, there was no way to teach the new converts what it meant to be a Quaker. When the pastoral system was adopted, a typical Bible school system was present, but no mechanism for transmitting the culture was in use, leading to the weakening of Christian Quakerism. In the twentieth century, the Sunday school or Bible school system became firmly entrenched in American pastoral ecclesiology, with yearly meetings producing materials for use in weekly classes.[522]

Leadership

There has been a dramatic rise over the last few decades in the emphasis on training and education within businesses and organizations.[523] While early leadership theory stressed a micro-managing approach that left the employee as simply a cog in a wheel, there is now great pressure and incentive to facilitate education, training, improvement, and innovation in both individuals and the collective organization.[524] Employee education and training have been shown to positively impact the public sector and nonprofit organizations.[525]

To achieve this, one organizational theory posits that the ultimate goal is for an organization to become a "learning organization," which involves an emphasis on individual and corporate learning based on organizational goals in order to facilitate continuous improvement that leads to a competitive advantage.[526] This learning/training can be formal, but can also be spontaneous and organic;[527] learning can be technical, but can also cover interpersonal relationships, organizational culture, teambuilding, or other "soft skills."[528] Regardless of the content, context, or modality of learning, the impetus for education/training is meant to be implemented and sustained by the leadership; otherwise, any new innovation and adaption emerging from education and training will be stifled by the managerial bureaucracy and static organizational culture.[529]

For employee (or member) learning and training to be effective, it must be connected to the overall goals of the organization.[530] Leaders must not only invest the resources to create formal training/education practices, but also foster a culture by which members feel empowered to initiate self-education and apply their learning toward organizational improvement. It is also vital for leaders to review training programs in order to optimize the return on the resources invested in such programs. This is true even if the training deals with intangibles such as adaption to the organizational culture and other employee outcomes that are not easily measured.[531] The greatest compliment given to employee education and training within learning organizations is that the "focus is on a company's only appreciating asset—its people."[532]

Evangelism, Outreach, and Service

The goal of evangelism is to draw people to the point of conversion, by which they may experience the gift of an eternal salvation and a radical transformation of life in the present. This evangelistic drive is supported scripturally and theologically, through the understanding that "this gift of becoming 'children of God' is available in the here and now of human historical existence with the surety that this eternity life continues through death into God's unending 'now.'"[533] It is through the reaching out and the walking with that people become introduced to and acquainted with the life-giving grace of God, and if they so choose, begin a journey of discipleship. However, it is necessary for individual Christians and communities of faith to communicate this gospel, for "how can they hear without someone preaching to them?" (Romans 10:14). It was this impetus that helped spread Christianity from Palestine to the Roman world within a few generations.

While this mission of the church has not changed, the church faces more nuanced and segmented populations than ever before. For example, though the term "teenager" did not even become popular until World War II,[534] it is now a differentiated demographic, with economic (through the purchasing power of parents) and cultural power.[535] While the concept of teenager may seem commonplace to us, it should serve as a reminder that demographic concepts can change relatively quickly (think of the "tween" arising now in popular culture, or the issue of delayed adulthood in post-adolescents). Beyond demographic categories, there have also been philosophical and epistemological shifts occurring in American society, including the rise of postmodernism, which includes skepticism regarding authority, received wisdom, absolute truths, and metanarratives (a major challenge to the mostly modernistic American church).[536] If the church is not mindful of these diverse populations, opportunities to reach them will be missed.

Additionally, the church must come to terms with its use of popular culture with regard to evangelism and outreach. Some argue that popular culture should be leveraged by the church to reach people, while others wonder if there should be discernment as to the rightness or wrongness of the cultural element, not just potential effectiveness at making the church appear relevant.[537] Either way, sensitivity should also be used regarding the already present cultural symbols found in the church and its liturgy. Tee Gatewood argues that "the church is a missionary community whose mission expands across cultural lines and national borders."[538] In order to achieve this, Christians and the church must undo ethnocentrism, recognizing the value and necessity of learning, appreciating, and communicating through culture.

Pastoral Paradigm

Despite the Quaker movement's origins in Spirit-led ministry and preaching, as well as through lives that communicated a testimony of Christian discipleship, evangelically-minded Friends in the twentieth century fell prey to the modernist understandings of evangelism, based on systematic and strategic inputs into the surrounding community. Under this paradigm, each member of the community is the responsibility of some church, which is "failing in its evangelistic task if it does not go out to discover, and bring into Christian fellowship, these un-churched persons."[539]

While these methods are not inherently wrong, and were often beneficial for church growth, they are unsuitable for Christ-centered Quakerism for several reasons. First, the adoption of modern evangelistic techniques marginalized the "life testimony" principles that communicated the gospel. Second, many of these methods were based on an attractional model, by which one sought to draw people to the church. The trouble is that this model may no longer be missiologically suited for American society. From the perspective of the unchurched, these attractional outreach programs can undercut or demean any relationships built, making it seem that relationships were formed only for the purpose of church growth.

However, hope still lies with Christ-centered Quakerism, for its foundation is based on principles that speak to the condition of this generation. By seeking to genuinely live out the commands of Jesus, we communicate to others that we take scripture seriously. By focusing on hospitality, relationship, and the betterment of the community, one can share the gospel relationally—which seems to be the premiere avenue of persuasion in this postmodern society. Thus, by our lives and service, done out of obedience to God and not out of any quid pro quo, Christ-centered Quakerism can evangelize to both the unchurched and those disenfranchised from the established church. For Christ-centered Quaker churches, evangelism will not occur through traditional modern methods, but through traditional early-church methods.

One of those lost methods from the early church—which should really be reinterpreted as an essential character trait of all believers—is hospitality.[540] This hospitality must not be a mere utilitarian practice in order to gain converts, but a Christ-like concern for others.[541] It is, according to Diana Butler Bass, "a central practice of the Christian faith—something Christians are called to do for the sake of that thing itself."[542] By regaining a sense of welcoming, openness, and community, the church proclaims an alternative narrative to the paradoxical one found in contemporary society: highly-connected and information rich, yet disconnected and intentionally opaque. The church can reach people by offering what they desperately crave but cannot find: love, trust, comfort, and community. Through the simple act of taking seriously the biblical passages that describe the church as a family and a united fellowship, Christ-centered Quakerism will have gone a long way toward reaching a disaffected and disenfranchised world.

The ministry of service should also be elevated within the hierarchy of spiritual activities (a hierarchy that many churches deny having). Pastors should encourage both organic, personal service and formal corporate efforts to serve others. Service in either form should avoid both the intent and the appearance of having a transactional nature. Elton Trueblood pointed out this danger when he wrote,

> The stranger who is visited by a representative of the Church frequently gets the impression that he is being viewed as a prospective customer, a potential addition to the numbers or the income,

> rather than a person who is approached for his own sake. Part of the shame of the contemporary Church is that it seems to be motivated by self-interest. We need to be reminded that the Church exists for men and not men for the Church.[543]

Though the cup of cold water should be given in Jesus' name, it should not have any obligation of reciprocal response attached. Whether a person immediately responds in faith to an act of evangelistic service is irrelevant. It is through a selfless life that one communicates the gospel and opens opportunities for deeper encounters with people within which Christ can be shared.

Finally, relation of the local church to missions, though a topic better explored in a Quaker ecclesiology, is still relevant to pastoral theology, for part of the vision and mission of the church (which the pastor helps discern, communicate, and mobilize) involves participation in the broader work of the church in reaching lost people throughout the world. The pastor's enthusiasm and support (or lack thereof) will often have an influence on the congregation's views and support of missions. Pastors must utilize their opportunities of teaching, preaching, and casting vision in order to rally the congregation around supporting missionaries and missionary endeavors.

Bible and Theology

It is not a stretch for Christopher Wright, speaking of missions and evangelism, to say that it is "what the Bible is all about."[544] The meta-narrative of scripture finds its culmination in Christ Jesus, and through him, "The God of Israel would also bring about all that he intended for the nations; . . . the eschatological redemption and restoration of Israel would issue in the ingathering of the nations."[545] The good news of this salvation and restoration through Jesus Christ is not automatic or universal, but comes through the reception and acceptance of the gospel by those who encounter its message (Romans 10:14–15).

To help facilitate this encounter with the gospel, the church should look to the foundational text that outlines its missional and evangelistic direction: Matthew 28:16–20. Christ commands the disciples to evangelize, disciple, and teach those whom they encounter. The end goal is nothing less than the salvation and redemption of all the nations

This direct commission by Christ, coupled with the meta-narrative of scripture, teaches that the church must have as its goal that "the good news of the salvation made possible by the work of Jesus Christ must be expressed in all the languages and cultures of the world."[546] Evangelism and missions should not be limited in focus to a mere spiritual salvation (something the American church has overemphasized),[547] but a recognition that salvation renews, recreates, and restores all facets of one's existence and continues to do so. As Michael Jenkins describes Paul's teaching, this redemption "is for humanity and creation [and] is not 'spiritual' in any Platonic sense; it is *embodied* redemption, *historical* and *particular*.[548] The gospel is not merely about an eternal afterlife, but an abundant life presently (John 10:10); the church's evangelism should reflect this. As with the early church, evangelism is only the first step in a path of discipleship, community, and spiritual growth of believers.

Historic Friends

The common cultural archetype of the Quietist Quaker has given rise to the notion of the Friends movement as always having been insulated from the outside world and uninterested in evangelism. While this may have possibly been true at some points in our history, the evidence is overwhelming that the Friends movement was founded in a missionary spirit—one that was revived in the nineteenth century and, hopefully, will be energized as Christ-centered Quakerism takes hold of its inheritance as a missional movement.

The Friends movement spread on the efforts of traveling ministers—local ministers who felt the leading to travel to other monthly meetings, yearly meetings, or foreign fields. Traveling ministers traveled under the blessing and affirmation of their home meetings, which granted each a certificate that introduced and legitimized their ministry to the receiving monthly meetings.[549] These ministers, embodying the principle of the equality of all people, did not hesitate to visit world leaders, such as Sultan Mohammed IV, Peter the Great, Pope Pius VII, and others.[550] These traveling ministers preached wherever they could, often in open air settings. Early Friend John Audland recorded, in his journal, an evangelistic preaching endeavor:

> The Word of the Lord came to me, and I was like a drunken man because of the Lord. . . . Such a dreadful voice ran through me as I never felt before, and the terror of the Lord took hold upon many hearts, and the trumpet sounded throughout the city.[551]

This specific missionary journey was quite effective, Charles Marshall noting that "many were effectually convinced, and from darkness to light turned, after which our meetings grew larger and larger."[552] Other missionary endeavors faced great hardship: Katherine Evans and Sarah Cheevers languished in prison for over three years during the Roman Inquisition,[553] while, in England, "Punishments over and above imprisonment were severe . . . [including] whippings, ear croppings, piercing of the tongue with a hot iron, and execution."[554] Not even the executions of Marmaduke Stephenson, William Robinson, William Leddra, Mary Dyer, and others could dampen the missionary zeal of early Friends. There are records of missions throughout England and Europe, with William Crouch writing,

> As it pleased the Great Disposer of all things, according to his own goodwill and pleasure, to order his servants and handmaidens into divers and sundry parts of this nation, so according to his own secret will and counsel, he moved in the hearts of many of his servants to visit foreign nations, as Holland and Germany, and other of those eastern countries, and also the English colonies and plantations abroad.[555]

Though this missionary zeal diminished during the era of Quietism,[556] forms of traveling ministry and evangelism were revived into the early twentieth century, and many faced similarly difficult conditions.[557] However, these missions were also fruitful, with Friends ministries planted throughout the world.[558]

In the twentieth century, the literature emphasized the necessity of evangelism by the local church. Because of the low turnout and spiritual vitality of the local congregations, there was recognition that, before the church could evangelize the unchurched, it must first evangelize its own members who had fallen away, in order to restore a healthy, active, and attractive community of faith.[559] It appears that resistance to strategic evangelistic actions at this time stemmed from an idealized notion of early Friends meetings as being so filled with "evident spiritual power" that no outreach was necessary—people would simply be drawn to the worship and convinced.[560]

This belief was fallacious for two reasons. First, this view, influenced by Quietism, appears to have clouded the view of historic Quakerism, which grew out of intense evangelistic efforts, and not just mere meetings for worship. Second, even if the spiritual power emanating from worship services was sufficient to attract people toward conversion, it was clear that the current makeup of Friends worship was deficient, for no such conversions were occurring. While the recognition of the need for evangelism in the local church is admirable, perhaps a more suitable course of action would have been to revisit the state of worship and discipleship in the local Friends church.

Leadership

The struggle of every organization is to spread beliefs to more people.[561] Vast sums of money are spent on marketing and advertising to cause people to purchase, use, or affiliate with a product, service, or movement. Ironically, despite an entire industry dedicated to the task of marketing and advertising, the act of popularization for something often occurs organically and spontaneously, passing from one person to another. This by-product of a mass-connected world means that passive modes of advertisement, such as billboards and commercials, are not adequate in this new marketplace.[562]

But what does work? Online sharing is an easy way to spread information, and it costs the sharer little or nothing.[563] The trick is to make the digital messages compelling enough that the person receiving them will want to pass them on to their acquaintances. Derek Thompson, writing about what makes something a "hit," notes,

> Every time you pass along a piece of information in a social network—online or offline—its ultimate popularity depends on whether your audience decides to tell other people, *their* audience, about it.[564]

Unfortunately, there is often no way of knowing what will catch society's attention, and attempts to use previously popular messages and memes are often viewed as fake or manipulative.

Word-of-mouth is an extremely powerful but greatly underused method of spreading information.[565] Research has revealed the impact of social media and online word-of-mouth to be vastly exaggerated. Despite the ubiquitous presence of digital connection in contemporary society, only 7 percent of word-of-mouth occurs online.[566] The clear majority occurs in the old-fashioned way, through offline conversation.[567] There are implications for this, especially in a society where people are increasingly insulated from in-person interactions with one another. Organizations that can foster an energized fan base, who feel strongly enough about a product to speak about it to others in an authentic way, will see a much stronger response than through traditional advertising.

If an organization facilitates, as part of its mission, in-person interactions and community, the potential response is even greater.

It is important to realize that, when one interacts with someone new, "What happens *at the moment of contact* defines the relationship."[568] Success during this critical moment depends on both the content and the delivery of the salesperson.[569] Therefore, to maximize this pivotal interaction, as well as all subsequent interactions, it is important to emphasize relationship instead of task.[570] Relating to Judith Glaser's example of sales representatives, this meant a shift from merely selling to a collaborative partnership with the consumer that helps solve the consumer's problem.[571] It is through the leveraging of this problem-solving relationship with the customer that an organization can gain a competitive advantage.[572] Customer service is paramount, regardless the type of business.[573] Leaders who are intentional about improving customer service will, in turn, improve customer satisfaction and, subsequently, customer loyalty.[574]

Worship

The pastor's role in worship is to actualize the conceptual theology of a church's purpose—worshipping its Creator.[575] At its heart, the corporate worship of God is derived from the fellowship of Christians within a community of faith.[576] According to Emil Brunner, "Fellowship is nothing other than the existence with each other whose ground is God's existence with us."[577] The pastor, working with others, often acts as the facilitator and perhaps the leader of the worship service, both practically and *pro forma*.[578] The pastor should seek cooperation among those participating in the worship service, making sure the service is congruent with the message of the sermon and vision of church, as well as ensuring doctrinal cohesion of the various worship elements.[579] At its heart, organizing or leading worship is another form of pastoral service, or pastoral care, though it is often not viewed as such.[580]

Pastoral Paradigm

It is not beneficial to be prescriptively specific regarding elements found in a worship service (besides open worship). The three broad areas explored in this section are corporate worship, silence, and freedom of gifts.

Corporate Worship

Corporate worship, or the consistent gathering of the church for worship, is an important aspect of the life of the believer and the church. This topic will be explored more fully in chapter 10.

The pastor must communicate the importance of corporate worship to believers, as well as help facilitate a worship service that is glorifying to God and meaningful to the participants. Negative memories of being guilted into mandatory church attendance can make this a difficult conversation for some. What will separate this discussion from that type of experience will be a shift from the negative consequences of truancy to the positive benefits of corporate worship on both personal spiritual growth and the health of the community of faith.

The hope and prayer is that, because the pastor is also emphasizing both the importance of community and the mandatory mission of the church, members will themselves recognize and be convinced of the worth of worship, perhaps even resulting in an experience of dynamic, Spirit-filled worship that ignites a hunger for further fellowship and ministry participation. Regardless, a Christ-centered Quaker pastor should seek to convey that one's Christian faith is not a singular endeavor, but one that reaches its fullness when experienced within the Body of Christ.

Above all else, the pastor must facilitate a consistent, corporate gathering for worship, in order that the congregation may, as Steve Kang and Michael Feldman elegantly described it, "remember, rehearse, and respond to what God has done in Jesus Christ and God is doing in this world . . . [and] surrender the patterns of this world that are deeply ingrained . . . and affirm [its] allegiance to God by the power of the Holy Spirit."[581]

Silence

For most of the twentieth century, there has been recognition of the backlash against lifeless silent meetings, to the point where, in some Friends churches, any form of silence is unfamiliar and greeted with suspicion. Unfortunately, this condition has been present literally since the twentieth century began,[582] making any efforts at introducing open worship much more difficult. Compounding the obstacle of unfamiliarity is the difficulty of the discipline. As Robert Barclay noted, "There can be nothing more opposite to the natural will and wisdom of man than this silent waiting upon God."[583] Silence and stillness have never been easy, and the pervasively-connected society of the twenty-first-century makes this discipline all the more difficult. A Christ-centered Quaker pastor must work to reintroduce the concept of silence to corporate worship.

One way to integrate this ethos of early Quaker worship into the worship series is by connecting it with the spiritual and biblical discipline of corporate prayer. The notion of corporate prayer, framed as corporate silence (perhaps with an opening and closing prayer to bracket it) would introduce this vital discipline without alienating those unaccustomed to it. This method also helps introduce the free, participatory vocal worship, which is another unfamiliar practice for most congregations. By framing open worship as silence punctuated by vocal prayers from anyone in the sanctuary (as they are led by God), the pastor takes a wholly unfamiliar practice and makes it decidedly familiar. From this starting place, the pastor and leadership can continue to educate the congregation regarding the theological and biblical foundations of open worship, and begin leading to longer, freer sections of open worship in the service. The goal is not to replace all the elements of the service with open worship, but to provide the necessary space for the congregation to slow down, center, and listen to what the Holy Spirit has to say.

Freedom of Gifts

It is worth noting that even though the pastor should encourage the faithful use of people's gifts during worship, as well as their obedience to the call to speak, one should not have as a goal the sharing by every person in the congregation.[584] Not everyone has the gift of vocal ministry in equal measure, and the driving force should be obedience to God's leading, rather than any democratic notion of full participation.[585] Additionally, it is not fair to assume that vocal ministry is the height of spiritual gifting. Instead, a Christ-centered pastor must be humble, flexible, and open-minded enough to recognize the place of all forms of gifting within the church generally and the worship service in particular. There may be gifts that have never been expressed in a church's worship service before (e.g., dance, art, poetry, etc.). However, this does not mean they do not have a place, but merely that they were either ignored or suppressed in the past. While discernment is always necessary, it is probable that increased and diverse participation within your congregation will benefit and strengthen the worship and fellowship of the church.

Bible and Theology

Corporate Worship

Though under-emphasized in American Christianity, it must be understood that "the worshipping life of the Christian, whilst profoundly personal, is essentially that of a person who is also a member of a group."[586] The biblical record, along with the writings of the church fathers, articulates a paradigm in which spirituality and ecclesiology are intertwined. One's participation in the Kingdom of God and a life of following Christ is seen within the context of a community of faith. For example, one can extrapolate from Paul's command, in 1 Corinthians 5, for the incestuous member of the church to be cast out and handed "over to Satan," that participation in the corporate worship and fellowship of the church was of the highest spiritual value.[587]

But what was the structure of this worship? The regular meeting together of the church for worship centered around three main elements: prayer, ministry of the Word, and Eucharist.[588] The ministry of the Word (preaching) is covered extensively above but it is relevant here to say that the teaching and preaching of scripture was one of the focal points of early Christian worship.[589] Eucharist, though of highest importance in Christian worship for all of church history, will also not be explored, because of Friends' unique understanding of Eucharistic communion, a spiritual communion with God that can occur at all times.

Music also appears often in the New Testament in relation to worship (Ephesians 5:18–20; Colossians 3:16; 1 Corinthians 14:15),[590] and its continued presence in Christian worship throughout history evidences the assertion that "so natural is the association of music and worship, that it hardly occurs to anyone to ask why it exists."[591] However, as with a physical Eucharist, music in the early church will not be fleshed out here. This is not only because of early Quakers' disavowal of worship through music, but also because of the lack of specificity in the biblical record. These, along with the wide spectrum of biblical worship prescribed by denominations today, make an exploration of this topic here unhelpful.

However, even though the early Friends movement radically departed from the familiar forms that make up worship, there is still a worship act that unifies Quakers with the rest of historical Christendom and the contemporary Quaker church. Underlying these elements was prayer, which in Acts appears almost any time the faithful gathered. This should not be surprising, for, according to Franklin Segler and Randall Bradley, "Prayer is the soul of worship; in fact, the terms *prayer* and *worship* are often used interchangeably since worship and prayer are communion with God."[592] Corporate, public prayer was seen in Acts, where the followers of Jesus assembled daily for this purpose.[593] Later in Acts, the church gathered for corporate prayer in response to the imprisonment of Peter (Acts 12:12), as well as other instances of persecution or key moments for the church.[594] Whether the miraculous release of Peter was on account of this intercession, the point was that those who were closest to Jesus responded to difficult situations through gathered prayer.[595] Additionally, the gathered fellowship spurred on the faithful to the spiritual disciplines of prayer, as seen in the Didache, where they are called to pray the Lord's Prayer three times daily.[596] Regardless of the presence or absence of music, Quaker and early Christian worship shared the same foundation and purpose.

Silence

In most churches, sermons, prayers, and scripture form the backbone of liturgy.[597] In contrast, silence is rarely an element promoted or practiced as part of liturgy. To be fair, silence, as a specific element of worship, is not found in the biblical record. While there are mentions of times for and the value of silence in a person's life (Ecclesiastes 3:7; Proverbs 17:28), the Hebrew and early Christian culture, with their expectation of vocalized prayer, did not have much use for silence.

However, this does not mean that the Quaker emphasis on silence is antithetical to the biblical record of worship. Boris Paschke has shown that, while prayers in the New Testament were typically directed at God, there are no instances of praying to the Holy Spirit found in the New Testament.[598] But there are several instances where the Holy Spirit illumines, empowers, and leads people (Acts 1:2; 4:8; 9:31; 10:44; 13:3; 16:16). However, it is usually during times such as waiting, fasting, and worship, that the Holy Spirit alights upon the believers (e.g., the Acts 13:1–3 call of Paul and Barnabas by the Holy Spirit being revealed during worship and fasting). As confirmed by Jesus in John 3, the Holy Spirit is not at humanity's beck and call, but illumines and inspires in such a way that obedience requires a listening and humble spirit. One can argue that open worship, facilitated through silence, is the ultimate form of that humility. The silencing of one's mouth is almost symbolic of the silencing of one's desires, both done in order to better hear what God may say. In this way, the aims of open worship correspond to the aims of the early church—a humble expectancy of leading and inspiration from the Holy Spirit.

Freedom of Gifts

The typical order of worship found in many Protestant worship services is not found in any biblical text.[599] Regardless of how informal the service at one's church may be, it would not compare to the freedom of early church worship. The biblical and historical sources point to an early church liturgy that, while following a liturgical structure, also allowed for flexibility and extemporaneous expression, such as the songs and prayers.[600] Frank Viola and George Barna provide an excellent description of New Testament worship services: "The meetings of the early church were marked by every-member functioning, spontaneity, freedom, vibrancy, and open participation."[601]

Those in favor of a more structured worship and polity make a claim that New Testament ecclesiology is not prescriptive, but merely an outcome of extraordinary circumstances, only held together by a superabundance of the Holy Spirit's blessing.[602] However, there is nothing in the biblical record that supports a cessation of the Holy Spirit's activity or leading, especially when one believes in the indwelling of the Holy Spirit at salvation and the free expression of gifts as led by the Holy Spirit. Scripture calls believers and the church to not "quench the Holy Spirit" (1 Thessalonians 5:19). If one believes that the Holy Spirit has provided gifts to believers, to be used within the Body of Christ, then one can assume that at least some of these gifts were meant for use during worship. By unnecessarily restricting the liturgy and limiting what is considered acceptable, a church can essentially quench the Spirit's action within a congregation.

Lest anyone think that liturgical anarchy is the answer to perceived restrictions, it is important to review 1 Corinthians 14:26–33, in which Paul confronts issues of free expression, restriction, and decorum in worship. Because this was a letter, the modern reader does not have an exhaustive explanation as to the liturgical difficulties the Corinthian church was facing. However, Paul addresses some key themes. What is most relevant is the balance Paul strikes between the polyparticipatory charismatic freedom and the necessary order for edifying worship.[603]

Therefore, it can be reasonably claimed that early Friends worship was closer to the New Testament example than other contemporary worship forms. As such, Christ-centered Quaker worship, based on the ideals of historic Friends, would be similarly aligned with the early church.

Historic Friends

Corporate Worship

Marjorie Glines Brown correctly asserted that "the experience of worship lies at the heart of Quakerdom."[604] However, this experiential worship is not supposed to be a singular affair, for, according to Michael Birkel, "Quakerism has always placed a high value on group experience in the spiritual life."[605] The individualistic, experiential religion of early Quakers never overcame the necessity for corporate worship. George Fox and other Quaker leaders regularly gathered people together, often wherever was convenient,[606] in order to preach, teach, worship, and conduct business. Early in the movement, the elders at Balby exhorted,

> That the particular meetings by all the children of Light, be duly kept and observed, where they be already settled, every first-day of the week; except they be moved to other places. And that general meetings be kept in order and sweet in the life of God, on some other day of the week than on the First-day, unless there be a moving to the contrary: that so in the light and life, the meetings may be kept, to the praise of God.[607]

The ministers and elders of each meeting sought to communicate and set by example the importance of attending worship. However, Geoffrey Plank identified the tension in this endeavor, for "Quaker ministers sought to uphold their responsibilities and instill a sense of obligation in others without conveying that attendance was routine."[608] Regardless of intent, the social pressure of early Quaker communities made weekly attendance virtually mandatory, though freedom of silent worship helped mitigate any perception of repetitiveness.

Even though communal worship was a key factor in early Quakerism, this passion for community appeared to decline over the centuries. According to statistics from the Five Years Meeting (forerunner to Friends United Meeting), in 1945, over two-thirds of the membership were not regularly attending worship services.[609] In contemporary Friends churches, it is safe to claim that the levels of desire for corporate worship mirrors that of other Protestant services. This means that Christ-centered Quaker churches will have to alter the current ecclesiological trajectory in order to regain this important aspect of Christian life.

Silence

The importance of silent worship within the early Quaker movement was based on a theological and experiential presupposition that "communication with the divine occurs in communal silence."[610] While Friends have been caricatured as abandoning all forms of structure or formality in their worship, the truth is that even traditional silent worship requires some semblance of formality. However, the key is that one does not enter into worship with a spirit of formality and distance, but naturally, as one experiences relationship with family.[611] While the silence was understood as preparatory for vocal ministry, even when no word was spoken aloud, the silence could also be understood as a form of personal and corporate prayer. Early Quakers understood prayer also occurred outside the formal spoken variety, with Isaac Penington describing true prayer as "the breathing of the child to the Father which begat it, from the true sense of its needs, for the supply of those needs."[612] When early Friends gathered in silence, they were united in worship and prayer, seeking to individually and corporately receive the truths of God.

Freedom of Gifts

As mentioned earlier, the emphasis on the personalized nature of the Quaker expression of Christianity has muddied the waters regarding the tension between structure and freedom within Quaker worship. The initial reaction by some Friends is to reject any form of order or structure as anathema to Quakerism, while others marginalize the freedom and openness present in historic Friends meetings, making contemporary programmed Quaker worship nearly indistinguishable from other evangelical worship services.

Even though the pastoral system is well-established in American Quakerism, that does not mean it is automatically superior to pastor-less unprogrammed worship. Such a dichotomy is unnecessary, for "it is clear that the issue is not whether worship can only occur in a programmed meeting under the direction of the pastor or in an unprogrammed meeting, for both can be held under the inspiration of the Holy Spirit."[613] Regardless of the structure of the worship (either programmed or unprogrammed), it would be beneficial to heed the early Quaker John Banks's exhortation:

> In all your meetings together to do service for the Lord, his truth, and people, and to see that good order be kept in the churches of Christ, wait diligently to be endowed with power and wisdom

from above, which is pure, and peaceable; that by the same you may be guided to judge of and determine all that you have committed to your trust and charge, whether in things spiritual or temporal.[614]

Leadership

Creating an organizational leadership treatment of worship is exceptionally difficult, because it has no direct counterpoint in leadership studies. While teambuilding and other related ventures could be substituted, nothing exists that would do justice to the holistic concept of worship. However, as changes do occur in the culture and praxis of their churches, pastors will need to have wisdom and discernment, as well as an understanding of organizational dynamics.

This makes one aspect of organizational leadership relevant to Christ-centered Quaker pastors, regarding the introduction of new elements: organizational change. A pastor seeking to introduce new elements into the worship service, and thus reshape, however subtly, the ethos and practice of worship, is like any leader attempting to implement change into an organization. Like the business leader, the pastor will have obstacles, resistance, and setbacks, partly because of a psychological phenomenon known as "the exposure effect," by which people prefer things (shapes, landscapes, songs, voices, etc.) to which they have the most exposure.[615] New elements are often unconsciously resisted, regardless of their validity, for the simple fact that they are new. One way to mitigate this and other obstacles is by transitioning slowly—paradoxically, familiarity can be key to innovation.[616] Using the example of music, Derek Thompson noted that, to expose listeners to new music effectively, there must be familiar songs interspersed among the new.[617] This familiarity helps ease the listener into new music, whereas entirely new playlists often fail to engage a response.[618] In the same way, drastic changes in worship, unless absolutely necessary, should not be implemented by the pastor or leadership team. Rather, well-paced, incremental changes should be instituted, allowing for acclimation and acculturation.

Doctrinal Purity

Christian doctrine is understood as the collected and accepted beliefs of the Christian faith,[619] useful for teaching new converts, guiding members and congregations, and defending against false teachings and beliefs.[620] Denominational doctrine refers to the specific beliefs of the denomination that separate it from other Christian movements, as well as theological and practical guidelines for members of the denomination. Both Christian and denominational doctrines play a role in shaping the ecclesiology and pastoral theology of both church and denomination.

The pastor's duty is to teach and preach the convictions of the specific denomination in which the pastor serves, the broader convictions of the religious movement in which the pastor belongs, and the orthodox truths foundational to Christianity.[621] This maintenance of doctrinal consistency, in theory, will benefit the congregation as both believers and members of a specific religious movement,[622] even in the face of challenges from within the congregation or from without.[623]

Pastoral Paradigm

The education, training, and expectation of personal study of the pastor (both in sermon preparation and general continuing education) should not be understood as prerequisites for positional authority, but as tools to sharpen the pastor's faith and understanding and to use in equipping the saints. The pastor, as both facilitator of gospel proclamation and the shepherd of the congregation, should seek the well-being of others, which includes their proper understanding of God and of grace. In this aspect of ministry, the pastor may feel tempted to view themselves as the sole arbiter of biblical truth. Also, even the most well-intentioned pastor and congregation may allow a subtle drift to occur, in which, over time, the pastor may unknowingly be held up as the premier scriptural authority. This trajectory must be resisted; the pastor must recognize themselves as a servant.

Because of the transcendent culture of universal ministry, there is an expectation that all members of the congregation will exercise their gifts in order to positively impact the Kingdom (see "Equipping the Saints"). Thus, the need for doctrinal clarity is greater than in other denominations. In a church or denomination in which the ecclesiological expectations are an authoritarian clergy and a passive laity, laity are not expected to serve outside the church in any meaningful way and the need for doctrinal clarity is diminished. As long as the congregation remains under the control of the clergy, then they can be guided toward the truth.

In Christ-centered Quakerism, however, the opposite danger exists. Because each person is expected to express their gifts (and identity as a minister) both in and out of the church, and because these gifts are considered equal in the

Body of Christ, the consequences of inconsistent theology are enormous. These consequences are magnified further when one considers the decision-making polity of Friends, by which a minority of members can thwart or stall church business. An empowered and enfranchised congregation must be educated and informed, so as to rightly discern God's leading. While there are many paths, programs, and processes for teaching doctrine, the pastor should be chief promoter of these efforts, whatever they may be.

Bible and Theology

There are theological truths, inherent in Christianity, that transcend any theological or ecclesiological nuance that separates the various denominations. Historically, these core truths have been used to discern which beliefs or understandings about God are considered "orthodox."

These orthodox beliefs of the church must be an expression of the Trinitarian understanding and experience of God.[624] Any church that marginalizes or denigrates the divinity or authority of Christ loses the very truth that validates its existence as a church, for "there would be no Church without Jesus."[625] This emphasis on orthodoxy stretches back to the early church, which was forced to articulate its theology and doctrines in the face of widespread growth, persecution, and heresy. While different religions, philosophical schools, and mystery cults vied for adherents in ancient Rome, the overall atmosphere was one of open-minded tolerance—there was plenty of room for everyone's belief, as long as it was subsumed under obedient patriotism. Christianity, however, did not work well within this context. According to Ramsay MacMullen, "Christianity . . . presented ideas that demanded a choice, not tolerance."[626] This was not an intolerance based on uncaring arrogance, as many have seen in the church throughout history, but one of survival.

Historic Friends

Despite some histories that seek to portray the ethos of Quakerism as one distinct from Christianity,[627] the evidence is overwhelming that the early Friends movement was firmly orthodox in its belief and grounded in scripture. William Penn provides an articulate exposition of the theological foundation of Friends:

> Which doctrine of repentance leads to justification; that is, forgiveness of the sins that are past, through Christ the alone propitiation, and the sanctification or purgation, of the soul from the defiling nature and habits of sin present, by the Spirit of Christ in the soul; which is justification in the complete sense of that word: comprehending both justification from the guilt of the sins that are past, as if they had never been committed, through the love and mercy of God in Christ Jesus; and the creature's being made inwardly just, through the cleansing and sanctifying power and Spirit of Christ revealed in the soul; which is commonly called sanctification. But none can come to know Christ to be their sacrifice, that reject him as their sanctifier: the end of his coming being to save his people from the nature and defilement, as well as the guilt of sin.[628]

Or more concisely from Penn regarding orthodox Christian doctrine, "It is the only door to true Christianity, and the path which the ancients ever trod to blessedness."[629] This sentiment has been validated by other works that emphasize the place of Quakerism within the orthodox Christian stream, such as Robert Barclay's *Apology* and George Fox's "Letter to the Governor of Barbados."[630] These Christian roots, however, have been dislodged in the perceptions of many through a marginalization of this Christian history, as well as by the presence of post-Christian Quakers in academic and popular literature and media.[631]

Even within orthodoxy, however, the emphasis, by Friends, on the Holy Spirit has seemed to some to communicate a marginalization of the Bible, but this is not the case. The Quakers' emphasis on the illuminating, informing, and leading of the Holy Spirit, meant to be a course correction for Western Christianity, has been misinterpreted as a denigration of the validity and authority of scripture. There is overwhelming evidence that early Quakerism was founded on and informed by the Bible, illumined by the Holy Spirit. As explained by Edward Grubb,

> Friends never thought of questioning the inspiration and authority of the Bible, the Divinity of Christ, His Incarnation, or the reality of His Atonement as the means of reconciling man to God.[632]

The prime example of articulated orthodoxy is found in George Fox's "Letter to the Governor of Barbados," where Fox outlines how Quakerism resides safely within the avenue of orthodoxy, as well as affirming the authority of scripture.

Some have argued that early Friends viewed the Bible's authority as having internal authority (the personal effect on the believer) rather than any external authority (authority granted to it by being inspired by God).[633] Not only is this argument tenuous (disconnecting Penn from the rest of early Quakerism), but it is also unnecessary. Clearly the words and message of scripture had a transformative effect on the lives, ministry, and writings of early Quakers. Robert Barclay and Isaac Penington both created catechisms to instruct others in the Quaker faith; Barclay's catechism utilized only scripture as authoritative evidence for the justification of Quaker principles.[634]

In addition to a proper understanding of scripture, early Quakers had to eventually address the seemingly inevitable conflict between personal leadings or revelations and the authority of scripture, as well as the authority of the monthly, quarterly, and yearly meetings. Nowhere is this more clearly seen than in preaching during the meetings for worship, by which the individual leadings and proclamations may conflict with the testimony of scripture, and thus lead to heterodox beliefs within the congregation. An example of this is found in the Balby Elders' epistle, in which they offer guidelines of how to respond to preaching that transgresses orthodox boundaries:

> Let the person or persons in whom the seed of God is burthened, speak in the light (as of the Lord they are moved,) in meekness and godly fear, to him; but let it be done in private, betwixt them two, or before two or three witnesses, and not in the public meetings, except there be a special moving so to do.[635]

However, the ministers themselves engaged in maintaining doctrinal consistency, especially in the Second Day Morning Meeting (also known as Second Morning Meeting, or Morning Meeting), which first formed in London in 1670. The main purpose of this meeting was to monitor and control local and traveling ministry, as well as maintain the doctrine and practice of the movement, by which the "writings of adversaries and apostates were sought out and answered."[636] Specifically, the tracts and writings produced by members of the movement were reviewed and were approved, had revisions recommended, were rejected, or in the rarest of occasions, were banned.[637] George Fox, who himself had a paper held up for questioning by the Second Morning Meeting,[638] articulates the underlying philosophy guiding these ministers who proclaimed and protected the truths of God:

> For it hath been the work of all the false teachers and ministers to drive away from God, and his truth, and his light, and those have been the devil's servants, and the wages he gives them is death. [However,] this hath been the way of all true ministers, 'to seek that which was lost, and that which was driven away;' as you may see Christ and the apostles, and all the true prophets did.[639]

While it is true that not all Quakers accepted the authority of Second Morning Meeting,[640] it does provide as an example of efforts to maintain the doctrinal consistency of the early Friends movement.

One major event in Quakerism's history that dealt directly with doctrinal consistency is the Hicksite separation of 1828. Elias Hicks, a country Quaker, began having an unsettledness toward new elements such as camp meetings being brought into the Friends Church.[641] This unsettledness crystallized into a doctrinal framework that stressed the "overriding importance of behaviour over belief,"[642] and included heterodox views, including a disbelief in the divinity of Christ, no necessity of atonement, and a diminished authority of scripture.[643] In response to Hicks and his followers, the rival group, known as the Orthodox, became vociferous in their theological claims: a "vision of Christ and the authority of Scripture that echoed those of other Protestants."[644] The Hicksites and the Orthodox split soon after. While some have claimed (not without merit) that this was merely a socio-economic split in American Quakerism,[645] this motive should be understood as secondary to the issue of doctrinal differences that separated the Hicksites and the Orthodox Friends.

This concern for an orthodox theological foundation continued into the twentieth century, when ministry leaders, concerned about the lessening emphasis on evangelical beliefs, met at Cheyenne, Wyoming, in 1927 to discuss a potential response.[646] Out of these discussions emerged the Association of Evangelical Friends, which sought to organize around the protection of the Christian tenets of the Friends movement.[647] While the potential issues regarding this realignment were addressed in an earlier chapter, the intention behind it (the maintenance of orthodox theology) are in line with the actions of the early Friends movement.

Leadership

For an organization to succeed in its mission, it must always maintain its core values. Lest anyone think that ossification and parochialism are the antidote to this constantly-shifting world, it must be pointed out that successful organizations adapt to their surroundings to survive. Thus, paradoxically, the key to lasting success for any organization is the ability to preserve core values while at the same time adapting to changing circumstances.[648] Looking at the Friends movement, one should see that orthodox Christianity is a core value, while the expression of those values (in worship, service, etc.) should remain flexible and adaptable. It was when these Christian core values were threatened or marginalized that the very soul of the movement was also threatened. This can also occur at the level of the local church.

No matter how strong the emphasis on core values and mission, an organization's culture will suffer if those values are not lived out in the daily routine of the organization and its members.[649] If members fail to buy into the culture of an organization, their actions and attitudes may threaten or undermine the organization's mission. In order to prevent these threats to the culture and mission of an organization, the leadership must respond quickly to deviations from the established culture and communicate which actions or attitudes are considered transgressive.[650] According to business experts Robert Sutton and Huggy Roa, "Supervisors of the most productive units . . . confronted problems more directly and quickly, issued more verbal and written warnings, used formal punishments more often, and promptly fired employees when warnings failed."[651]

The church, unlike other organizations, must live in the tension of being a community that welcomes and forgives, while at the same time holding its members and leaders accountable. For the most part, responses to issues of doctrinal consistency, when linked to the correction of clergy or members, strike many as dictatorial or heavy-handed. However, this should be leavened by the understanding of the place doctrine holds in the context of the work and worship of the church and the continuation of the church's mission.

Chapter Nine
Lead

Philosophically and theologically, the notion of pastoral leadership is rooted in the example of Christ as both servant and shepherd.[652] In fact, Kenneth Gangel described pastoral leadership as pastors exercising "leadership as servants and stewards, sharing authority with their followers and affirming that leadership is primarily ministry *to* others, modeling *for* others, and mutual membership *with* others in Christ's body."[653]

However, in addition to the understanding of the pastoral leaders as humble servants, there is also an implicit and explicit agreement that the congregation will follow the leadership of the pastor.[654] This submission, whether functional (as an expedient to achieve the church's goals) or ontological (where the pastor is more spiritual or holy than a layperson), has the potential to create an artificial divide between the clergy and the laity, especially if leadership is unethical.[655] However, any praxis of pastoral leadership is predicated on the assumption that the congregation will follow the pastor's vision.[656] Within this delicate relationship, any ambiguity or lack of communication can create a ripple effect in the authority and leadership of the pastor, which may have a negative effect on the church overall.

Organizational leadership, in ministry context, involves the pastor in a cooperative context with the other leadership elements of the church, including, but not limited to, elders, church boards, deacon boards, and other committees that provide vision and leadership for the church.[657] Once those aims have been clarified and codified, leadership also involves effective communication of ministry goals to the congregation and other church leaders.[658] This vision-casting and communication must be linked with effective recruitment and volunteer organization in order to accomplish organizational goals.[659]

However, unlike traditional organizational leadership, pastoral leadership is imbued with a divine calling, mission, and purpose. It recognizes the need for effective organizational leadership to achieve the aims to which God has called the church, while humbly acknowledging that it is God who brings the harvest.[660] Pastoral leadership is "waiting and watching, attending to what God is doing and helping others to also attend to what God is doing."[661]

Vision and Innovation

This section, along with the following two ("Church Mission" and "Strategy"), will include some extra clarification, for not only are they linked practically, but also because vision, mission, and strategy are often undifferentiated as topics, and thus used interchangeably to describe the same thing. This inaccuracy may deprive pastors and churches of opportunities for creativity and obedience to God as they seek to live and act as the body of Christ on earth.

Here, casting a vision for a church is understood as a process involving creativity and revelation. This is the process by which pastors prayerfully seek out the Lord's leading regarding the direction of the church. This is also a time to dream big, to receive or create a vision of what could be—an audacious goal that may seem impossible to achieve. This is a time of freedom, to break the shackles of what has always been done in order to unleash the creative possibilities for the community of faith. It is a time to be inspired.

The goal of visioning should be the transformation of the church through a closer encounter with God and transformation of the world through its encounter with God through the church. This transformative encounter should be understood as not just tweaking member and church practices, but is "something more like death and resurrection" of the way things are done. A transformative vision of the church may be as simple as "taking Scripture, worship, prayer, theology, and church itself more seriously."[662]

Pastoral Paradigm

The pastor is released to not only engage in ministry activity, but to also engage in ministry contemplation. This contemplation is facilitated through prayer, the worshipful study of scripture, and reflective thought on the truths of God and the context/needs of the church and community. It is through this intentional contemplation and reflection that the pastor can both conceive of and receive a vision of God's plan for the church. These ideas can then be brought forward to the leadership teams, committees, and congregations for communal discernment and reaction.

In order to provide the clearest revelatory conduit between the pastor and God, they must seek after holistic health. Spiritually, the pastor must be grounded in God's truth and rooted in a personal relationship and sacramental life with Christ. This spiritual depth mitigates the temptation of worldly ambition, which may drive visions of numeral, financial, and architectural success. These successes, though often shrouded in sanctifying rationalizations, may in fact be antithetical to the plans and will of God.

Physical and emotional health are also key to proper vision-casting. The physical and emotional demands of ministry are great and can take a toll on a pastor's health and effectiveness unless active measures for self-care are taken. A pastor's capacity to see the grand plans of God and the possibilities present for the church is greatly diminished by fatigue and discouragement.

The emphasis on the creative process of the pastor should not mislead the reader; vision-casting is not a single-player activity. Vision is not only the responsibility of the pastor, but also of the entire congregation. The pastor has been released to prayerfully consider the strategic possibilities of the church; they do so in service of the church, as it serves the Lord. However, this position to start or enact this creative process does not grant the pastor authority to unilaterally cast the vision, mission, and direction of the church. A mistake that pastors can make is not allowing members of the congregation or pastoral staff to share other creative ideas or perspectives. Rather, the pastor presents ideas and possibilities to the church and facilitates the generative process of gathering congregational ideas and vision. During this process, pastors should be careful not to be biased toward their own ideas, nor become defensive at honest resistance to their ideas. What matters is that a God-inspired vision for the future of the ministry is conceptualized, not from whom this vision emerged.

Bible and Theology

The three biblical events in Acts that correspond to this leadership framework are the Ascension (mission), Pentecost (vision), and the Choosing of the Seven (strategy). It is apparent that Pentecost occurred after the Ascension, thus potentially distorting the framework presented, as we begin with vision. However, it will be argued that these three events follow the same trajectory, if not the chronology. Reversing the order does injustice neither to the framework nor to the biblical text and may actually improve understanding of the ecclesiological development of the early church.

When Jesus presents the call to be "witnesses . . . to the ends of the earth" (Acts 1:8), it would not be a stretch to assume the disciples were either befuddled or overwhelmed by this commission (an idea that will be explored further in "Church Mission"). The disciples were drawn largely from the lower ranks of society, with the exception of some wealthy, cosmopolitan members (mostly women) who appeared to financially support the incipient movement (Luke 8:1–3). At this stage, the idea of traversing the known world, spreading the good news of a risen Messiah, would have been quite a paradigm shift. This is seen from the disciples' dogged adherence to the old narrative of messianic expectations: "Lord, are you at this time going to restore the kingdom to Israel?" (Acts 1:6). At this point, while the commission may have been given (Matthew 28:16–20), the followers of Christ may not have been able to see how or when that mission would be carried out.

All of that changed at Pentecost. The Holy Spirit fell, and at once the followers of Jesus saw the vision of the Kingdom of God, a kingdom expanding not through violence, destruction, and worldly might, but through peace, re-creation, and the redemptive power of Christ. What they saw was a glimpse of a future eschatological reality—a reversal of Babel[663] and the gathering of "every tribe, tongue, and nation" (Revelation 7:9). They would have known of this reality from the prophets (Isaiah 2:2) as well as from Joel, whom Peter references in his sermon. The presence of glossolalia provided a vision of boundaries overcome by the power of God, and signaled a spiritual revival so effervescent that words of praise flowed out of them in words that they themselves did not understand. The vision cast before the church was one of a boundary-less community of faith, gathered from all over the world to praise God for the victory of Christ.

This vision, supplemented by others (as in Acts 10, when Peter is called to remove further boundaries to church fellowship), allowed the early church and its leadership to see the possibilities present in their obedience to the risen Messiah. And it is here that the Great Commission/Ascension Commission were truly understood by the followers of Jesus. The leaders now had a vision of what could be, and empowered by the Holy Spirit, could begin implementing the *missio Dei*.

Historic Friends

One famous event in the history of George Fox and Quakerism is the ascent of Pendle Hill; it also serves as an excellent example of a ministry leader's vision. In Fox's case, it could also be called an actual vision, an opening or revelation from God. Because of its brevity, and the textual and editorial differences between the editions of his journal, two versions of his account will be quoted in their entirety:[664]

> And so we passed on warning people as we met them of the day of the Lord that was coming upon them and as we went I spied a great high hill called Pendle Hill and I went on the top of it with much ado it was so steep: but I was moved of the Lord to go atop of it; and when I came atop of it I saw Lancashire sea: and there atop of the hill I was moved to sound the day of the Lord and the Lord let me see atop of the hill in what places he had a great people.[665]

> As we travelled we came near a very great hill, called Pendle Hill, and I was moved of the Lord to go up to the top of it; which I did with difficulty, it was so very steep and high. When I was come to the top, I saw the sea bordering upon Lancashire. From the top of this hill the Lord let me see in what places he had a great people to be gathered.[666]

The divine leading of this action should be taken at face value, for it was no small task to ascend the hill—it was not a place frequented by people for pleasure, and took away from Fox's pressing mission of ministering to the surrounding communities.[667] It was at the top of the hill that Fox received his vision of possibility. The "great people to be gathered" were the people waiting to hear the message of Christ through Fox, and Fox himself received a "wholly new conception of his work in the world."[668] As for "sounding" the day of the Lord, the majority opinion is that this is a prophetic enactment of Joel 2:1–2.[669]

John Punshon offers a potential alternative: "The usage may be that of sounding the depths—as at sea—as if Fox was working out the implications, or estimating the significance of his calling."[670] Regardless, these reactions point to a sense of divine imperative on his current and future work.

While it is impossible to know the personal effect this ascent had on Fox (for his journal provides only a narrative description without reflection), some have written about the profound practical effect of this vision. Elvira Vipont wrote that Fox appeared to react to this mountaintop experience as if "he had suddenly received a new sense of direction in his wandering life."[671] Elton Trueblood went even further when he wrote, "From that day forward, Fox was both resolute and successful."[672] It can be cautiously stated that this broad vision of possibilities did not appear to hinder his missionary journey, but perhaps even spurred it on. It should also be noted that this vision was not a tactical map, but an eye-opening glimpse into what God had in store for him, and, as such, stands as a prime example of the power and purpose of vision.

Leadership

A leader must be visionary. While that statement may seem overblown, the reality is that effective leaders "are the thinkers and the doers who envision what a better future looks like and take actions that lead themselves—and others—toward it."[673] For a leader, having vision involves sensing opportunities and threats in the environment, setting strategic direction, and inspiring others to look beyond current practice.[674] It is this capacity that separates leaders from managers;

according to Herminia Ibarra, "A leader without vision is merely an excellent manager."[675]

Among the problems that make people hesitant to label themselves "creative" or to engage in creative endeavors is that there is a poor understanding of the term "creativity."[676] According to Jonah Berger, "*Creativity* is a catchall term for a variety of distinctive thought processes."[677] Rather than being merely a divine gift or inherent skill, it should be understood as a process that can be developed and experienced by all. Todd Henry, an expert on creativity, writes that "anyone can improve his ability to generate good ideas consistently if willing to be a little more purposeful in how to approach the creative process."[678] A focused effort on creative vision is important, for when issues arise, there are far more plentiful options than one realizes.[679] The trick is to recognize those options.

Proper facilitation of vision and creativity involves leaders keeping non-judgmental and discerning communication open between themselves and others and allowing various inputs to inform the discussion.[680] Coupled with this willingness to hear alternative perspectives should be the leader's personal humility. A leader should also avoid having their vision be disregarded by an organization that does not or cannot understand it. A leader should have the courage to stand up for their vision.

There are times when a leader can't wait for a mountaintop experience of insight. When a crisis hits an organization—one that requires a major organizational shift to survive—the leadership team must summon creativity and innovation in a short amount of time. This situation is not entirely antithetical to innovative thinking, for as Shane

Snow astutely observed, "Creativity comes easier within constraints."[681] Tougher situations require creative solutions, and organizations that successfully solve difficult problems will often do so through a radically innovative solution out of necessity.[682] While leaders should not simply wait until a crisis to think creatively about their organization, they can know that when a crisis does hit, they can respond with creative and innovative solutions.

There is no single right way to facilitate organizational creativity; the literature points to neither a backburner nor a persistent focus approach to creativity.[683] One example that has been successfully utilized by organizations could be called "free time." Corporations such as Google and 3M have created cultures in which a portion of an employee's time is free for them to explore concepts and side projects (usually called 20 percent time or 15 percent time).[684] Counterintuitively, this free time has benefited both companies in significant ways, such as in the creation of such products as Post-It Notes and Gmail.[685] A leader committed to creativity and innovation will not micro-manage others' time, but create an atmosphere in which workers are given the space and time to think deeply about their organization, its future, and their role in making that future a reality.

Church Mission

If the vision of a church is the glimpse of possibility, the mission of a church is the conceptual clarity needed to undertake steps toward fulfilling that vision. To understand the term "mission" best, one should move away from the Christian definition of the word and into the world of business. The mission of the church should not be understood as merely the missionary activities of the church, but instead as the thing that drives the purpose and existence of the church, much like the mission of a business or organization. It is important to realize that the "mission is less what the church does than who God is."[686] A pastor should seek to instill an understanding of the nature of God, so out of that understanding can flow an obedience and purpose as the church seeks to serve those who are marginalized in society. As Stewart Newman notes, "What the church is and what its nature obligates it to do give meaning and value to the service to be engaged upon by its members."[687]

The most common way a church articulates its mission is through a mission statement which "defines the purpose of an individual, group, business, or institution."[688] Related to the vision of the church and pastor, the mission statement "puts the feet to that vision and sense of purpose."[689] A church mission statement should seek to articulate not just the end results of the activities it engages with, but also methods used in those activities (i.e., not just what the church will accomplish, but how it will do it).[690]

Too often, however, churches have mission statements that are either unknown to many in the congregation, or bear little to no resemblance to the actual activities and direction of the church.[691] Thus, it is a good idea to revisit the mission statement, seeking to discern whether the church needs to adapt to fit the current statement, or create a better one. The mission statement should integrate the vision of the church, the gifts and talents of the congregation, and internal and external goals of the church.[692]

A mission statement is valuable for several reasons. First, it is a continuation of the vision-mission-strategy paradigm that helps pastors engage, reengage, or redirect church activities. Second, the mission statement can act as a benchmark and filter for church ministries and activities. If a ministry or activity does not fit within the mission of the church, it may have to be phased out, so that resources and efforts can be utilized for the greatest effect. Third, it is an aspirational statement that should inspire the efforts of the congregation, who see their passions and calling within the mission of the church.[693] Fourth, a mission statement, if communicated well, can even be an evangelical tool, inviting people who feel called or drawn to the community and mission of the church. In all these ways, the mission of the church pushes and guides the church toward becoming a witness of Christ in everything it does.

Pastoral Paradigm

It is not enough for the pastor to simply dream big about their ministry. After a time of visioning by the pastor and the congregation, there must be a process of encapsulating that vision through the conceptualization and articulation of a mission statement. For many pastors, a mission statement may already be in use by the church. In this case, the pastor and leadership must engage in self-analysis to see if the church's activities and intentions line up with the mission statement, and whether it's used during decision-making processes. There are six possible results:

1. The activities of the church align with the mission statement, and no changes need to be made.

2. The activities of the church align with the mission statement, but the statement should be changed to push the church into greater ministry.

3. The activities of the church align with the mission statement, but the mission statement is inadequate and must be changed in order to improve church ministry.

4. The activities of the church do not align with the mission statement, but the mission statement is strong, so the church must change to align with the mission statement.

5. The activities of the church do not align with the mission statement, and the mission statement is acceptable, but both the mission statement and the ministries of the church would benefit from revision.

6. The activities of the church do not align with the mission statement, and the mission statement is weak, so the mission statement must be changed (which may lead to a revision of church activities).

Because this mission will drive the actions and intentions of current and future church ministries, it is imperative that there is buy-in from church members (a concept that will be explored further in "Communication and Collaboration"). This personal investment in the church's mission will keep it at the forefront of church activities, as well as help prevent deviation from it. Once the congregation owns this mission, the leadership of the church can begin to identify strategic ways to fulfill this mission.

Bible and Theology

To better understand the mission of the church, one has to explore the New Testament understanding of the church (*ekklesia*). In fact, the term *ekklesia* carries this goal-oriented connotation. This term, used by Paul and other New Testament writers, would have been quite familiar to any Roman audience.[694] Though its standard definition referred "to any aggregation of persons whose 'togetherness' was the result of being gathered around a common purpose or cause,"[695] the meaning most familiar to the New Testament audiences was the public assembly, or the gathering of the city members to vote or enact town policy.[696] At that time, "Public assemblies were the way in which the free male populace participated in the civic life of the city."[697]

For early Christians, rather than a town council meeting to discuss and decide civic matters, the *ekklesia* was a group gathered to enact kingdom matters. There is no record as to how the first church responded to this innovative utilization of government terminology, though we see that the term stuck.

It is important to understand the original meaning of *ekklesia* for two reasons. First, it represented a shift away from the worship of Yahweh in the temple to the worship of God through the relationality of Christ manifest in the community of Christians.[698] "The divine indwelling in the midst of a believing community makes it appropriate to speak of the community as a living Temple, the sacred place where God can now be found."[699] Second, and more important than the paradigmatic shift away from temple worship, was the connotation of mission and action inherent in *ekklesia*.

But what was the mission of the early church? The Great Commission stands as the ultimate mission of the *ekklesia*, both at the time of the apostles and continuing today. This ministry is an expansion of their previous commission to reach out to the "lost sheep of Israel" (Matthew 10:6), but still includes Israel, as it radiates outward to include all nations ("people groups").[700] The purpose of this ever-expanding missional activity was to "make disciples," which included being both followers of Christ and members of the *ekklesia*. Christ also provides the means by which one can be initiated into salvation and the family of God—through baptism and through learning the commands of Jesus.[701]

While it is anachronistic to apply the framework and standards of a mission statement back onto the words of Christ, it is fascinating how well the Great Commission fits the form. The Great Commission provides a directive ("go") as well as a purpose/goal: "Make disciples of all nations." This mission is ambitious, yet Christ provides action steps through which to begin working for this goal (baptizing and teaching). Finally, Jesus provides the inspirational impetus for the seemingly outlandish goal of making disciples of all nations, proclaiming his power and authority at the beginning, as well as his faithfulness and continuing inspiration at the end. Armed with this knowledge and experience of Christ's authority, the apostles can thus minister with boldness and confidence.[702] Overall, the Great Commission stands as an excellent example of a mission statement, and should stand as an example for pastors and congregations creating their own.

Historic Friends

Early Friends saw themselves within the apocalyptic meta-narrative of God, by which they, through their faithful obedience, could guide the nations back to true, primitive Christianity. After Fox's vision on Pendle Hill, where he saw the people waiting to be gathered, he left that hill with what could be considered his marching orders[703]—to gather these people. Out of the vision emerged his mission.

Joining him in this mission was a gathering of convinced Friends who were equally compelled to spread this truth of their experience of Christ throughout England.[704] This informal group was called the "First Publishers of Truth," or the "Valiant Sixty,"[705] and were men and women of different levels of education, training, and social standing.[706] What knit them together was their convincement of the truth and the mission of God to restore people's relationships with Christ. This helped create a movement that was tightly knit and passionate in its mission. It is this mission-centricity that allowed early Friends to suffer persecution, punishment, and death, all the while keeping faith in Christ and his commands.

This same spirit should guide the contemporary Friends church. As Elton Trueblood noted,

> What the world desperately needs is a redemptive fellowship centered in Jesus Christ, as an antidote to the evils of civilization. The problem is not that of organizing a congregation, which is easy, but rather that of seeing to it that the salt does not lose its savor.[707]

Leadership

The crafting of an organization's mission (or mission statement) is paramount to achieving both aims and excellence. A great leader helps define an organization's mission and communicates it profusely.[708] To facilitate the mission statement acting as a guide for organizational decisions, the leader should have this mission statement displayed in the office, printed in reports and correspondence, and easily accessible on the organization's website and social media.[709]

Counterintuitively, an effective mission should be simple, moral (to give meaning to employees' work), and unattainable.[710] The unattainability of an organization's mission may strike the reader as odd, but this allows the organization to continuously strive to fulfill the mission in creative ways, without ever reaching the point where either the mission would have to be changed or complacency would set in. However, having an aspirational mission does not mean it should seek to achieve excellence in all potential areas at all times, for that would be both unachievable and unbelievable, harming the morale of the members who recognize the folly of their efforts. When crafting an overarching mission, it is important for organizations to focus on key areas of excellence, rather than try to be everything to everyone.[711]

A mission statement should provide clarity for decisions, helping prevent organizations from getting bogged down in decision-making over issues that should be clearly seen as either mission-critical or not.[712] This is more important than is first realized, for many organizations and leaders overestimate their ability to recognize and discern which actions or issues fall within the scope of their mission. Daniel Goleman expounded on this danger when he wrote that "attention in organizations, as with individuals, has a limited capacity. . . . Organizations, too, have to choose where to allocate attention, focusing on this while ignoring that."[713] While organizations often appear to make rational decisions based on objective interpretation of available information, this is often not the case; organizations have a limited scope of perspective and information, as well as an inability to rationally approach every possible decision.[714] When faced with time or pressure constraints, leaders will often make decisions from this position of weakness which, in organizational theory, is called "bounded rationality."[715] From another perspective, the situation is even more dire, where "firms are guided by long-held organizational habits, patterns that emerge from thousands of employees' individual decisions."[716] In this perspective, there are no truly rational decisions, but only the habitual responses created by the chaos of unchecked random decisions throughout the organization.

Whatever the perspective, the need for a mission statement is clear. Organizational success will occur when an organization's mission is driven by the organization's core values.[717] It acts as a filter that allows the leadership to judge the appropriateness of a course of action by comparing it to the core values and mission communicated through the mission statement. This step in the decision-making process can go a long way toward saving time, energy, and resources from being wasted on efforts that ultimately do not align with the purpose of the organization. If these efforts fail, they drain the energy needed for success. If they succeed, they draw the organization away from its original intent. Peter Greer and Chris Horst wrote of this mission drift found in many organizations, where "slowly, silently, and with little fanfare, organizations routinely drift from their original purpose, and most will never return to their original intent."[718] While a mission statement alone cannot prevent this, it can aid a leader in keeping the proper course of an organization.

Strategy

If vision is the prophetic possibility of a church, and mission is the conceptualized core of the church journeying toward that reality, then strategy should be understood as the specific steps toward achieving that mission. This discussion will involve the time, resources, personnel, and organizational changes necessary to implement the mission of the church. Since the mission of a church is never completed through just one ministry, this discussion often engages the complex interplay between multiple ministries occurring in the local church, as well as the resource needs of each of these ministries. The tension between needs of personnel, resources, and emphasis highlights the necessity of a strategic framework to help direct tactical discussions.

Pastoral Paradigm

Strategic thinking may not be the strong suit of a pastor without education or experience in strategic planning. So, it is at this point that a pastor may want to look outside of the church for expertise regarding the strategic application of the church's mission. A pastor should never copy another church's vision or mission, for these emerge from the very DNA of the church, and any transplanted mission is likely to be rejected. However, once a church has discerned its own unique mission, it is perfectly acceptable to study how other communities of faith have tried, failed, and succeeded at putting feet to their faith. There are many published works that outline how other churches have attempted to conceptualize, begin, and sustain new ministries. A pastor can learn from the successes of these examples and use them as aids to help think through the practical application of their church's mission.

As always, it is important for the congregation to discuss the practical changes that may be necessary. It may seem redundant to have these discussions after forming the vision and mission. However, congregations (and their leadership, for that matter) are not always rational agents. People may be fully supportive of the mission of the church in the hypothetical, but balk at the practical implications of that mission. One way to avoid this disconnect is through what pastor Josiah Williams (Derby Friends Church) calls "throwing it all in the pot," through which everything the church does is reviewed and scrutinized by the congregation, in order to see what God is cooking up. This avoids any whiff of favoritism or agenda, but allows all to have a voice in deciding whether continued emphasis on a specific ministry aligns with the church's mission and whether it should remain in the church's strategic plan.

Not only will such congregational input help clarify the intent of this strategic planning, but it may also reveal some blessings that were hidden in the congregation. Often, there are businesspeople in the congregation who have ample abilities in strategic planning and organizational leadership as well as people who are unsure of their role and participation in the church. If a pastor finds a combination of the two, they may be able to utilize the talents of the person without taking them away from another ministry. Making use of the expertise of the congregation can help pave the way for clearer strategy of ministry.

Bible and Theology

An example of the strategy of the early church can be found in Acts 6. This chapter is important because it articulates two primary missions of the Jerusalem *ekklesia*: ministry of the word and taking care of widows (who were destitute, isolated, and targets of abuse and neglect).[719] It came to light in Acts 6 that some widows were being overlooked in the distribution of food. This inequity highlighted racial prejudices that were hurting the witness of the church.[720] The material support of these marginalized people was important to the church, and logistical issues were taken very seriously.

The strategy that emerged was to separate the leadership and oversight of these two ministries. The apostles would continue in their ministry of the word and of prayer, while seven *diakonai* (directly translated as "servant," though this belies deeper connotations that also make this the root of the term "deacon") would oversee the distribution of material resources. The plan evidently worked, with both ministry elements achieving their aims without drawing or draining resources from the other.[721] It can be argued that the strategic decision to separate the ministries provided the means to achieve both goals, whereas a lack of strategy could have contributed to failure of both aims of the church's mission: lack of food for those who needed it the most and a weakened witness to Jerusalem.

Historic Friends

Following the proposed paradigm, one can see how the vision of George Fox led to the mission of the Valiant Sixty. As Quakerism progressed and coalesced, it became clear to Fox that, in order for this God-mission to be sustainable, there needed to be a strategic plan that unified Quakers and aligned their efforts. Beginning in 1667, Fox began promoting an organizational structure for the movement, with "monthly and quarterly meetings to provide poor relief, discipline members, supervise marriages, and keep written records."[722] These local meetings would help provide mutual restraint against improper actions by Friends, as well as keep record, through the use of a clerk, of the sense of the meeting—the decision reached in peaceful unity.[723]

Many disagreed with this new system, finding it antithetical to their perceived understanding of Quakerism. Fox, supported by Robert Barclay, William Penn, and others, defended this move as a necessary strategy to keep the Friends movement from dissolving into chaos. Robynne Healey noted, "The structure that was imposed effectively brought what threatened to become an unruly flock into a framework where control was centralized and monitored."[724] Significantly, it also allowed Quakerism to utilize its resources and members for mutual support, as well as to help facilitate the achievement of its mission to spread the truth of primitive Christianity revived.

Leadership

An effective leader recognizes the value of strategy in assisting the achievement of organizational goals, for "the purpose of strategy is to motivate [people] to act."[725] However, the praise of strategic planning must be tempered with some cautions. The notion of a single strategy that will account for the success of all organizational goals must be disabused as it often takes multiple strategies to achieve outcomes.[726] Also a leader must be flexible and willing to divert from the plan when necessary when engaging in ministry in a messy world. Norman Rosenthal, who has written extensively about adversity and one's response to it, offered this helpful tip: "Most things don't have to be perfect . . . so cut corners if you must, as long as you don't sacrifice the essence or core of your work."[727] A leader should have a strategy and plan, but be willing to adapt as situations develop.

Further, a strategy that attempts to account for every possible contingency will soon become overly complicated. This may actually hinder action, as it is difficult both to communicate and implement. The key to an effective strategy is simplicity.[728] Nor does a strategy need to be groundbreaking. A leader does not have to engage in radical innovation to sustain organizational success and keep people happy. Research reveals that consistency in providing expected service and fulfilling basic promises is a large factor in maintaining loyalty (which often contributes to organizational success).[729] And when a strategy succeeds, humility is required in order to avoid being deceived by one's own genius. Most successes involve some form of randomness, with a strategic reason being supplied only in hindsight.[730] Finally, a leader cannot rest on their laurels regarding successful strategic innovation. Organizations cannot expect past invention and innovation to sustain their successes for long.[731] A successful strategy is successful only for so long. A leader must always create the space for a new vision, articulated mission, and an implemented strategy, so an organization will not get stuck in the past.

Communication and Collaboration

One of the steps of effective pastoral theology is communicating the intended philosophy and praxis to the congregation.[732] A common mistake is to understand effective pastoral communication as necessary only from the pulpit. Rather, it is important for the pastor to effectively communicate the purpose and aims of the church in all situations. The goal of such communication is to gain support and participation from members, in order that the church may proceed in its continuing mission to reach people and build up the body of Christ.

Pastoral Paradigm

Because the practical application of a church's mission will have a direct effect on the congregation, it is important that the congregation buys into any strategic changes, for that will provide the support (financially, philosophically, and physically) that brings these strategic aims to fruition. Congregational support is especially necessary if these strategic aims require the dissolution of present ministries in the church.

The best way to gain this buy-in is through honest, transparent conversation between the pastor and congregants. Whether involving members or staff, it is through these formal meetings and informal conversations that pastors can communicate a safe, trusting environment, along with their

God-given hopes and dreams for the future of the church. A pastor should not be hesitant to speak about this vision, regardless of any skittishness over members who may be in opposition. This form of thinking only leads to further distrust, back-channel dealing, and hard feelings on both sides. It is better to be open about any future plans, trusting in the Holy Spirit to bring unity.

Bible and Theology

A major portion of the New Testament—the apostolic epistles—acts as an example of communication and collaboration. Paul was a prolific letter-writer, who sought to encourage, exhort, and at times, combat through the power of the written word. His skill in this medium was well-known and often compared against a relatively weak presence in person (2 Corinthians 10:10). In these epistles, we see "official correspondence, directed to a variety of immediate and urgent problems confronting the newly established Christian congregations."[733] These issues reveal the efforts required of Paul to help maintain orthodoxy and fellowship within these churches. The preservation, utilization, and later canonization of these letters point to their value, not just to the original audience, but to the greater church as well.

Historic Friends

The early Quakers were also prolific letter-writers: more than five hundred of Margaret Fell's letters exist, while George Fox is said to have written more than three thousand letters in his lifetime.[734] It is through these letters that Quakers were able to teach, correct, and encourage one another in England and across the Atlantic. They also serve as what Matthew Horn described as a "texted authority," a peripheral supplement to the personal authority of the Quaker leaders and a boundary to the primacy of personal experience of individual Quakers.[735] It is through voluminous correspondence that ecclesiological innovation of the monthly meeting was communicated and defended by Fox and others. However, Quaker correspondence did not limit itself to internal missives, but also used external communiques, especially when Quaker leaders needed to articulate beliefs or combat slander or libel against the movement.[736] While large amounts of epistolary correspondence were not unusual in seventeenth-century Puritan England, the value of early Quaker letters in uniting geographically-separated Friends cannot be overstated in its impact on the unity and perseverance of the movement, especially during times of persecution.

Leadership

Those who have high interpersonal skills and social/emotional intelligence will experience greater success than those who don't[737] since the outcome of those abilities is effective collaboration—one of the most important leadership competencies.[738] Judith Glaser claims that the differentiation between the successful and the unsuccessful can be attributed to the ability to converse in a productive, engaging, and collaborative way.[739] According to the corporate consulting firm VitalSmarts, "Individuals who are the most influential—who can get things done *and at the same time* build on relationships—are those who master their crucial conversations."[740] However, even leaders who do not naturally possess these social skills can achieve successful teamwork and cooperation through intentional efforts at communication, along with having the mindset always geared toward collaboration.[741]

Effective communication of an organization's mission best occurs with the collaboration of those who have high levels of respect and influence within the organization. Some people have higher social capital than others, causing them to act as arbiters of what is acceptable or unacceptable in a given situation, as people will follow the in example. Unfortunately, many leaders do not take into account the opinions and perspectives of such stakeholders.[742] A good leader, however, will use stakeholders to help communicate and model the mission and vision, so that others will observe and model themselves accordingly.[743] Leaders should then seek to reach out to all levels of an organization, creating platforms (i.e., structured times or procedures) to facilitate internal conversation and collaboration both among co-workers and between the leader and workers.[744]

The role of leadership involves communicating vision to the rest of the organization. The right vision, no matter how obvious it may be to the leader, is useless if it cannot be communicated in a way that brings about agreement and buy-in.[745] A leader must convey or instill ownership of that mission into its members.[746] Charlene Li has summarized this leadership imperative: since "information is the lubricant of any organization," every leader must understand that communication is key to success.[747]

Administration

Practical theologian Don Browning refers to the concrete leadership and administrative actions of the pastor as "strategic practical theology," an area "where ministers and lay persons who think about the practice of the church really function."[748] Such managerial leadership involves administrative duties, including matters of correspondence, finances, budgets, and church grounds, as well as other routine tasks that fall under the purview of the pastor.[749] While some churches provide staff workers to complete these tasks, the responsibility and oversight of the duties are still the responsibility of the pastor.[750] However, in many churches, the pastor is the sole employee of the church, and except for volunteers, these duties are carried out by the pastor. If volunteers are available, then it is the pastor's duty to organize and monitor the tasks being accomplished,[751] ensuring that the church functions at the operational level.

Pastoral Paradigm

At every size of church, a pastor is a manager, for they are often in charge of the day-to-day running of the church. In a small church this can be as simple as turning on the lights, managing the thermostat, making sure the church doors are open on Sunday mornings; at a megachurch, this may mean overseeing multiple staff while creating policy and procedures. In terms of management, pastors also oversee the facilities, programs, and special events. This management role is distinct from leadership in the sense that leadership involves vision casting as a means of influencing others. To make sure that a funeral proceeds smoothly, for instance, is an act of management, rather than pure leadership. Thinking of the front of the church as a stage, the pastor is often the stage manager, making sure that people, places, and things are in the right places at the right times.

One potential issue is that pastors, either because of education, ego, or both, feel themselves above such trivial things as management, and there may be opportunities to enlist those with such giftings to help share the administration. However, there may still be times when a pastor has to empty a wastebasket; no amount of education, stature, status, or skill in preaching is ever going to remove that fact. Thus, regardless of church size, pastors should study management literature in order to help improve the daily processes of the church, so that it can better function in its core mission—proclaiming the Kingdom of God as the Body of Christ.

Bible and Theology

While "management" and "administration" appear, in American culture, to be terms devoid of spirituality, it is not the case in the New Testament. In 1 Corinthians 12:28, Paul lists as one of the spiritual gifts of the Holy Spirit the gift of *kubernesis*, which can be translated as administration, governance, or guidance, and was sometimes used to describe a ship's captain.[752] The connotation appears to be one that describes effectively administrating as well as guiding the local church. While it is not explicated in detail, its presence in Paul's list acts as evidence that the early church recognized the charismatic gift exercised by those who helped govern and guide the *ekklesia*.

Historic Friends

The growth of the Friends movement experienced its share of early crises, which led to the introduction of an organizational strategy that sought to provide boundaries for both orthodoxy and orthopraxy. This organizational structure also provided ways for Friends to manage and distribute resources to those in need. In addition to the meetings for worship and meetings for business, there was also a women's meeting established, where Friends women led efforts in "visiting the sick and feeble, and ministering to their necessities, as also to look after the widows and orphans."[753] Additionally, the quarterly gatherings of these meetings also sought out the spiritual health of Quaker women specifically, utilizing the queries.[754]

While these women's meetings were meant to act as parallel to the men's meetings, they did not possess the same power or authority. Because of this, it was noted by some in the movement that, although the duties of the women's meetings were important, they were secondary to the power to make decisions regarding the trajectory and priorities of Quakerism—which was the authority of the men's meeting.[755] While it could be claimed that this separation was meant to subdue women in the movement, this structuring also provided organizational authority and efficiency to the work that women, such as Margaret Fell were doing. The management and administration of these resources provided support and relief to many, fulfilling the gospel command to help the "least of these."

Leadership

While leadership and management are two separate fields, each with its own corresponding expectations and literature, it is important for a leader to be able to act as an effective manager (either temporarily or permanently). As with leadership, management is a field where one can benefit greatly from both positive and negative examples. As far as negative managerial strategies to avoid, one only has to look at the history of management in the twentieth century. The old view of management was a micromanagement paradigm of obedience: obedience of the worker to the management and obedience of management to the aims of the system, and that "management wins when it can get the most work for the least pay."[756] This management style was very alluring for, as Laslo Bock noted, "command-oriented, low-freedom management is common because it's profitable, it requires less effort, and most managers are afraid of the alternative."[757]

However, the negative effects of micromanagement have been well-documented. Research has shown that there is a correlation between job demands (expectations required of the position), level of control (ability of the employee to make decisions), and one's productivity and health.[758] A low-demand, low-control job does not benefit a person, for the work is unimpressive and the person is often bored and uninvolved. A high-demand, low-control job can have a negative effect on productivity and health concerns, including elevated rates of cardiovascular disease.[759] What is surprising, though, is that a highly demanding job can lead to increased productivity and health benefits if a person feels they have a relatively high level of autonomy and decision-making ability. Workers will experience increased productivity and health in spite of the demanding work.[760] It is when one feels powerless that both productivity and health decrease,[761] making it important that those under one's leadership feel trusted and autonomous.

In addition to people, a manager is also in charge of processes, procedures, and other operational functions. A managerial leader will seek to improve organizational efficiency through improvement at the level of these operations. Within the paradigm of vision-mission-strategy, management acts just below strategy, seeking to modify operations and processes in order to best achieve outcomes. Part of fostering excellence is highlighting bright spots or best practices that occur within an organization.[762] These bright spots can be used as an example and a prescriptive measure to improve performance in the rest of the organization.[763] The benefit of highlighting internal excellence, rather than examples from other organizations, is that it is less likely to suffer rejection, for it is an *insider*, rather than an *outsider* example.[764] Also, when improving the efficiency and effectiveness of an organization, it may only take a few minor changes in key areas to make a major difference. For example, after extensive research, a hospital that had suffered from poor customer scores made the following changes to the advised staff/patient interaction: "Smile, make eye contact, identify yourself, let people know what you're doing and why, and end every interaction by asking, 'Is there anything else that you need?'"[765] These seemingly minor changes in fact changed everything—service quality scores increased, and the hospital soon became best in its class.[766]

Ultimately, a leader must not fall into the trap of excelling at day-to-day management while ignoring higher level strategic thinking and activities necessary to stay relevant in one's position.[767] What separates a leader from a manager is that, for a leader, management is a means to an end. As such, proper management and administration will help an organization achieve its goals more efficiently and effectively, and should be taken seriously by all leaders.

Chapter Ten
Shepherd

The dominant image of pastoral care is the word "shepherd,"[768] an image epitomized in Jesus.[769] Jesus even described himself as the "good shepherd" (John 10:11). Inherent in shepherd imagery are the notions of feeding the sheep (John 21:15), protecting the sheep (John 10:9), and closeness and familiarity with the flock (John 10:27). Properly understood, these ancient images provide a reference to appropriate pastoral care.

Pastoral care is understood as "the aspect of the ministry of the Church which is concerned with the well-being of individuals and of communities."[770] While many conceive of pastoral care as consisting solely of counseling and visitation, this is not accurate, as pastoral care consists of any act of service to individuals, families, congregations, or communities.[771]

Spiritual Growth and Discipleship

One of the chief goals of a pastor is to facilitate the spiritual growth of the people in the congregation. Although a vague term, "spiritual growth" is best understood as synonymous with "spiritual formation,"[772] which is the process of growth in holiness, maturity, and knowledge of and a relationship with Jesus Christ, throughout the different stages of life.[773] While spiritual formation is ultimately an individual endeavor, the church and pastor can provide resources and guidance to increase and improve the process.[774] While spiritual formation is the dominant term to describe the paradigm, the idea of growth is important to maintain here to communicate the increasing nature of spiritual formation which is a goal of pastoral leadership. Spiritual growth can be facilitated through broad measures (vision casting, preaching, etc.), as well personal interactions, such as discipleship.

Discipleship is understood as a fulfillment of Jesus' command to "go and make disciples of all nations" (Matthew 28:19), which occurs through spiritual growth by means of a personal, formative relationship between a student and a teacher.[775] The teleology of discipleship is a deeper relationship with Christ, increased understanding of biblical and theological truths, and a better praxis for living based on Christian teaching.[776] Discipleship also occurs through spiritual direction, which can be classified as a subset of pastoral counseling. Spiritual direction involves intentionally listening and engaging in a life of another, seeking to discern ways to guide them into greater spiritual health.[777] The goal of discipleship is to set believers on a trajectory toward a deepening relationship with Christ, a faithful obedience to God's will and word, an increasing *shalom* in all facets of life, and the tools necessary to go and make disciples themselves.

Pastoral Paradigm

A pastor's goal for discipleship ministries should be to help develop Christians who are not dependent on the pastor for the elementary basics of Christian faith and practice, but are able to experience increasing personal spiritual growth and obedience. While the pastor should engage in personal discipleship when possible, it is more beneficial to also establish a discipleship ministry in the church. This ministry seeks to ensure that those new to the faith are not adrift in the congregation, but have someone to journey alongside them as they grow in Christ. For discipleship to effectively occur, the disciple must be willing to learn from a self-chosen teacher,[778] who is willing to journey with the disciple during one or more informal stages of spiritual growth.

Bible and Theology

In the gospels, action often characterizes discipleship,[779] a lifestyle that reflects the disciple's obedience to God. Different texts provide shades of nuance regarding the understanding and practice of discipleship. The Gospel of John, for example, provides the example of discipleship as "simply being and remaining (*menein*) with Jesus" (1:39).[780] However, this concept grew into a fleshed out understanding of spiritual growth and enculturation into the faith community. The early church followed a model of discipleship that provided both spiritual formation and future leadership for the growing church.[781] Perhaps one difference between the early church and contemporary discipleship is the goal: Instead of a deeper, meaningful, personal relationship with Christ being the end or purpose (as one sees in the contemporary church), the goal of both the disciplers and disciples in the early church was a recognition and use of their gifts to build up the church.[782] This corporate mentality could be regained with great benefit to the church, as it would help link a Christian's journey with Christ to their local community of faith—a connection that has been lost.

Historic Friends

Given the newness of the Friends movement, coupled with often intense persecution of its members, it is not surprising that the leaders exhorted care over fellow members. George Fox, writing in 1652, began a letter with a call for the recipients to "watch over the weak, and see how the plants of the Lord grow."[783] This encouragement is seen in other letters, as when he calls Quakers to "watch over one another in love, and stir up that which is pure in one another, and exhort one another daily."[784]

Spiritual growth was of utmost importance to the early Quakers; the movement, in fact, emerged as a reaction to those who knew the scriptures and participated in the rituals, yet had no personal relationship with Christ Jesus, and thus no spiritual vitality in their lives. As Isaac Penington wrote:

> A man may read the letter of Scriptures diligently, and gather a large knowledge from there, and feed greedily there; but it is only dead spirit which feeds in this way, but the soul underneath remains lead, barren, hungry, unsatisfied, which, when it awakes, it will feel.[785]

While not maintaining any positional authority, the early Friends ministers felt a godly expectation to "comfort and strengthen [God's] flock."[786] Carole Spencer's research revealed that one of the aims of spiritual growth in the early Friends movement was holiness, as they understood it.[787] This is confirmed by early Quaker writers, such as William

Penn, who wrote that "the knowledge and obedience of the doctrine of the cross of Christ is of infinite importance to the souls of mankind."[788] Penington paints an even more vivid image of the daily wrestling with sin and obedience:

> That which destroys you, and separates you from the living God, will be daily wrought out, and the heart daily changed into the image of him who is light. And you will be brought into unity and fellowship with the light, possessing it, and being possessed by it. This is your salvation.[789]

Leadership

In a society that may be on a course toward becoming post-Christian, there is a staggering amount of self-improvement material that still references some form of spirituality as a component of betterment. Even secular texts recognize the evidence that true life change is often dependent on a recognition of a higher power. Specifically, research of alcoholics in recovery revealed that the key factor of maintaining sobriety was the belief that a higher power was giving them strength to make it through the stressful periods that led other alcoholics to relapse.[790] Understandably, "Researchers hated that explanation . . . God and spirituality are not testable hypotheses."[791] As such, leaders of organizations rooted in or related to religion, such as pastors, have a decided advantage in helping people improve their lives.

However, even absent religious elements, secular leaders can still guide others toward personal betterment. The key task of leaders, regarding both individuals and organizations, is "creating and fueling a virtuous circle."[792] A leader should work to "give people new habits that help them figure out where to go on their own."[793] Jim Loehr and Tony Schwartz extol the importance of the creation of positive, habitual behaviors, which they call "ritual."[794] They define a positive ritual as a "behavior that becomes automatic over time—fueled by some deeply held value."[795] However, overreliance on ritualistic achievement can sometimes mask larger issues that should have been addressed such as self-sabotaging behavior or moral licensing, behavior, in which a person who does a small act of kindness will often fail to do a larger act of kindness (or even rationalize an act contrary to their values).[796] Though illogical, such self-sabotaging behaviors did occur in participants studied.[797] For pastors, scrupulously regarding a narrow range of Christian behaviors can mask or even promote unchristian behavior amongst members of the congregation.

There are various schools of thought regarding individual growth and life change. Some argue that major change occurs when *behaviors* change, and these vital behaviors should be the focus.[798] Others claim that it takes a paradigm shift in thinking (such as finding a purpose for one's life or finding religion), which will subsequently drive behavioral change. Most often, it is a mixture of both. Even the most strident behaviorists recognize that people are more likely to change or sustain new behaviors when those behaviors are linked to a larger moral vision.[799] The main problem with behavior change is that many people are provided an outcome to advise, rather than a behavior as a method for achievement (e.g., eat fewer calories than you burn—good explanation of how the weight is lost, but no specific behaviors or directions to eat those fewer calories).[800] Successful behavior change should be facilitated through effective communication of broad goals and purposes, which drive specific behavior change, accompanied by specific actions and strategies to achieve desired outcomes.

One way to influence positive behaviors through specific strategies and actions is through vicarious experience, by which a person models what positive behaviors look like.[801] The subjects exposed to this modeling can learn from the successes and failures of the model, and often adjust their behaviors accordingly.[802] This strategy is often more effective than verbal persuasion, which, despite its ineffectiveness in changing expectations or behaviors, is one of the most common tools utilized.[803] A related version of this is the power of pairing, placing together people of differing abilities and experience so that each can learn from the other.[804]

Regardless of the strategy, by helping a person improve merely one habit or area of life, a leader can facilitate a chain reaction of betterment throughout the person's whole life. These improvements do not even have to be momentous, but can be rather pedestrian changes. For example, "Studies have documented that families who habitually eat dinner together seem to raise children with better homework skills, higher grades, greater emotional control, and more confidence. . . . Making your bed every morning is correlated with better productivity."[805] In the same way, a leader should always have their eyes open for ways to leverage small changes and habits into a virtuous cycle of improvement for others.

Equipping the Saints

Ephesians 4:12 calls pastors to "equip the saints for the work of ministry." It is best understood as an ecclesiological continuum, where, at one end of the spectrum, the pastor and leadership are tasked with teaching and training the congregation how to minister.[806] At the other end of the spectrum, the notion of equipping the saints for ministry can be understood as an ecclesiology where the congregation, rather than a professionalized clergy class, are tasked with performing acts of worship and ministry.[807] Regardless of one's definition of "equipping ministry," Randy Berkner argued that, because of the overreliance on the shepherd motif, the paradigm of equipping the saints has been underutilized, in spite of its importance as an aspect of pastoral leadership.[808] A pastor should seek to discern the gifts, skills, and passions of the members of the congregation, and place them where those gifts, skills, and passions can be actualized for the good of the church.[809]

Because of differing denominational views, the literature regarding pastors as equipping the laity is not as abundant as other domains, but equipping ministry is highly relevant to Quaker history and theology, given that the notion of equipping those of ministry would be appropriate within a movement where each member was viewed as an active minister.

For a Christian to be properly equipped for a life of faithful obedience and ministry, it is not enough to provide biblical teaching and tips for Christian living. The church must also help each Christian discover some key components about themselves. These components, once known, can be fostered, developed, and utilized by the community of faith in order to glorify God, bless the community, and reach more people.

Pastoral Paradigm

Even though God has gifted each member of the church in order that all may serve and minister,[810] many have not recognized their gifting or passion, and many do not even know how to do so. Because of this, the pastor must give time and energy to prayerful discernment of the members of the congregation, seeking to discover giftings and talents that the people have and that the church needs. A class, sermon series, or other endeavor that helps people discover their gifts should be implemented as well. At first, having people utilize their gifts may require some convincing, but hopefully, as more people exercise their gifts and calling in the church, new Christians will experience a culture in which the expectation is participation, rather than reception.

In addition to spiritual gifts, there are also natural talents that people possess. The pastor should make sure that each believer recognizes the sermon of self—the gospel message that can be proclaimed through their daily actions and attitudes. Through excellence and integrity, every Christian, in the tradition of Quaker forebears, can communicate Christ through their labors. Additionally, certain talents or skills, such as carpentry or electrical expertise, can be exercised by members to benefit the church. In fact, the pastor could seek to foster a church culture where, in addition to monetary offerings, those with various specialized skills can "tithe their talents."[811] This allows Christians to see their talents from a divine perspective, so that the plumbing work done in service to the Lord is held in equal esteem to the preaching from the pulpit.

Bible and Theology

Ephesians 4:1–16 provides a concise summary of the purpose of spiritual gifts in the early church. In the passage there is a call for unity in the church, a unity made possible by the Holy Spirit. The purpose of these gifts is for their use, in order "to equip his people for works of service, so that the body of Christ may be built up" (Ephesians 4:12). Taken to its logical conclusion, Paul's description of the "body of Christ" is harmed if the structure of worship and church mission inhibits the expressions of gifting by all the members.[812] This would also explain why Paul wrote so passionately about the need for orderly worship in the Corinthian church, so that all of God's gifts may be utilized for the edification of the church and for the glory of God.

The Bible is also clear that, although God calls some to leave their jobs in order to serve the Lord exclusively, there are also opportunities for God's people to glorify God through their vocations. The best example of this is found in Exodus 31:1–6, in which the Lord reveals to Moses those within the community who had the skills and talents to create the tabernacle:

> Then the Lord said to Moses, "See, I have chosen Bezalel son of Uri, the son of Hur, of the tribe of Judah, and I have filled him with the Spirit of God, with wisdom, with understanding, with knowledge and with all kinds of skills—to make artistic designs for work in gold, silver and bronze, to cut and set stones, to work in wood, and to engage in all kinds of crafts. Moreover, I have appointed Oholiab son of Ahisamak, of the tribe of Dan, to help him. . . .

While not a part of the priestly tribe that ministered on behalf of the people, these two craftsmen were essential to the future worship of Yahweh. Their talent, though perhaps not considered religious by the Levitical taxonomy of the day, was, in a sense, sanctified through their obedient exercise for the Lord.

Historic Friends

The building up and equipping of the saints in the early Friends movement was not only a mission of self-interest, for the benefit of Quakerism, but meant to allow Christ's light to shine in all places. Elton Trueblood recognized the power of Christian witness, regardless of vocation, when he wrote, "If the central Christian convictions are accepted seriously, every major human enterprise takes on new excitement."[813] This is seen in early Friends theology and ecclesiology, in the concept of "universal ministry." Quakers understood this as a recognition that God uses all types of people to minister. As time progressed, this concept of universal ministry expanded beyond the idea that anyone could speak or minister in the specific sense, to a broader understanding that one's life could communicate the gospel. Regardless of occupation, a life lived in integrity, simplicity, peace, and faith is a life of faithful witnessing.

Another core conviction was that the local meeting should manifest a "wide participation and shared leadership."[814] Even following the adoption of the pastoral system, there was an idealized understanding of the pastor's role regarding the building up of members for ministry:

> This specialized ministry of which we speak must also wage a constant battle against the tendency

of Protestant ministers to become merely professional holy men, performing all the religious tasks of the community, thus relieving the rest of the congregation for purely secular pursuits. This ministry must be one of equipping "God's people for work in his service" (Eph. 4:12 NEB). This kind of minister will seek constantly to work himself out of a job. He will train others to offer public prayer, to lead prayer meeting, to evangelize, to visit the sick, to counsel the troubled, and to participate in other aspects of the universal ministry.[815]

Unfortunately this ideal did not manifest itself in most pastoral Friends churches, but instead devolved into an active clergy/passive laity paradigm that is still present among many Quaker churches.

Leadership

This task of developing people under one's leadership begins with discernment, as a leader should focus on recognizing people's talent or potential, and then help foster and develop those talents.[816] The ability to recognize and develop talent outshines the leader's personal talent, for the work of the group multiplies effectiveness.[817] There may also be latent or hidden talent possessed by members of an organization, which can be discovered by the leader. However, in those scenarios as well, discernment is required to find those who don't fit the common molds with their competencies and skills.[818] Regardless, the potential rewards of these untapped resources are immense.

Visitation

Visitation is the act of the pastor visiting a person while in the role of pastor.[819] While it is most commonly associated with home visits, pastoral visitation is not limited to the home, but is open to several contexts—some planned, others extemporaneous—but all in the role of pastor.[820] Such contexts include hospital, prison, nursing homes, hospice, school, and the homebound.[821]

The goal of visitation is to provide prayer and counseling, a proxy connection between the church and those visited, and pastoral care and fellowship.[822] Visitation also fulfills the biblical command to visit the sick, the poor, and those in prison (Matthew 25:31–40). Unsurprisingly, pastoral visitation has the potential to have a positive impact on those being visited.[823] This is especially true during situations of intense stress or trauma, such as life-threatening illnesses, accidents, or end-of-life situations.[824]

Because of the time and travel commitments involved, pastoral visitation can also detract from other areas of church activity. Paul Perl noted that pastors who spent a larger proportion of their time in pastoral visitation and counseling spent less time in administrative duties and church meetings.[825]

Pastoral Paradigm

One of the foundations of Quakerism is that there is not a divide between the sacred and the secular; God is immanent in creation. In the same way, one's faith should not experience a separation between Sunday and the rest of the week. To facilitate this, the ministry of the church should extend past the walls of the church on Sunday morning and into the community during the rest of the week. While there are many ways to achieve this (some covered in this book), one of the main ways the pastor can be a representative of Christ to both the congregation and the community is through visitation.

To be fair, anyone in the congregation can and should practice visitation ministry. However, the pastor has some definitive advantages, in this culture, that improve visitation ministry. One, if the pastor is financially released for ministry, then they can visit at times when most of the congregation would be at work. Second, in medical facilities, a minister can often visit patients at times and places that are off-limits to a normal visitor. Third, at times of tragedy, a properly trained minister will have the tools necessary to engage those affected by tragedy. Thus, the pastor may never remove the obligation of visitation, but they can expand its effectiveness through the equipping of others.

Bible and Theology

Paul's missionary journeys can act as an example for the ministry of visitation. While Paul was prolific and powerful in his written correspondence, even he made known his desire and plan to visit the churches in person (Romans 1:10; 2 Corinthians 13:1; 1 Corinthians 16:1). Paul seemed to recognize the value of personal interaction for both growing in fellowship and correction. Paul's several missionary journeys allowed him to establish and revisit congregations throughout his travels. It was only when he was under arrest that the letters became the primary source of instruction and correction.

Historic Friends

Though the traveling ministry was explored in chapter 8, one further point remains relevant here. The itinerant ministry of early Quakerism is an aspect of Quaker ecclesiology that has been underrepresented in religious research and literature, especially when compared to Methodist circuit riders or Jesuit missionaries, two other similar historical ministries that have received much attention. The suffering and sacrifice experienced by Friends ministers abroad should stand as an example for all Christians.

Leadership

There is not a direct equivalent in organizational leadership to the dynamic of the pastor visiting congregants. However, the tangential area of workplace interaction provides a point of similarity. Effective leaders and managers, when studied, achieved much by simply walking around and engaging in seemingly serendipitous encounters with workers.[826] These encounters allowed the leader to learn more about the workers, reinforce a goal and priority, and preempt any potential issues before they grew.[827] A leader should never be isolated from those in the organization, but should seek to be a presence in all areas, in order that they may see in person what is occurring at the level of operations.

Counseling

People request pastoral counseling for a variety of reasons, including, but not limited to, decision-making, depression or guilt, crises, failure, conflict resolution, marriage counseling, and addiction problems.[828] While a pastor can be fully certified as a counselor or therapist, most are not, and such pastoral counseling is a nonmedical service. However, a pastor's informal relation to therapy allows many people to utilize their services who may not participate in formal therapy, although pastors do refer parishioners to professional therapists in certain cases.[829] A majority of pastoral counseling involves short-term encounters with parishioners or others.[830] The hope is that the pastoral counselor will provide insight into the person's condition, as well as biblical and helpful ways to improve that condition, usually through an increased understanding of and relationship with God.[831]

The need for a spiritual perspective is often felt most urgently during times of suffering and tragedy. However, any pastor offering care during tragedies would be wise to heed Jim Horsthuis's assertion that "suffering is a pastoral problem that defies rational explanation."[832] Pastors should not seek to immediately provide a rational, theological answer to senseless suffering, but instead should seek to be both a physical presence of care and support as well as a symbol of God's presence during times of trial. It is during these times that pastors must divest themselves of any positional distance and suffer with those who are suffering, seeking to help to bear the burdens of the afflicted.

Pastoral Paradigm

A Christ-centered Quaker pastor will find themselves called upon to counsel people from within and outside the congregation. While spiritual counseling can occur in the formal setting of the church office, the pastor will often have informal encounters during daily interactions with congregants.

Whether formal or informal, these encounters will cover a spectrum of issues, from commonplace to tragic circumstances. Regardless, the pastor is expected to be a representative of God, offering spiritual wisdom and, if nothing else, a presence of peace. Effective pastoral counseling requires a commitment to confidentiality, a willingness to journey with people through pain, healing, and restoration, and courage to speak necessary words of truth, however painful it may be at the time.

The most common forms of pastoral counseling are pre-marital counseling and funeral-related grief counseling. Before officiating a wedding, it is customary for the pastor to request that the couple participate in pre-marital counseling. This is a chance to impart godly wisdom and advice, as well as to suss out any potential issues that may occur between the soon-to-be-wed couple. These counseling sessions can help provide the tools and foundational work for a stronger, healthier marriage. Officiating a funeral presents other opportunities to offer the comforting presence of Christ to those experiencing loss. While, in some situations, there will be formal grief therapy sessions, it is more likely that the pastor will provide counsel and comfort informally, during interactions with the bereaved before, during, and after the funeral.

Outside the congregation, the pastor may be called upon to officiate weddings and funerals of people who are not members of the congregation (this is especially true in small towns). These events are both opportunities and obligations to counsel those who would not normally be in contact with or influenced by the church. Even though the lack of previous contact and relationship may make the counseling process more difficult than with a church member, potential positive impact from these interactions cannot be discounted.

While many pastoral counseling encounters fall into these common categories, it is important for the pastor to always remember the boundaries of their expertise, as well as the of proper education and training in counseling and psychology. The myriad of issues facing individuals, relationships, and families can quickly surpass and overwhelm any pastor's knowledge of pop psychology and common sense. Pastors must not let ego or pride deceive them into thinking that their competence covers every possible contingency. In certain situations, the most pastorally beneficial service is to communicate one's inability to resolve the issue, and to offer to help connect the person with a local mental health professional. Above all, the pastor must hold the health and safety of those they counsel as the highest priority.

Bible and Theology

Because of the relatively recent emergence of psychology, psychiatry, and other related fields of mental health, there is not a direct equivalent found in scripture. However, one could argue that Jesus' healing of the sick acts as a significant parallel example. In the gospels, those who were infirm often faced suffering, isolation, disruption of their lives, and no hope of recovery. When he encountered such people, Jesus was moved by intense compassion (*splanchnizomai*) and healed them, and contrary to the dominant religious dogma, assigned no blame nor spiritual cause to their infirmity. While these healings do act as evidence for Jesus being the Messiah, their inclusion in the gospels represents more than simple historical record or apologetic proof. Rather, it shows the heart of God toward humanity. It is incumbent upon every Christian, when encountering a person dealing with suffering, to "go and do likewise."

Historic Friends

Because there was no frame of reference regarding modern mental health in seventeenth-century England, Quaker records do not record anything related to it. However, there is one tangential piece of evidence that may be of some value. George Fox, in his journal, recounts frustration and spiritual anguish he experienced from the lack of vitality he found in the established churches of his youth.[833] However, when he received the divine revelation that "there is one, even Christ Jesus, that can speak to thy condition," his journal records that his "heart did leap for joy."[834]

Leadership

While a business leader may not have the same encounters as a pastor, they still have to lead and manage organizations filled with people—people who have issues, hang-ups, and conflicts. It is important that a leader be appropriately aware of the life situations of those in their organization. Often, many issues or complaints a person has can be resolved simply through active listening, even if the issue itself isn't resolved. Active listening is the empathic process of being fully present, attentive, and nonjudgmental to the speaker during the conversation, seeking to empower the other person by making them feel heard.[835]

Active listening does not have to be an overthought, robotic practice, but should be understood as simply being patient and present in conversation. Even minor changes can have positive results. For example, simply repeating what a person has said communicates that they are being heard, and studies have shown, increases positive interaction and outcomes.[836] A successful resolution may hinge solely on simply "paying attention to people's feelings and needs, and showing concern."[837] Key facets of effective conversation are building rapport, listening without judgment, asking discovery questions, reinforcing success, and dramatizing the message.[838] Another succinct description of active listening and effective conversation is to be sincere, be curious, and be patient.[839]

Open and transparent conversation can also help remove anxieties held by members of the organization, especially anxieties related to the unpredictability of the company or the future of the person's employment. When faced with unpredictability, anxiety grows.[840] In the absence of other inputs, such as communication from a leader or clarification of the future, anxious people naturally seek out ways, which are not always healthy, to alleviate their anxiety. Studies have shown that performing actions or tasks (even unrelated to the anxiety source) reduces anxiety,[841] but can become compulsive behaviors and lead to possible dysfunction. Even perfectionism can morph into a mental affliction—obsessive-compulsive personality disorder—by which obsession with detail and perfection can cause life disruption.[842] Additionally, "compulsive working," and "excessive devotion to job and productivity to the exclusion of relationships and downtime,"[843] is a rarely successful attempt to work one's way out of anxiety. The many mental concerns relating to the workplace points to the necessity of a leader being aware of the health of those under their leadership.

Above all, a leader must recognize, in others and in themselves, that many mental afflictions require extensive professional therapy to address.[844] Such illnesses are not simple matters to be joked about or dismissed. While the leader may not have the resources to provide services for workers suffering from such illnesses, they can at least be understanding and as accommodating as possible.

Conclusion

As mentioned in the introduction, this book is not meant to be a comprehensive exploration of a Quaker pastoral theology. Rather this book is meant to orient contemporary Friends pastoral theology and practice toward a trajectory that maintains its faithfulness to scripture, strengthens its Quaker heritage, and increases the effectiveness of pastoral leadership. It is not possible to articulate a complete, Christ-centered Quaker pastoral theology, not just because of the space constraints of this book, but because there is still much work to be done in understanding the pastoral role within Quakerism.

However, the goal of this book is two-fold: One, that this book will provide a pastoral paradigm for new, current, and future Friends pastors; two, that this book will also spur on a broader conversation regarding pastoral expectations within churches, yearly meetings, and between yearly meetings. These conversations can help clarify the pastoral position, allowing for further pages to be written on the subject.

A pastoral theology should never exist for its own sake, but for the benefit and service of the church, and for the glory of God. In the same spirit of humility, this endeavor seeks to serve the Body of Christ, by allowing Quaker communities of faith to be served and led by pastors of increasing effectiveness. An oft-misunderstood truth is that a stronger pastorate should not equal a weaker congregation. On the contrary, a stronger pastor should result in a better servant, an "approved worker who is not ashamed" (2 Timothy 2:15). This servant of Christ should live out their calling as a shepherd, leader, and proclaimer of the gospel—in humility, community, and contentment. Blessed with pastors such as these, the possibilities for American Quakerism to impact this world are endless. I pray we all have both the boldness and obedience to take the critical first steps to realize the dream of a vibrant, resurgent Quaker church.

Derek Brown, Ph.D.
Haviland, KS

Index

A

Advices, 24, 174–175
Alaska Yearly Meeting of Friends, 109, 110, 115–116, 118, 120, 123, 125–127
Albia Friends Meeting, 49
Alvesson, Mats, 93
America, 9, 11, 13, 17, 19, 21, 45, 52, 66, 96, 99, 149, 169, 173
Anglican, 26, 42, 55, 61–62, 70–74, 76–78, 165, 167–166
Arizona, 111–112
Ascension, 215, 216
Association of Evangelical Friends, 112, 207
Atlantic, 236
Audland, John, 183
Augustine, 172

B

Babel, 216
Balby Elders, 205. *See also* Elders at Balby
Banks, John, 198
baptism, 42, 46–47, 172, 225
Baptist, 100
Barclay College, 7
Barclay, Robert, 42, 56–61, 70–74, 78–80, 173, 189, 204–205, 232
Barna, George, 194
Becker, Penny, 95
Belleville, Linda, 147
Berger, Jonah, 219
Berkner, Randy, 252
Bible, 169
Birkel, Michael, 67–68, 132, 170, 196

Bock, Laslo, 241

Brace, Laura, 75–76

Bradley, Randall, 193

Brister, C. W., 32

Browning, Don, 168, 238

Brown, Marjorie Glines, 196

Brunner, Emil, 187

Byars, Ronald, 155

C

California, 111

California Yearly Meeting, 82, 110–111, 113

Calvary Chapel, 7

Cambridge, 55, 58

Canada, 112

Catholic, 44, 135, 162

Center Quarterly Meeting, 112

Chapman, Raymond, 70

Cheevers, Sarah, 184

Cheyenne, Wyoming, 207

Christianity, 9, 11–12, 16–17, 20–21, 31, 35, 63–62, 70, 93–94, 97, 99, 107, 131, 135, 157, 161, 166, 172–173, 177, 191, 198, 200, 202–204, 208–207, 226, 232

church fathers, 30, 172, 191

Church of England, 28, 70, 73, 75

Civil War, 114

Colorado, 111–112

Communion, 66, 136, 192–193

Congregationalist church, 173

Cooper-White, Pamela and Michael, 132

Cope, Jackson, 164

Crouch, William, 184

D

Dandelion, Pink, 64, 66, 72

Derby Friends Church, 230

Dingemans, Gisjbert, 31

distinctives (Quaker), 9, 43, 103, 131

Douglas, Alaska, 110

Dyer, Mary, 148, 184

E

Eastern Region Yearly Meeting. *See* Evangelical Friends Church—Eastern Region

ecclesiology, 7, 10, 15, 34–35, 43–45, 48, 51, 61, 70, 73–74, 90, 99, 103, 130,

131, 141–142, 162–163, 165, 175, 181, 191, 195, 200, 252, 255, 259

elders, 25, 27–29, 47, 67–74, 117–120, 127, 147, 166, 196, 212

Elders at Balby, 196. *See also* Balby Elders

Elliott, Errol, 16

England, 43, 52, 61, 75, 148, 184, 226, 236, 263

Eshcol, 46

Eucharist, 42, 62, 162, 192

Europe, 184

evangelical, 7, 9, 17–20, 29, 65–66, 82, 94, 101, 103, 131, 140, 178, 198, 207, 222

Evangelical Friends Church International, 18, 110–112

Evangelical Friends Church—Eastern Region, 109, 112, 115, 117, 120, 121, 122, 124, 127

Evangelical Friends Church—Mid America Yearly Meeting, 109, 111, 114, 116, 119, 120, 122, 125, 128

Evangelical Friends Church—Southwest, 109, 110–111, 115, 117, 118, 120–123, 125–127

Evans, Charles, 164

Evans, Katherine, 184

F

facing bench, 29

Fairfield Quarterly Meeting, 112

Faith and Practice, 13, 23, 24, 28, 67, 68, 109, 114–116, 120, 122–127, 129, 166, 174–175, 247

Feldman, Michael, 189

Fell, Margaret, 42, 146, 148–149, 235, 240

Five Years Meeting, 110, 111, 113, 197

Florida, 112

Fox, George, 21, 42–43, 48, 55–61, 70, 72, 76–78, 105, 139, 163, 165, 196, 204–206, 216–218, 226, 232, 235, 248, 263

Frame, Nathan and Esther, 48, 69, 75

Friends United Meeting, 18, 111–114, 197

G

Gallagher, Carol, 145

Gangel, Kenneth, 211

Gatewood, Tee, 178

Germany, 184

Glaser, Judith, 187, 236

Goleman, Daniel, 227

Graves, Michael, 65

Great Commission, 172, 216, 225

Greer, Peter, 228

Grubb, Edward, 204

Gurneyite, 112

Gurney, Joseph John, 47

Gwyn, Douglas, 63, 64, 78, 164

H

Hall, Christopher, 30

Hamm, Thomas, 46, 47

Harold, Henry, 47

Hatch, Mary, 102

Healey, Robynne, 148, 232

Henry, Todd, 219

Hesper, Iowa, 46

Heusel, Lorton, 49

Hicks, Elias, 206

Hicksite, 206

Hinshaw, Seth, 19, 52–53

Holland, 184

Holy Spirit, 11, 20, 26, 28, 34, 53, 57, 60, 117–118, 120, 133, 135–136, 154, 163–164, 172, 174, 189–190, 194–195, 198, 204, 215, 235, 239, 254

Hoover, J.Y., 46, 67–68, 74

Horn, Matthew, 236

Horst, Chris, 228

Horsthuis, Jim, 260

I

Ibarra, Herminia, 38, 219

Idaho, 109

Illinois, 112

Indiana, 113

Indiana Yearly Meeting of Friends, 27, 48, 52, 53, 81, 109, 112–115, 115, 116, 119, 121, 123, 126, 128

Ingle, H. Larry, 58, 71, 78

Iowa, 113

Iowa Yearly Meeting of Friends, 82, 109, 111, 113–115, 117, 119, 123, 126, 128

Israel, 7, 171, 181, 215, 225

J

Jenkins, Michael, 34, 182

Jerusalem, 171, 231

Jesuit, 59, 259

Jesus, 21, 25, 46, 54, 60, 72, 77, 79, 101, 106, 132, 135, 145, 148, 159, 159–161, 172, 179, 181–182, 189, 193–194, 202–203, 215–216, 225–226, 245–248, 262–263

Jones, Rufus, 64

K

Kadesh, 46

Kang, Steve, 189

Kansas, 110–111

Kansas Yearly Meeting, 7, 23, 25, 81–83, 86–90, 111, 113

Kenworthy, Amos T., 47

Kotzebue, Alaska, 110

Kotzebue Sound Mission, 110

L

LaMothe, Ryan, 33

Lancashire, 217

Leddra, William, 184

Liberty Monthly Meeting, 84

Li, Charlene, 237

Liston, Gregory, 9

Loehr, Jim, 250

London Yearly Meeting, 174

Lord's Prayer, 193

M

MacMullen, Ramsay, 202

Macquarrie, John, 30

Mardock, Hubert, 98

Marshall, Charles, 184

Massachusetts General Court, 148

McPherson, Jesse, 49

Messiah, 160, 215–216, 262

Methodist, 75, 95, 259

Miami Quarterly Meeting, 112

Michigan, 74, 112

Mid-America Yearly Meeting, 111. *See also* Evangelical Friends Church—Mid America

Midwest (United States), 46, 48

Miller, Calvin, 156

Minutes, 24, 44, 53, 86, 89

Missouri, 111

Mohammed IV, Sultan, 183

monthly meeting, 21–23, 26, 28, 45, 54, 68, 82, 119, 121, 128, 134, 139, 174, 183, 236

Mosaic covenant, 159, 171

Mudge, Lewis, 30

N

Nayler, James, 58, 105, 166

Nazareth, 172

Nebraska, 112

Nebraska Yearly Meeting, 111

Nevada, 111

New Jersey, 112

Newman, Stewart, 93, 221

New Testament, 34, 145, 159–160, 172, 192, 193–195, 224, 235, 239

New York, 112

Noblesville Friends Church, 49, 159, 171

North Carolina, 82, 112, 114–116

North Carolina Yearly Meeting of Friends, 82, 109, 112, 114–115, 116, 119, 121, 123, 126, 128

Northwest Yearly Meeting of Friends Church, 109, 114–116, 119–120, 125, 127

O

Ohio, 112–113

Ohio Yearly Meeting, 112

Oklahoma, 111

Oregon, 109

Oregon Yearly Meeting, 110, 113

Orthodox Friends, 207

orthodoxy, 94, 99, 101, 103, 133, 202, 204, 235, 240

orthopraxy, 240

Oxford, 55, 58

P

Palestine, 177

Paris, 61

Paschke, Boris, 193

Peake, Frank, 56

Pendle Hill, 216–217, 226

Penington, Isaac, 173, 197, 205, 248

Pennsylvania, 42, 112

Penn, William, 42, 59–60, 203–205, 232, 248

Pentecost, 49, 215

Perl, Paul, 257

Peter the Great, 183

Pinnock, Clark, 136

Pius VII, Pope, 183

Plank, Geoffrey, 196

Plugh, M. H., 63

Polling, James, 30

postmodernism, 178–179

practical theology, 8, 31–32, 95, 98, 133, 142, 168, 238

professionalized clergy, 27, 43, 48–49, 52–61, 64, 75, 82–83, 252

Programmed Worship, 29, 62, 65–66, 84, 198

Promised Land, 159

Protestant, 15, 18, 21, 23, 44, 63, 93, 135, 153, 163, 194, 197, 207, 256

Prusak, Bernard, 132

Publishers of Truth, 226

Punshon, John, 20, 218

Puritan, 42, 62, 164, 165, 173, 236

Q

Quarterly Meeting, 22–23, 27, 48, 105, 113, 232

Queries, 24, 115, 174–175, 240

Quietist, 102–103, 105, 175, 183

R

recorded minister, 25–27, 29, 44, 48, 157

Reformation, 62, 162

Religious Society of Friends, 16, 42

Roa, Huggy, 208

Robinson, William, 184

Rocky Mountain Yearly Meeting of the Friends Church, 109, 111, 114, 117, 118–123, 125, 127

Roman Empire, 157

Roman Inquisition, 184

Rosenthal, Norman, 233

Rowntree, John Wilhelm, 49

S

Sanders, Amos, 49

Schwartz, Tony, 250

275

Second Day Morning Meeting, 206
Segler, Franklin, 192
Shana, David Le, 175
Shawnee, 111
silence, 28, 44, 63–65, 188–190, 193, 197
Snow, Shane, 219
social gospel, 17, 20
South Carolina, 114
Southwest Yearly Meeting. *See* Evangelical Friends Church—Southwest
Spencer, Carole, 248
spiritual formation, 154, 245–247
Springfield Monthly Meeting, 82
Stephenson, Marmaduke, 184
Sutton, Robert, 208
Swarthmore Hall, 148

T

Terrell, Luramall, 49
testimonies (Quaker), 9, 10, 11, 16, 18, 20, 24, 43, 54, 96, 99, 101, 103, 115, 131, 150
Texas, 111
Thompson, Derek, 186, 200

Tjørhom, Ola, 35
Torah, 77, 171
Trinitarian, 11, 18, 202
Trinity, 21
Trueblood, Elton, 19, 60, 180, 218, 226, 255

U

United Kingdom, 56
United Methodist Church, 95
United States, 31, 112
Unprogrammed Worship, 28–29, 62–66, 83, 198
Utah, 111

V

Valiant Sixty, 226, 232
Vatican II, 33
Viola, Frank, 194
Vipont, Elvira, 218
Virginia, 112
Voltaire, 60

W

Washington, 109
Wesleyan Holiness, 46, 69

Western Yearly Meeting of Friends, 109, 113–116, 119, 121, 123, 126, 128

Westminster Assembly of 1643–1653, 173

Williams, Josiah, 230

Williams, Walter, 24

Wilmington College, 112

Wilmington Yearly Meeting of Friends, 109, 112–113, 115–116, 119, 121, 123, 126, 128

World War II, 177

Wright, Christopher, 181

Y

Yahweh, 224, 255

Yolen, Jane, 63

Scripture Index

Old Testament

Genesis
5:2 149

Exodus
31:1–6 254

Deuteronomy, 159
6:7 171
11:19 171

Nehemiah
8:5–8 171
8:7–8 171

Proverbs
17:28 193

Ecclesiastes
3:7 193

Isaiah, 160
2:2 216

Joel, 216
2:1–2 217

New Testament

Matthew
5–7 159
5:17 160
10:6 225
10:8 77
13:10–12 161
25:31–40 257
28:1–10 145
28:16–20 .... 172, 182, 215
28:19 246

Mark
5:24–34 145

Luke
8:1–3 215
10:38–42 145

John, 247
1:39 247
3 194
4 145
8:1–11 145
10:9 245
10:10 182
10:11 245
10:27 245
15:15 16
20:17 149
21:15 245

Acts, 60, 145, 192, 215
1:2 194
1:6 215
1:8 215
4:8 194
6 231
6:12 160
9:31 194
10 216
10:44 194
12:12 193
13:1–3 194
13:3 194
16:16 194
18 145

Romans, 146
- 1:10 258
- 10:14 177
- 10:14–15 182

1 Corinthians
- 1 149
- 5 191
- 11:3–4 146
- 11–14 162
- 12:28 239
- 13:3 164
- 14:15 192
- 14:26–33 195
- 14:34 146
- 16:1 258

2 Corinthians
- 10:10 235
- 12:9 149
- 13:1 258

Ephesians
- 4:1–16 254
- 4:12 252, 254, 256
- 5:18–20 192

Colossians
- 3:16 192

1 Thessalonians
- 5:19 195

1 Timothy
- 2:12 146
- 4:1-2 124
- 5:17 124

2 Timothy
- 2:15 268

Hebrews
- 4:12-13 124

1 Peter
- 2:5 43

Revelation
- 7:9 216

Endnotes

Introduction

1 Smith, *Philosophy of Ministry*, 23.
2 McCracken, *Hipster Christianity* 12.
3 Newman, *Free Church Perspective*, 3.
4 Liston, *Anointed Church*, 2.
5 McCracken, *Hipster Christianity*, 13.
6 For an in-depth exploration of the representation of Quakerism in arts and culture, see James Emmett Ryan, *Imaginary Friends: Representing Quakers in American Culture, 1650–1950*.
7 Berger, *Contagious*, 7.
8 Ibid., 7–9.
9 Sutton and Rao, *Scaling Up Excellence*, ix.
10 Biffi, *Casta Meretrix: "The Chase Whore"*, 11.

Chapter 1

11 Russell, *History of Quakerism*, 30; Trueblood, *People Called Quakers*, 4.
12 Barbour and Frost, *Quakers*, 28; Cooper, *Living Faith*, 1.

13 Elliott, *Whither Bound Quakers*, 3.
14 Bronner, *Quakerism and Christianity*, 10.
15 Tongue, *Vocation of Friends*, 44.
16 Ingle, *Quakers in Conflict*, 12–14; Le Shana, *Quakers in California*, 35.
17 Brooks, *Road to Character*, 30.
18 Swift, *Joseph John Gurney*, 177.
19 Williams, *Rich Heritage*, 169.
20 Mccracken, *Hipster Christianity*, 75.
21 Punshon, *Patterns of Change*, 15.
22 Gwyn, *Unmasking the Idols*, 4.
23 Trueblood, *Total Gospel*, 3.
24 Hinshaw, *Message and Mission*, 10.
25 Newby, *Teachings of Evangelical Friends*, 6.
26 Punshon, *Patterns of Change*, 10.
27 For example, the term "Christ-centered" could unintentionally lead to a form of Unitarianism, focusing solely on Christ the Son, at the expense of other members of the Trinity. Byars, *Lift Your Hearts*, xii.
28 Vipont, *Story of Quakerism*, 97.
29 Abbott, Chijioke, Dandelion, and Oliver, *Historical Dictionary*, 185.
30 Brinton, *Quaker Practice*, 27.
31 Collier, *Quaker Meeting*, 21ff.
32 London Yearly Meeting, *Christian Faith and Practice*, sec. 348–58.
33 Kansas Yearly Meeting, *Discipline* (1940), 51.
34 Stranahan, *History of Friends*, 17.
35 Abbott, Chijioke, Dandelion, and Oliver, *Historical Dictionary*, 235.
36 Jones, *Later Periods of Quakerism*, 110.

37 Lucas, *Quaker Story*, 43.
38 Abbott, Chijioke, Dandelion, and Oliver, *Historical Dictionary*, 310.
39 Jones, *Later Periods of Quakerism*, 183.
40 Kansas Yearly Meeting, *Minutes* (1900), 64.
41 Evangelical Friends Church Southwest, *Faith and Practice*, 11.
42 Williams, *Rich Heritage*, 93.
43 Kansas Yearly Meeting, *Discipline* (1892), 98.
44 Hoover, *History of the Life*, 45.
45 Hamm, "Chipping at the Landmarks, 136–59; Kansas Yearly Meeting, *Discipline* (1886), 11.
46 Gurney, *Peculiar People*, 73.
47 Hamm, *Quakers in America*, 86; Vipont, *Story of Quakerism*, 142; Woodman, *Quakers Find a Way*, 46.
48 Gurney, *Peculiar People*, 228; Punshon, *Portrait in Grey*, 141.
49 Punshon, *Portrait in Grey*, 141.
50 Wood, *Distinguishing Doctrines*, 16–17.
51 Indiana Yearly Meeting, *Discipline* (1864), 103.
52 Ibid.
53 Harvey, *Rise of the Quakers*, 68; Nuttall, *Refreshing*, 13ff; Trueblood, *Studies*, 16.
54 Brinton, *Prophetic Ministry*, 19.
55 Mudge and Poling, *Formation and Reflection*, xiii.
56 Macquarrie, *Faith*, 12.
57 Gamertsfelder, *Systematic Theology*, 7.
58 Hall, *Learning Theology*, 10.
59 Pinnock, *Flame of Love*, 12.
60 Plantinga, Thompson, and Lundberg, *Christian Theology*, 18.
61 Willard, *Knowing Christ Today*, 154.

62 Ibid., 197; Strong, *Systematic Theology*, 17.
63 Farley, "Interpreting Situations," 1.
64 Dingemans, "Practical Theology," 82.
65 Ibid., 84; Grethlein, *Practical Theology*, 5.
66 McKim, *Westminster Dictionary*, 215.
67 Dingemans, "Practical Theology," 84.
68 Browning, *Practical Theology*, 3.
69 Lovin, "The Real Task," 126.
70 Cahalan and Mikosi, *Opening the Field*, 2.
71 Schneider, Wittberg, Unruh, Sinha, and Belcher, "Comparing Practical Theology," 408.
72 Pattison, *Challenge of Practical Theology*, 11.
73 Forrester, *Truthful Action*, ix.
74 Farley, "Interpreting Situations," 3.
75 Ibid.; Pattison, *Challenge of Practical Theology*, 247.
76 Brister, *Pastoral Care*, 8.
77 Adams, *Shepherding God's Flock*, 5; Byrum, *Christian Theology*, 2; Miller-McLemore, "Pastoral Theologian," 813–15.
78 Ingram, "Leadership, Democracy, and Religion," 119–29; Steele, *On the Way*, 124.
79 LaMothe, "Broken and Empty," 452.
80 Jenkins, *Church Faces Death*, 36.
81 Becker, "Understanding Local Mission," 273.
82 Rightmire, "Subordination of Ecclesiology," 27.
83 For example, Stramara, "Toward a Charismatic Ecclesiology," 218–46; Fiddes, "Christian Doctrine," 195–219.
84 Tjørhom, "Better Together," 284–85.
85 Elliott, *Whither Bound Quakers*, 6.
86 Burns, *Leadership*, 1.
87 Dickson, *Humilitas*, 33.

88 Bacon, *Elements of Influence*, 12.
89 Sears, quoted in Elashmawi and Harris, *Multicultural Management*, 9.
90 Patel, *Interfaith Leadership*, 12–13.
91 Dickson, *Humilitas*, 43.
92 Goleman, Boyatzis, and Mckee, *Primal Leadership*, 5.
93 Kohles, Baker, and Donaho, *Transformational Leadership*, 273.
94 Batten, *Tough-Minded Leadership*, 35.
95 Yukl, *Leadership in Organizations*, 3.
96 Malphurs, *Values-Driven Leadership*, 22.
97 Maxwell, *Developing the Leader*, 1.
98 Seidman, *HOW*, xxv.
99 Ibid.
100 Hershey and Blanchard, *Management*, 5.
101 Ibid.
102 Ibarra, *Act Like a Leader*, 36.
103 Steers, *Organizational Behavior*, 298; Goldhaber, *Organizational Communication*, 59.
104 Williams, *Human Behavior*, 25.
105 Ibid.; Forsyth, *Introduction*, 8.
106 Ibid.

Chapter 2

107 Jones, *Life and Message*, 4–5; Van Etten, *George Fox*, 21.
108 Braithwaite and Hodgkin, *Message and Mission*, 22–24; Fox, *Journal*, 13; Fox, "Epistle 265," 11.
109 Douglas, *George Fox*, 16–17; Sharman, *George Fox*, 84–86.
110 Barbour, *Quakers in Puritan England*, 47; Marsh, *Popular Life*, 67; Wildes, *Voice*, 75–76.
111 Fisher, *Quaker Colonies*, 8–11; Glines, *Undaunted Zeal*, 390–95.

112 Gurney, *Observations*, 4–5; Miller, *Friends and Their Beliefs*, 5; Woodward, *Timothy Nicholson*, 17–20.
113 Shideler, "Concept of the Church," 67–81.
114 Brinton, *Prophetic Ministry*, 14; Dandelion, *Liturgies of Quakerism*, 23–25.
115 Comfort, *Just Among Friends*, 9–10.
116 Clarkson, *Portraiture of Quakerism*, 124–27.
117 Evans, *Concise Account*, 138–40.
118 Whitmire, *Plain Living*, 23.
119 Hobart, *Can Quakerism Speak*, 8–9.
120 Fox, "Epistle 266," *Works*, 8:11–12; Ingle, *First Among Friends*, 57–58.
121 Cadbury, *Character*, 30–31; Indiana Yearly Meeting, *Discipline* (1905), 61–62.
122 Collier, *Quaker Meeting*, 1–2; Emmot, *Story of Quakerism*, 85–89; Osborn, *Journal*, 4.
123 California Yearly Meeting, *Friends Worship*, 22; Sheeran, *Beyond Majority Rule*, 4–6; Vipont, *Story of Quakerism*, 98.
124 Lucas, *Quaker Message*, 29; Pollard, Pollard, and Pollard, *Democracy*, 46–51.
125 Fendall, Wood, and Bishop, *Practicing Discernment*, 83–84; Junior, *Monthly Meeting Chronicle*, 7.
126 Holden, *Friends Divided*, 19.
127 Brinton, *Prophetic Ministry*, 15; Wood, *Distinguishing Doctrines*, 16.
128 Le Shana, *Quakers in California*, 30.
129 Hamm, *Quakers in America*, 94; Trueblood, *Incendiary Fellowship*, 112–14.
130 Le Shana, *Quakers in California*, 99. For example, the evangelist Allen Jay, see Jacob, *Builders*, 198–99.
131 Hamm, "Chipping at the Landmarks," 146.

132 Hoover, *History of the Life*, 88.
133 Jackson, *Quaker Preachers*, 23.
134 Harold, "Early Activities," 4.
135 Allman, *Pioneer Friends Preachers*, 64; Jacob, *Builders*, 198.
136 Le Shana, *Quakers in California*, 39.
137 Hamm, "Chipping at the Landmarks," 147.
138 Le Shana, *Quakers in California*, 40.
139 Punshon, *Portrait in Grey*, 201.
140 For example, this is seen in the inclusion of the pastoral position in Iowa Yearly Meeting, *Book of Discipline*, 81.
141 Frame and Frame, *Reminiscences*, 444–45, 530–31.
142 Heusel, *Quaker Pastorate*, 7.
143 Friends United Meeting, *Foundations for Membership*, 11.

Chapter 3

144 Hinshaw, *Spoken Ministry*, 105–106.
145 Ibid., 105.
146 Kansas Yearly Meeting, *Minutes* (1873), 14; (1874), 9; (1875), 9; Indiana Yearly Meeting, *Discipline* (1864), 81; (1839), 75; Kansas Yearly Meeting, *Discipline* (1884), 117; (1896), 122. What is fascinating about the Kansas Yearly Meeting disciplines above is that the call to support the minister is very clearly articulated (and italicized) as *"while they are engaged in this work,"* which points to a continued tension regarding the financial support of pastors.
147 Indiana Yearly Meeting, *Discipline* (1854), 80.
148 Fox, *Journal*, 10.
149 Peake, "Reflections," 99.
150 Ibid.
151 Barclay, *Apology*, 316.
152 Fox, *Works*, 16.

153 Barclay, *Apology*, 11.
154 Fox, *Works*, 15.
155 Ingle, *First Among Friends*, 43.
156 Barclay, *Apology*, 298.
157 Nayler, *Works*, 17–18.
158 Penn, *Brief Account*, 59.
159 Foster and Smith, *Devotional Classics*, 218.
160 Penn, *Brief Account*, 42.
161 Ibid., 2.
162 Ibid., 39.
163 Trueblood, *Robert Barclay*, 1.
164 Ibid., 3.
165 Ibid. A description of the Scots College that Barclay attended in Paris can be found in Halloran, "Spirited Scottish Students."
166 For an anthology chronicling the continuity of presence of Anglican clergy in village life, see Chapman, *Godly and Righteous*.
167 Gwyn, *Apocalypse*, 59.
168 Plugh, "Meaning in Silence," 208.
169 Ibid.
170 Ibid.
171 Daniels, "A Convergent Model," 4; Volf, *After Our Likeness*, 224ff.
172 Yolen, *Friend*, 165.
173 Stuard, "Women's Witnessing," 11–13; Mack, *Visionary Women*, 133.
174 Jones, *Faith and Practice*, 58.
175 Dandelion, *Liturgies*, 32.
176 Gwyn, *Apocalypse*, 168–69.
177 North Carolina Yearly Meeting, *Three Hundred Years*, 49–50.

178 Hamm, *Quakers in America*, 83.
179 Graves, "Ministry and Preaching," 288.
180 Ibid., 288.
181 Ibid.
182 Ibid.
183 Ibid.
184 Dandelion, *Introduction*, 208.
185 Ibid.
186 Ibid.
187 For example, see California Yearly Meeting, *Friends Worship*, 15ff.
188 Iowa Yearly Meeting, *Discipline* (1891), 16–17.
189 Birkel, *Silence and Witness*, 99.
190 Hoover, *Life and Labors*, 48.
191 Ibid., 53.
192 Birkel, *Silence and Witness*, 99.
193 Frame and Frame, *Reminiscences*, 426.
194 Hamm, *Quakers in America*, 21.
195 Braithwaite, *Beginnings of Quakerism*, 3–4, 84.
196 Birkel, *Silence and Witness*, 17; Marsh, *Popular Life*, 56–57; Punshon, *Patterns of Change*, 36.
197 Chapman, *Godly and Righteous*, viii.
198 Ibid.
199 Barclay, *Apology*, 311.
200 Ingle, *First Among Friends*, 43.
201 Fox, *Works of George Fox*, 4:18.
202 Barclay, *Apology*, 260–61.
203 Dandelion, *Liturgies of Quakerism*, 28.
204 Barclay, *Apology*, 19.
205 Ibid., 286.
206 Le Shana, *Quakers in California*, 34.

207 Hoover, *Life and Labors*, 164–65.
208 Frame and Frame, *Reminiscences*, 122.
209 Braithwaite, *Beginnings of Quakerism*, 458–59; Evans, *Friends in the Seventeenth Century*, 613–15.
210 Brace, *Idea of Property*, 17ff.
211 Ibid., 17.
212 Ingle, *First Among Friends*, 58.
213 Brace, *Idea of Property*, 17.
214 Ibid.
215 Fox, *Works*, 17.
216 Fox, *Some Principles*, 21.
217 Ibid.
218 Fell, "Epistle to Friends," 49.
219 Fox, *Works*, 12.
220 Gwyn, *Apocalypse*, 27.
221 Ingle, *First Among Friends*, 80.
222 Barclay, *Apology*, 323.
223 Ibid., 324.
224 Brace, *Idea of Property*, 18.
225 Barclay, *Apology*, 324.
226 Penn, *Brief Account*, 39.
227 Barclay, *Apology*, 20.
228 North Carolina Yearly Meeting, *Carolina Quakers*, 62.
229 Jones, *Quakers of Iowa*, 107. I came across this fact and subsequent source in Le Shana, *Quakers in California*, 110.
230 Haworth, *Springfield*, 32.
231 Le Shana, *Quakers in California*, 120.
232 Kansas Yearly Meeting, *Minutes* (1891), 26–27, 37; (1893), 6; (1894), 37; (1895), 8; (1896), 7; (1897), 29.
233 Ibid., (1897), 70.
234 Ibid., 71.

235 Barna and Viola, *Pagan Christianity*, 33.
236 Dyer and Hoch, *Alva Friends Meeting*, 2.
237 Indiana Yearly Meeting, *Minutes*, 32
238 Iowa Yearly Meeting, *Minutes*, 13.
239 Kansas Yearly Meeting, *Minutes* (1886), 42; (1887), 37; (1888), 59; (1978), 24.
240 Ibid., (1884), 40–41; (1952), 34–35; (1954), 43; (1955), 36; (1956), 39–40.
241 Ibid., (1891), 37.
242 Ibid., (1890), 23.
243 Ibid., (1957), 43; (1958), 40; (1959), 43; (1969), 45.
244 Ibid., (1962), 39.
245 Ibid., (1965), 43–44; (1968), 37, 40. The 1968 minutes are a fascinating example of both encouragement and concern regarding church finances. While a concerted stewardship effort had increased giving and pastoral support slightly, there were still concerns over some signs of decline and apathy regarding future growth.
246 Ibid., (1930), 17.
247 Ibid., (1925), 30.
248 Ibid., (1958), 40.
249 Ibid., (1914), 38.
250 Ibid., (1921), 19.
251 Ibid., (1978), 24.
252 Ibid., (1925), 30.

Chapter 4

253 Newman, *Free Church Perspective*, 60.
254 Alvesson, "Organizational Culture," 44.
255 Ibid.
256 Newman, *Free Church Perspective*, 86.

257 Strawbridge, "Word of the Cross," 61.
258 Gwyn, *Idols*, 4.
259 Seidman, *HOW*, 49.
260 Becker, "Understanding Local Mission," 269.
261 Cartledge, "Practical Theology," 268.
262 Browning, *Fundamental Practical Theology*, 7; Mudge and Poling, *Formation and Reflection*, 104.
263 Punshon, *Patterns of Change*, 20.
264 Johnson and Johnson, *Joining Together*, 5. According to Johnson and Johnson, a "group" is defined as any interdependent gathering of people. All organizations are groups, but not all groups are organizations.
265 Glaser, *Conversational Intelligence*, 25; Berger, *Contagious*, 96; Morgan, Lynch, and Lynch, *Spark*, 121.
266 Henry, *Accidental Creative*, 26.
267 Johnson and Johnson, *Joining Together*, 7.
268 Newman, *Free Church Perspective*, 3.
269 Kao, *Jamming*, 81.
270 Ibarra, *Act Like a Leader*, 4.
271 Ibid.
272 Mardock, *Adventures*, 5.
273 Lovin, "Real Task," 125.
274 Ibid., 128.
275 Newman, *Free Church Perspective*, 11.
276 Hatch, "Dynamics," 658.
277 Mayers, *Christianity Confronts Culture*, 98.
278 Vanhoozer, *Everyday Theology*, 24.
279 Odom, Boxx, and Dunn, "Organizational Cultures," 158.
280 Ibid.; Sutton and Rao, *Scaling Up Excellence*, 91; Mudge and Poling, *Formation and Reflection*, 103–19.
281 Berne, *Structure and Dynamics*, 15.

282 Akerlof and Kranton, *Identity Economics*, 4.
283 Hatch, "Dynamics," 660.
284 Newman, *Free Church Perspective*, 11.
285 Hurst, *Crisis and Renewal*, 1.
286 Hatch, "Dynamics," 667.
287 Ibid.
288 Phillips, "Ancient and Comely Order," 96.
289 Ingle, *Quakers in Conflict*, 4.
290 Sinclair, "Approaches," 66.
291 Ibid.
292 Ibid.
293 Ibid., 131.
294 Hallett, "Symbolic Power," 133.
295 Ibarra, *Act Like a Leader*, 143.

Chapter 5

296 Beebe, *Garden of the Lord*, 26.
297 Ibid.
298 Hinshaw, "Five Years Meeting," 96.
299 Roberts, *Tomorrow*, 22.
300 Alaska Yearly Meeting, *Discipline*, 3.
301 Ibid.
302 Evangelical Friends Church—Southwest, *Faith and Practice*, 10.
303 Hinshaw, "Five Years Meeting," 104.
304 Evangelical Friends Church—Mid America, *Faith and Practice*, 5.
305 Ibid.
306 Ibid.
307 Dandelion, *Introduction to Quakerism*, 165.

308 Evangelical Friends Church—Mid America, *Faith and Practice*, 5.
309 Rocky Mountain Yearly Meeting, *Faith and Practice*, 5.
310 Roberts, "Evangelical Quakers," 112.
311 Rocky Mountain Yearly Meeting, *Faith and Practice*, 5.
312 Hamm, *Quakers in America*, 48–49.
313 Evangelical Friends Church—Eastern Region, *Faith and Practice*, 5.
314 Wilmington Yearly Meeting, *Faith and Practice*, 8.
315 Yearly Meeting Centennial Committee, *Wilmington Yearly Meeting*, 4.
316 Hieronimus, *Friends in Tennessee*, 10.
317 Ibid., 34.
318 Jones, *Quakers of Iowa*, 38.
319 Iowa Yearly Meeting, *Discipline*, 1–2.
320 Jones, *Quakers of Iowa*, 38.
321 Newman, *Procession of Friends*, 122.
322 "Churches," Iowa Yearly Meeting of Friends, accessed June 15, 2017, https://www.iaym.org/churches.
323 Coffin, "Western Yearly Meeting," 9–11, http://muse.jhu.edu/article/404608/summary.
324 Western Yearly Meeting, *Semi-Centennial Anniversary*, 96.
325 Stanfield, "American Quakers," 35.
326 "Directory," Western Yearly Meeting, accessed June 7, 2017, https://www.westernyearlymeeting.org/meetingchurch-directory/.
327 Hinshaw, *Indiana Friends Heritage*, 2.
328 Indiana Yearly Meeting, *Faith and Practice*, 10.
329 "IYM Meetings & Churches," Indiana Yearly Meeting of the Religious Society of Friends, accessed

February 10, 2017, http://www.iym.org/site/cpage.asp?cpage_id=180039785&sec_id=180010756.

330 Moore, *Friends in the Carolinas*, 4–5.
331 North Carolina Yearly Meeting, *Carolina Quakers*, 37; Hinshaw, *Carolina Quaker Experience*, 138.
332 Rocky Mountain Yearly Meeting, *Faith and Practice*, 50.
333 Evangelical Friends Church—Mid America, *Faith and Practice*, 68.
334 Northwest Yearly Meeting, *Faith and Practice*, 63.
335 Evangelical Friends Church—Southwest, *Faith and Practice*, 57.
336 Iowa Yearly Meeting, *Discipline*, chap. 4:3, 6.
337 Western Yearly Meeting, *Faith and Practice*, 56; North Carolina Yearly Meeting, *Faith and Practice*, 75.
338 Indiana Yearly Meeting, *Faith and Practice*, 75.
339 Evangelical Friends Church—Eastern Region, *Faith and Practice*, 50.
340 Evangelical Friends Church—Mid America, *Faith and Practice*, 68.
341 Alaska Yearly Meeting, *Discipline*, 15.
342 Northwest Yearly Meeting, *Faith and Practice*, 64.
343 Wilmington Yearly Meeting, *Faith and Practice*, 41; Indiana Yearly Meeting, *Faith and Practice*, 75.
344 Western Yearly Meeting, *Faith and Practice*, 37.
345 North Carolina Yearly Meeting, *Faith and Practice*, 75.
346 Evangelical Friends Church—Southwest, *Faith and Practice*, 56.
347 Ibid.
348 Ibid.
349 Alaska Yearly Meeting, *Discipline*, 14.
350 Ibid., 15.

351 Rocky Mountain Yearly Meeting, *Faith and Practice*, 50.
352 Evangelical Friends Church—Mid America, *Faith and Practice*, 68.
353 Northwest Yearly Meeting, *Faith and Practice*, 64.
354 Alaska Yearly Meeting, *Discipline*, 15.
355 Indiana Yearly Meeting, *Faith and Practice*, 76.
356 North Carolina Yearly Meeting, *Faith and Practice*, 72.
357 Iowa Yearly Meeting, *Discipline*, 3–4.
358 Wilmington Yearly Meeting, *Faith and Practice*, 38; Western Yearly Meeting, *Faith and Practice*, 35.
359 Evangelical Friends Church—Southwest, *Faith and Practice*, 56.
360 Northwest Yearly Meeting, *Faith and Practice*, 64.
361 Evangelical Friends Church—Mid America, *Faith and Practice*, 68.
362 Alaska Yearly Meeting, *Discipline*, 15.
363 Indiana Yearly Meeting, *Faith and Practice*, 75; North Carolina Yearly Meeting, *Faith and Practice*, 80.
364 Western Yearly Meeting, *Faith and Practice*, 37; Wilmington Yearly Meeting, *Faith and Practice*, 41.
365 Trueblood, *Studies*, 20–21.
366 Evangelical Friends Church—Southwest, *Faith and Practice*, 58.
367 Evangelical Friends Church—Eastern Region, *Faith and Practice*, 49.
368 Evangelical Friends Church—Mid America, *Faith and Practice*, 68.
369 Rocky Mountain Yearly Meeting, *Faith and Practice*, 50.
370 Southwest Yearly Meeting, *Faith and Practice*, 58.
371 Alaska Yearly Meeting, *Discipline*, 15.

372 Indiana Yearly Meeting, *Faith and Practice*, 75–76; North Carolina Yearly Meeting, *Faith and Practice*, 80; Western Yearly Meeting, *Faith and Practice*, 38; Wilmington Yearly Meeting, *Faith and Practice*, 41.
373 Evangelical Friends Church—Southwest, *Faith and Practice*, 57.
374 Evangelical Friends Church—Eastern Region, *Faith and Practice*, 49.
375 Alaska Yearly Meeting, *Discipline*, 15.
376 Ibid.
377 Rocky Mountain Yearly Meeting, *Faith and Practice*, 50.
378 Evangelical Friends Church—Mid America, *Faith and Practice*, 68.
379 Northwest Yearly Meeting, *Faith and Practice*, 64.
380 Iowa Yearly Meeting, *Discipline*, 4–7.
381 Indiana Yearly Meeting, *Faith and Practice*, 75; North Carolina Yearly Meeting, *Faith and Practice*, 79–80.
382 Western Yearly Meeting, *Faith and Practice*, 37; Wilmington Yearly Meeting, *Faith and Practice*, 41.
383 Evangelical Friends Church—Southwest, *Faith and Practice*, 56.
384 Ibid.
385 Ibid.
386 Evangelical Friends Church—Eastern Region, *Faith and Practice*, 49.
387 Rocky Mountain Yearly Meeting, *Faith and Practice*, 50.
388 Northwest Yearly Meeting, *Faith and Practice*, 64.
389 Alaska Yearly Meeting, *Discipline*, 15.
390 Evangelical Friends Church—Mid America, *Faith and Practice*, 68.
391 Indiana Yearly Meeting, *Faith and Practice*, 76.

392 Iowa Yearly Meeting, *Discipline*, 4–7; Western Yearly Meeting, *Faith and Practice*, 38.

393 North Carolina Yearly Meeting, *Faith and Practice*, 80; Wilmington Yearly Meeting, *Faith and Practice*, 41.

Chapter 6

394 Prusak, *Church Unfinished*, 9.

395 Cooper-White and Cooper-White, *Exploring Practices*, 12.

396 Birkel, *Engaging Scripture*, xx

397 Newman, *Free Church Perspective*, 32.

398 Ibid., 40–41.

399 Ibid., 40.

400 Ibid., 26.

401 Briggs, "Biblical Hermeneutics," 202.

402 Ibid.; Farley, "Interpreting Situations," 13.

403 Newman, *Free Church Perspective*, 49.

404 Browning, *Fundamental Practical Theology*, 116.

405 Punshon, *Patterns of Change*, 14.

406 Oden, *Living God*, 5; Stafford, *Theology for Disciples*, 34

407 Erickson, *Christian Theology*, 21; Byrum, *Christian Theology*, 1; Strong, *Systematic Theology*, 1; Gamertsfelder, *Systematic Theology*, 1.

408 McKim, *Westminster Dictionary*, 279.

409 Erickson, *Christian Theology*, 21.

410 Demerest, "Systematic Theology," 1064.

411 Plantinga, Thompson, and Lundberg, *Introduction to Christian Theology*, 3.

412 Hall, *Learning Theology*, 31.

413 Pinnock, *Flame of Love*, 12.

414 Berne, *Games People Play* (1964), 29.

415 Brooks, *Social Animal*, 179.

416 Mintzberg, *Power*, 22.
417 Bass and Riggio, *Transformational Leadership*, 6.
418 Northouse, *Leadership*, 226.
419 Williams, *Human Behavior*, 25.
420 Willink and Babin, *Extreme Ownership*, xii.
421 Bass and Riggio, *Transformational Leadership*, 6.
422 Lewis, *Transformational Leadership*, vi.
423 Lowney, *Heroic Leadership*, 1.
424 Pfeffer, *Power*, 5.
425 Kaplan, *Warrior Politics*, 53. Please note the explicit rejection of Judeo-Christian morality in the subtitle, replaced with an apparently more effective "pagan ethos."; Roberts, *Leadership Secrets*, (does this need a page number?)
426 Dickson, *Humilitas*, 66.
427 Pfeffer, *Power*, 11.
428 Klaus, *Brag!*, 6.

Chapter 7

429 Gallagher, *Family Theology*, 43.
430 Keener, "Matthew's Missiology," 13.
431 Fell, *Women's Speaking Justified*, 7.
432 *Christianity Today*, "Women," 74–75; Duff, "Ordination of Women," 95ff.; Thorley, "Junia," 18–29. Cf. Scaer, "Was Junias a Female Apostle?" 76; Wolters, "IOYNIAN," 397–408.
433 An example: Økland, *Women in Their Place*, 230. Økland argues that Paul addressed a broader issue of sacred space and order in worship, which reflected a broader cosmic order, rather than specific gender issues per se.
434 Hensley, "Σιγάω, λαλέω, and ὑποτάσσω in 1 Corinthians 14:34," 343–64; Spurgeon, "Pauline Commands and

Women," 317–33; Janzen, "Orderly Participation," 5570. For a different textual theory, see Marquardt, "The Peculiar Use," 289–303; Allison, "Let Women Be Silent," 27–60.

435 Fell, *Women's Speaking Justified*, 8.
436 Belleville, *Woman Leaders*, 19.
437 Plant, "Subjective Testimonies," 296.
438 Myles, "Monster to Martyr," 18.
439 Rapaport, *Naked*, 73–75.
440 Myles, "Monster to Martyr," 6.
441 Healey, *Quaker to Upper Canadian*, 25.
442 Fell, *Women's Speaking Justified*, 3ff.
443 Ibid., 3.
444 While contemporary American pastoral Quakerism must take responsibility for barriers that hindered female public ministry, such inequalities have existed throughout the movement. Western Yearly Meeting affirmed a recognized inequality by stating that "men ministers [are] taking more of the time of our Meetings for worship than is due them." Western Yearly Meeting, *Minutes*, (1880), 42.
445 Akerlof and Kranton, *Identity Economics*, 83.

Chapter 8

446 Craddock, *Preaching*, 27; Eswine, *Post-Everything World*, 145–46; Lose, *Confessing Jesus Christ*, 63ff.; Olford, *Anointed Expository Preaching*, 3–5.
447 Barna and Viola, *Pagan Christianity*, 85.
448 Chapell, *Hardest Sermons*, 12; Kent, *Pastor and His Work*, 87.
449 Lowry, *Homiletical Plot*, 24; Webb, *Preaching Without Notes*, 35–36.

450 Craddock, *Preaching*, chaps. 6–9; Eswine, *Post-Everything World*, 27–28; Hills, *Homeletics*, 72–94; Hybels, Briscoe, and Robinson, *Contemporary Preaching*, 74–75; Lowry, *Homiletical Plot*, 25–26; Stott, *Between Two Worlds*, 211–54; Webb, *Preaching Without Notes*, 38.

451 Allen, "Pulpit in the Round," 47–59; Stone, "Word and Sacrament," 444–63.

452 Loscalzo, *Sermons that Connect*, 148; McCracken, *Making of Sermon*, 68ff.

453 Foss, "Preaching for Discipleship," 164; Mawhinney, *Preaching with Freshness*, 82–87; Niles, *Preacher's Task*, 116; Shields, "Preaching and Spiritual Formation," 246–47.

454 Hybels and Bell, "Communicating Vision," 34ff.

455 Byars, *Protestant Worship*, 71.

456 The term *narrative preaching* has a broad range of meanings without a clear consensus as to which one is preeminent: Is it preaching as storytelling? Preaching over a narrative/life of a Bible character? The use of stories to illustrate the sermon? To clarify this, I have included *story* or *storytelling* next to *narrative* to show that, for this book, *narrative preaching* means utilizing the structures, methods, and concepts of stories in one's preaching. For a summary of these differing definitions, see Tucker, *Preacher as Storyteller*, 1–3.

457 Salmon, *Storytelling in Preaching*, 22. See also Eswine, *Post-Everything World*, 74–77.

458 Lord, *Finding Language*, 13.

459 Miller, *Preaching*, 12.

460 Jagerson, "Power of Narrative," 259–75; Wright, *Telling God's Story*, 13.

461 McClure, "Collaborative Preaching," 64.

462 Von Rad, "Ancient Word and Living Word," 4; Bennett, "Preaching Values in Deuteronomy," 45; Block, "Recovering the Voice of Moses," 385.
463 Sandy, *Plowshares & Pruning Hooks*, 131.
464 Gowan, *Prophetic Books*, 9.
465 Smith, *Prophets as Preachers*, 10; Zimmerli, *Fiery Throne*, 1–5.
466 Martin, *Worship in the Early Church*, 73.
467 Enoch, "Systematic Expository Preaching," 160; Kitchens, "Degree of Effectiveness," 187.
468 Wilder, *Early Christian Rhetoric*, 56.
469 Snodgrass, *Stories with Intent*, 2.
470 Witherington, *Paul's Narrative Thought World*, 205.
471 Cameron, *European Reformation*, 17.
472 McBrien, *Catholicism*, 398.
473 Barna and Viola, *Pagan Christianity*, 31.
474 Ibid., 34.
475 Wilder, *Early Christian Rhetoric*, 56.
476 Rowe, "1 Corinthians 12–14," 119–28; Schweizer, "Service of Worship," 402; Heil, *Letters of Paul*, 41.
477 Fox, "Epistle 267," 13–14.
478 Frye, *What Can I Believe*, 16.
479 Gwyn, *Apocalypse of the Word*, 128.
480 Evans, *Friends in the Seventeenth Century*, 61.
481 Cope, "Seventeenth-Century Quaker Style," 725.
482 Ibid., 725.
483 Graves, *Preaching the Inward Light*, 2.
484 Birkel, *Engaging Scripture*, 4–5.
485 Gwyn, *Apocalypse of the Word*, 180.
486 Dandelion, *Introduction to Quakerism*, 28.
487 Scott, "Ecclesiology and Mission," 321.
488 Eccles, *Art of Musick*.

489 Healey, *Quaker to Upper Canadian*, 29.
490 Plank, *John Woolman's Path*, 55.
491 Ibid., 92.
492 Ibid.
493 Berger, *Contagious*, 187.
494 Patterson, et al., *Influencer*, 57; Barker, *Barking*, 75.
495 Browning, "Practical Theology," 97.
496 Browning, *Fundamental Practical Theology*, 97.
497 Ibid.
498 Leithart, "Pastor Theologian," 11.
499 For a brief historical overview of Protestant Sunday schools, see Seymour, "Reforming Movement," 3ff.
500 Hayes, "Theological Foundations," 33.
501 Marmon, "Transformative Learning Theory," 428.
502 Birkel, *Engaging Scripture*, 42.
503 Tidwell, *Educational Ministry*, 19.
504 Christensen, *Word Biblical Commentary*, 80.
505 Longenecker, "Acts of the Apostles," 289.
506 Daniel, Wade, and Gresham, *Christian Education*, 19.
507 Cf. Volz, *Pastoral Life*, 98. Volz is unsure of whether a distinction can be made between *kerygma* (preaching) and *didache* (teaching). While understanding this hesitation to make an unnecessary categorical distinction, I believe there is sufficient evidence to warrant it. See also Keener, "Matthew's Missiology," 15–16.
508 Keener, *Gospel of Matthew*, 718.
509 Volz, *Pastoral Life*, 98. Volz is unsure of whether a distinction can be made between *kerygma* (preaching) and *didache* (teaching). While understanding this hesitation to make an unnecessary categorical distinction, I believe

there is sufficient evidence to warrant it: see also Keener, "Matthew's Missiology," 3–20.

510 Benson, *Christian Education*, 41–43.
511 Ibid.
512 Plimpton, *Mary Dyer*, 28.
513 Phelps, "Pastor and Teacher," 388; Stout, *New England Soul*, 104.
514 Vowell, *Wordy Shipmates*, 99.
515 Westminster Assembly, "Form of Presbyterial Church-Government," Church of Scotland, accessed July 15, 2017, http://www.freechurchcontinuing.org/about/government.
516 Barclay, "Catechism and Confession," 112ff; Coffin, *Mother's Catechism*; Philadelphia Yearly Meeting, *Brief Catechism*; Five Years Meeting, *Lessons in Friends History*.
517 Brown, *Quaker Queries*, iv.
518 Healey, *Quaker to Upper Canadian*, 29.
519 London Yearly Meeting, *Christian Advices*.
520 This is seemingly a problem whether the meeting is programmed or unprogrammed. See Collins, "Practice of Discipline," 136; Nelson, "Study," 71–72.
521 Le Shana, *Quakers in California*, 37.
522 See Iowa Yearly Meeting, *Bible School Lessons*; Iowa Yearly Meeting, *Bible School Lessons: Junior: Third Year*.
523 Kaur and Bhatia, "Involvement of Stakeholders," 3229.
524 For collective organizational improvement (instead of individual goals), see Humphrey, "Training the Total Organization," 57.
525 Tunio, Channa, and Pathan, "Training Practices," 197; Fry and Griswold, "Defining and Implementing," 311–12; Al-Refaie and Al-Tahat, "Effects of Knowledge Management," 387.

526 Jashapara, "Competitive Learning Organization," 52.
527 Kramlinger, "Training's Role," 46.
528 Kapp, "Manufacturing Organization," 49.
529 Giesecke and McNeil, "Learning Organization," 54.
530 Biech, "Learning Eye to Eye," 52.
531 Kaur and Bhatia, "Involvement of Stakeholders," 3229; Aziz et al., "Developing Organizational Training," 94.
532 Kapp, "Transforming Your Manufacturing Organization," 47.
533 Jenkins, *Church Faces Death*, 102.
534 Thompson, *Hit Makers*, 154.
535 Ibid.
536 Sim, "Postmodernism and Philosophy," 3.
537 McCracken, *Hipster Christianity*, 182.
538 Gatewood, "All Who Follow Jesus," 52.
539 Webb, *Fellowship Evangelism*, 6.
540 See Finger, "Theology of Welcome," 30; Pohl, *Making Room*, 7.
541 Bass, *Christianity for the Rest*, 81.
542 Ibid.
543 Trueblood, *Incendiary Fellowship*, 28.
544 Wright, *Mission of God*, 29.
545 Ibid.
546 World Evangelical Fellowship, "The Iguassu Affirmation," 18.
547 Ibid.
548 Jenkins, *Church Faces Death*, 23.
549 Plank, *John Woolman's Path*, 66.
550 Comfort, *Just Among Friends*, 81.
551 Audland, "Untitled Letter," 79.
552 Marshall, "Testimony," 81.

553 Evans and Cheevers, "Short Relation," 1; Palmer, Jr., "Cruel Sufferings," 11; Gill, "Evans and Cheevers," 258.
554 Healey, *Quaker to Upper Canadian*, 25.
555 Crouch, "Posthuma Christiana," 83.
556 Williams, *Rich of Heritage*, 124; Jones, "Quietism," 51.
557 Mardock, *Adventures*, 5.
558 For resources featuring examples of such Quaker mission fields, see Langford, *Fairest Isle*; Hilty, *Friends in Cuba*; Bears, *Urundi for Christ*; Steere and Steere, *Friends Work in Africa*.
559 Five Years Meeting, *Message of Christ*, 5.
560 Ibid.
561 Sutton and Rao, *Scaling Up Excellence*, ix.
562 Lee, "Marketing Is Dead."
563 Thompson, *Hit Makers*, 211.
564 Ibid., 215.
565 Manjoo, *True Enough*, 35.
566 Berger, *Contagious*, 10–11.
567 Ibid., 11.
568 Glaser, *Conversational Intelligence*, xx.
569 Van Edwards, *Captivate*, 40.
570 Glaser, *Conversational Intelligence*, xx.
571 Ibid.
572 Srivastava and Bhatnagar, "Customer Care Services," 2224.
573 Articles regarding customer service exist across nearly all fields. Examples include Rubin, "Taking Care of the Customer," 62–66.
574 Kuo-Chien et al., "Effect of Service Convenience," 1435; Scotti, Harmon, and Behson, "Structural Relationships," 195.

575 Segler and Bradley, *Christian Worship*, 81; White, *Christian Worship*, 34; Witvliet, *Worship Seeking Understanding*, 283.
576 Byars, *Christian Worship*, 13; Cherry, *Worship Architect*, 5.
577 Brunner, *Dogmatics*, 21.
578 Kent, *Pastor and His Work*, 82; Oates, *Christian Pastor*, 68ff.
579 Armour and Browning, *Systems-Sensitive Leadership*, 258; Callahan, *Dynamic Worship*, 22; Larsen, *Caring for the Flock*, 22–23.
580 Willimon, *Worship*, 47.
581 Kang and Feldman, "Transformed by the Transfiguration," 373.
582 Jones, *Practical Christianity*, 40.
583 Barclay, *Apology*, 330.
584 Nuttall, *Refreshing*, 23.
585 Ibid.
586 Underhill, *Worship*, 83.
587 Waters, "Curse Redux," 241; Schwiebert, "Table Fellowship," 164.
588 Byars, *Lift Your Hearts*, xii.
589 Byars, *Christian Worship*, 24–25.
590 Segler and Bradley, *Christian Worship*, 23.
591 Devan, *Ascent to Zion*, 148.
592 Segler and Bradley, *Christian Worship*, 119.
593 White, *Brief History*, 23; Holmås, "House of Prayer," 398–403.
594 Von Wahlde, "Theological Assessment," 524; Smalley, "Spirit, Kingdom and Prayer," 59ff; O'Brien, "Prayer in Luke-Acts," 112.
595 Martin, *Worship*, 30; Hinson, "Persistence in Prayer," 732.
596 *Didache*, accessed February 1, 2017, http://www.earlychristianwritings.com/text/didache-roberts.html.

597 Farrow, *Ascension and Ecclesia*, 4.

598 Paschke, "Praying to the Holy Spirit," 302.

599 Viola and Barna, *Pagan Christianity*, 50.

600 Segler and Bradley, *Christian Worship*, 28.

601 Viola and Barna, *Pagan Christianity*, 50.

602 Brachlow, *Communion of Saints*, 26.

603 Sampley, "First Letter," 967; Polhill, *Paul*, 248; Mitchell, *Rhetoric of Reconciliation*, 172–73.

604 Brown, *One Hundred Years*, 22.

605 Birkel, *Engaging Scripture*, 41.

606 Lavoie, "Reunified, Rebuilt," 24.

607 "The Epistle from the Elders at Balby, 1656," accessed March 1, 2017, http://www.qhpress.org/texts/balby.html#n6.

608 Plank, *John Woolman's Path*, 59.

609 Five Years Meeting, *Message of Christ*, 4.

610 Molina-Markham, "Being Spoken Through," 127.

611 Nuttall, *Refreshing*, 12.

612 Penington, "Short Catechism," 188.

613 Le Shana, *Quakers in California*, 125.

614 John Banks, *An Epistle on Good Order* (1684), http://www.qhpress.org/quakerpages/qwhp/goodorder.htm.

615 Thompson, *Hit Makers*, 29.

616 Ibid., 69.

617 Ibid.

618 Ibid.

619 Boettner, *Studies in Theology*, 83; Conner, *Christian Doctrine*, 11; Erickson, *Christian Doctrine*, 4; Strong, *Systematic Theology*, 1–2.

620 Brunner, *Christian Doctrine*, 54.

621 Stott, *Between Two Worlds*, 299.

622 Byrum, *Christian Theology*, 3; Strong, *Systematic Theology*, 17.
623 Bauman, *Contemporary Preaching*, 210; Strong, *Systematic Theology*, 18.
624 Zaprometova, "Eucharistic Mystery," 32; Byars, *Christian Worship*, 7.
625 Prusak, *Church Unfinished*, 9.
626 MacMullen, *Christianizing the Roman Empire*, 17.
627 Some examples of scholarship that seek to portray George Fox and early Quakes as proto-liberals: Rock, "George Fox," 269.
628 Penn, *Brief Account*, 23.
629 Penn, *No Cross, No Crown*, 1.
630 Stephen Angell's work regarding Fox's Barbados letter reveals some interesting textual variants among the early and subsequent copies. However, these variants, in my opinion, do not contradict the overall intent of Fox's correspondence. See Angell, "Early Version," 277–94.
631 For example, see Grant, "Understanding Quaker Religious Language," 260–76.
632 Grubb, *What is Quakerism*, 44.
633 Palmer, Jr., "Did William Penn Diverge," 62.
634 Barclay, "Catechism," iv; Penington, *Writings*, 112–26.
635 Fox, *Works*, 8:13.
636 Lloyd, *Quaker Social History*, 11.
637 Palmieri, "Quaker's Struggle," 101; Hagglund, "Quakers and Print," 483; Landes, *London Quakers*, 27.
638 Palmieri, "Quaker's Struggle," 101.
639 Fox, "Epistle 267," 13.
640 Landes, *London Quakers*, 27.
641 Wilbur, *Life and Labors*, 104.
642 Healey, *Quaker to Upper Canadian*, 154.

643 Hamm, *Transformation*, 15–16; Minear, *Richmond*, 3. To be fair, it must be noted that Hicks's views were not entirely consistent and did have some nuance. See Hamm, *Quakers in America*, 40–41.
644 Hamm, *Quakers in America*, 42.
645 Doherty, *Hicksite Separation*, 77.
646 Roberts, *Association*, 1.
647 Ibid., 7.
648 Collins, *Good to Great*, 195.
649 Stuart, "Core Values," 42.
650 Sutton and Roa, *Scaling Up Excellence*, 226.
651 Ibid., 232.

Chapter 9

652 Adams, *Shepherding God's Flock*, 6–7; Gangel, "Meaning of Leadership," 151; Hansen, *Art of Pastoring*, 154–55; Wilkes, *Jesus On Leadership*, 11–12.
653 Gangel, "Meaning of Leadership," 147.
654 Adams, *Pastoral Leadership*, 6–7; Prunty, "Jesus," 159; Richards and Hoeldtke, *Church Leadership*, 106.
655 Boehme, *Leadership*, 59ff.
656 Habecker, *Leading*, 79.
657 Anderson, *Leadership That Works*, 195.
658 Engstrom, *Gift of Administration*, 105; Estep Jr., "Decision Making," 235; Montoya, "Leading," 291.
659 Getz, *Sharpening the Focus*, 151; Kesler, *Being Holy*, 67; Leach, *Handbook of Church Management*, 72ff.
660 Robinson, "It's About God," 29.
661 Ibid.
662 Ibid.

663 Green, "In Our Own Languages," 213; Davis, "Acts 2," 30; Macchia, "Unity and Otherness," 5; Bonk, "Beyond Babel," 57.
664 The most relevant difference between the versions, for this book, is that some contain some combination of the presence or absence of the phrase "moved to sound the day of the Lord" and, following the phrase "a great people," an additional phrase, "to be gathered." There is not space to explicate the historical, textual, and editorial reasons for these differences, but simply to show they exist, and that the author, to be "better safe than sorry," will utilize the fullest version.
665 Fox, *Journal* (1998), 82–83.
666 Ibid., 150.
667 Vipont, *Valiant Sixty*, 18.
668 Trueblood, *People Called Quakers*, 22.
669 Fox, *Journal* (1998), 104.
670 Punshon, *Portrait in Grey*, 65.
671 Vipont, *Story of Quakerism*, 28.
672 Trueblood, *People Called Quakers*, 22.
673 Morgan, Lynch, and Lynch, *Spark*, 99.
674 Ibarra, *Act Like a Leader*, 41.
675 Ibid., 43.
676 Lehrer, *Imagine*, xvii.
677 Ibid.
678 Henry, *Accidental Creative*, 5.
679 Heath and Heath, *Decisive*, 49.
680 Kao, *Jamming*, 87.
681 Snow, *Smartcuts*, 165.
682 Ibid.
683 Lehrer, *Imagine*, 56.

684 Snow, *Smartcuts*, 111.

685 Ibid.

686 Binau, "Pastoral Theology," 14.

687 Newman, *Free Church Perspective*, 63.

688 Tenny-Brittian, "Why Most Church Mission Statements Aren't Effective."

689 Lazurek, "Create Your Church's Vision Statement," *Christianity Today*, March 30, 2015, womenleaders.com, http://www.christianitytoday.com/women-leaders/2015/march/create-your-churchs-vision-statement.html?paging=off.

690 Tenny-Brittian, "How to Write a Church Mission Statement," *Excellerate Church Software* (blog), http://www.excellerate.com/articles/how-to-write-a-church-mission-statement/.

691 Mancini, "6 Times When It's a Good Idea."

692 A mission statement cannot be considered effective unless it is the foundation of all planning and action, known and understood by the members of that organization (which then directs and leverages the resources/talents of those members). Ekpel, Enehl, and Inyang, "Leveraging," 139.

693 Buskirk, "The Value of a Mission Statement."

694 Collins, *Many Faces*, 1; MacCulloch, *Christian History*, 12.

695 Newman, *Free Church Perspective*, 56.

696 Hovorun, *Meta-Ecclesiology*, 4; Westhelle, "The Church's Crucible," 213.

697 Collins, *Many Faces*, 1.

698 Coloe, *Dwelling*, 2.

699 Ibid., 110.

700 Hendriksen, *New Testament Commentary*, 999.

701 Hagner, *Word Biblical Commentary*, 888.

702 Carson, "Matthew," 595.
703 Vipont, *Valiant Sixty*, 20.
704 Macy, *Stepping in the Light*, 34.
705 Barbour and Frost, *Quakers*, 29.
706 Braithewaite, *Beginnings of Quakerism*, 97.
707 Trueblood, *Incendiary Fellowship*, 29.
708 Goleman, *Focus*, 255; Li, *Open Leadership*, 27.
709 Wilson and Wauson, "Mission Statements," 86.
710 Bock, *Work Rules*, 34.
711 Thompson, *Hit Makers*, 64.
712 Heath and Heath, *Decisive*, 184; Wilson and Wauson, "Mission Statements," 86.
713 Goleman, *Focus*, 210.
714 Daft, *Organization Theory*, 449.
715 Ibid.
716 Duhigg, *Power of Habit*, 161.
717 Li, *Open Leadership*, 267.
718 Greer and Horst, *Mission Drift*, 15.
719 Spencer, "Neglected Widows," 732.
720 Sell, "The Seven in Acts 6," 60.
721 Nagel, "The Twelve and the Seven," 118. Nagel argues that the early church viewed the "ministry of the Word" as more important than the ministry of material care. While I concede that the early church may have thought this, I do not believe that it is a correct theological or ecclesiological perspective. Otherwise, the apostles might be accused of having the mindset of the Pharisees or Sadducees—of putting "religious" rituals ahead of care for the poor and marginalized. It is unlikely that Jesus would have approved.
722 Dunn, et al., *Papers of William Penn*, 327.
723 Barbour and Frost, *Quakers*, 67–68.

724 Healey, *Quaker to Upper Canadian*, 26.
725 Johansson, *Click Moment*, 83.
726 Patterson, et al., *Influencer*, 76.
727 Rosenthal, *Gift of Adversity*, 6.
728 Willink and Babin, *Extreme Ownership*, 140.
729 Sutton and Rao, *Scaling Up Excellence*, 226.
730 Thompson, *Hit Makers*, 170.
731 Seidman, *How*, 50.
732 Browning, *Fundamental Practical Theology*, 56.
733 Meeks, *Writings of St. Paul*, xiii.
734 Glines, *Undaunted Zeal*, xvii.
735 Horn, "Texted Authority," 290.
736 For example: Fox's Letter to the Governor of Barbados. See Gragg, "A Heavenly Visitation," 48.
737 Van Edwards, *Captivate*, 4.
738 Ibarra, *Act Like a Leader*, 14; Seidman, *How*, xxvi.
739 Glaser, *Conversational Intelligence*, xiii; Seidman, *How*, xxvi.
740 Patterson, et al., *Crucial Conversations*, 10.
741 Li, *Open Leadership*, 171.
742 Morgan, Lynch, and Lynch, *Spark*, 59.
743 Sutton and Rao, *Scaling Up Excellence*, 243.
744 Li, *Open Leadership*, 30.
745 Ibarra, *Act Like a Leader*, 36.
746 Van Edwards, *Captivate*, 215.
747 Li, *Open Leadership*, 56,
748 Browning, *Fundamental Practical Theology*, 55.
749 Chaffee, *Accountable Leadership*, 33; Anderson, Cousins, and DeKruyter, *Mastering Church Management*, 87; Ditzen, *Handbook of Church Administration*, 5ff.; Macnair, *Birth, Care, and Feeding*, 67; Welch, "Managing Buildings and Grounds," 367–68.

750 Pollock, "Managing the Church Office," 339ff.
751 Anthony, "Biblical Perspectives," 21; George and Logan, *Leading and Managing*, 123; Purcell, "Recruiting and Screening," 246; Rainer and Geiger, *Simple Church*, 169-70.
752 "Spiritual Gift of Administration," Spiritualgiftstest.com, accessed August 24, 2017, https://spiritualgiftstest.com/spiritual-gift-administration/.
753 Evans, *Friends in the Seventeenth Century*, 375.
754 Webb, *Fells of Swarthmore*, 356.
755 Ingle, "A Quaker Woman," 593.
756 Godin, *Linchpin*, 23.
757 Bock, *Work Rules*, 11.
758 Reinhold, *Toxic Work*, 23.
759 Ibid.
760 Ibid., 27.
761 Ibid.; Barker, *Barking*, 35.
762 Heath and Heath, *Decisive*, 73.
763 Ibid.
764 Ibid.
765 Patterson, et al., *Influencer*, 37.
766 Ibid.
767 Ibarra, *Act Like a Leader*, 29.

Chapter 10

768 Anderson, *They Smell Like Sheep*, 4; Larsen, *Caring for the Flock*, 51.
769 Larsen, *Caring for the Flock*, 51.
770 Campbell, *Dictionary of Pastoral Care*, 188.
771 Ibid.; Fowler, "Pastoral Care," 201.
772 Cully, *Education for Spiritual Growth*, 168.

773 Aleshire, *Faith Care*, 87; Elliot, *Liberty of Obedience*, 54ff.; Fawcett, *Understanding People*, 10; Morrow, "Introducing Spiritual Formation," 49; Stanger, *Spiritual Formation*," 13; Willard, *Renovation of the Heart*, 19.

774 Boa, *Conformed to His Image*, 437.

775 Barna, *Growing True Disciples,* 7; Eims, *Lost Art* 83; Hull, *Disciple Making Church*, 8; Kuhne, "Meaningful Relationship," 144.

776 Barna, *Growing True Disciples*, 20ff.; Cosgrove, *Essentials of Discipleship*, 15; Eims, *Motivational Leader*, 8. For a fuller articulation of the practical trajectory of discipleship, see: Steele, *On the Way*.

777 Hansen, *Art of Pastoring*, 155.

778 Milavec, "Modern Exegesis," 64.

779 J. Daryl Charles argues that this is the core characterization of discipleship in the gospel of Matthew. Charles, "Garnishing," 1.

780 Coloe, *Dwelling*, 39.

781 Newman, *Free Church Perspective*, 66.

782 Ibid.

783 Fox, "Letter 21," *Works*, 7:29.

784 Fox, "Letter 22," *Works*, 7:30.

785 Penington, "Short Catechism," 115.

786 James Backhouse, *Memoirs*, 56. Retrieved from https://archive.org/details/memoirsfrancish00backgoog.

787 Spencer, *Holiness: The Soul of Quakerism*.

788 Penn, *No Cross, No Crown*, 1.

789 Penington, "Short Catechism," 120.

790 Duhigg, *Power of Habit*, 84.

791 Ibid.

792 Sutton and Rao, *Scaling Up Excellence*, 70.

793 Duhigg, *Power of Habit*, 239.
794 Loehr and Schwartz, *Power of Full Engagement*, 14.
795 Ibid.
796 McGonigal, *Willpower Instinct*, 83.
797 Ibid.
798 Patterson, et al., *Influencer*, 23.
799 Ibid., 61.
800 Ibid., 27.
801 Ibid., 47.
802 Ibid.
803 Ibid., 50.
804 Sutton and Rao, *Scaling Up Excellence*, 203.
805 Duhigg, *Power of Habit*, 109.
806 Benjamin, *Equipping Ministry*, 12.
807 Johnson, *Recovery of Ministry*, 41.
808 Berkner, *Quantum Ministry*, 23.
809 Wilkes, *Jesus on Leadership*, 191.
810 Volf, *After Our Likeness*, 328–29.
811 McCracken, *Hipster Christianity*, 119.
812 Viola and Barna, *Pagan Christianity*, 76.
813 Trueblood, *Incendiary Fellowship*, 30.
814 Kenworthy, *Fourth Century of Quakerism*, 49.
815 Frye, *What Can I Believe*, 20.
816 Sutton and Rao, *Scaling Up Excellence*, 188.
817 Ibid.
818 Barker, *Barking*, 20.
819 Elder, "Making the Contact," 52.
820 Self, "Ministering in the Marketplace," 215.
821 Colson, "Building the Church," 215; Ellor and Tobin, "Beyond Visitation," 12; Milton, "What Are You Doing,"

450; Richmond and Middleton, *Pastor and the Patient*, 23; Spitale, *Prison Ministry*, 189ff.

822 Hansen, *Art of Pastoring*, 121-23; Sanders, "Why I Dread," 11–12; VandeCreek, "Parish Clergy's Ministry," 214.

823 Kuyper, "Home Visitation," 38; Milstein, et al., "Religious Practice and Depression," 81.

824 Scherzer, *Ministering to the Dying*, 105; Scherzer, *Ministering to the Physically Sick*, 55.

825 Perl, "Mainline Protestant Pastors," 177.

826 Ibarra, *Act Like a Leader*, 66.

827 Ibid.

828 Adams, *Insight and Creativity*, 14; Willimon, "Crisis and Conflict," 197; Worthington, *Marriage Counseling*, 103; Wright, *New Guide to Crisis*, 131.

829 Clinebell, *Pastoral Counseling*, 48, 314; Mason, Currier, and Curtis, *Clergymen*, 30; Oates, *Pastoral Counseling*, 161.

830 Oates, *Protestant Pastoral Counseling*, 113.

831 Adams, *Christian Counselor's Casebook*, 15–16; Anderson, *Christians Who Counsel*, 184.

832 Horsthuis, "Beyond Theodicy," 86.

833 Fox, *Journal* (1998), 8–9.

834 Ibid., 13.

835 Feinzig and Raisbeck, "If You Listen," 17; Tyler, "Reclaiming Rare Listening," 143; Senecal and Burke, "Learning to Listen," 37; Weger Jr., Bell, and Robinson, "Relative Effectiveness," 14; Ivey, et al., "Neuroscience of Listening," 19.

836 Vendantam, *Hidden Brain*, 31.

837 Goleman, *Focus*, 238.

838 Glaser, *Conversational Intelligence*, xxvii.

839 Patterson, et al., *Crucial Conversations*, 158.

840 Begley, *Can't Just Stop*, 73.
841 Ibid.
842 Ibid., 76–79.
843 Ibid., 85.
844 Ibid., 63.

Bibliography

Abbott, Margery Post, Mary Ellen Chijioke, Pink Dandelion, and John William Oliver. *Historical Dictionary of the Friends (Quakers)*. Lanham, MD: Scarecrow, 2011.
Adams, Jay. *The Christian Counselor's Casebook*. Grand Rapids: Baker, 1974.
———. *Insight and Creativity in Christian Counseling*. Philipsburg, NH: Presbyterian and Reformed Publishing, 1982.
———. *Pastoral Leadership*. Grand Rapids: Baker, 1975.
———. *Shepherding God's Flock*. Grand Rapids: Baker, 1983.
Akerlof, George and Rachel Kranton. *Identity Economics: How Our Identities Shape Our Work, Wages, and Well-Being*. Princeton: Princeton University Press, 2010.
Alaska Yearly Meeting of Friends. *Discipline: Faith and Practice*. Kotzebue: Alaska Yearly Meeting of Friends, 1988.
Aleshire, Daniel. "Christian Education and Theology." In *Christian Education Handbook*, edited by Bruce Powers, 13–28. Nashville: Broadman & Holman, 1996.
———. *Faith Care: Ministering to All God's People through the Ages of Life*. Philadelphia: Westminster, 1988.
Allen, O. Wesley. "Pulpit in the Round: The Authority of the Pastor-Preacher in a Conversational Homiletic." *Lexington Theological Quarterly* 39, no. 1 (2004): 47–59.

Allison, Robert. "Let Women Be Silent in the Churches (1 Cor. 14:33b–36): What Did Paul Really Say, and What Did It Mean?" *Journal for the Study of the New Testament* 10, no. 32 (February 1988): 27–60.

Allman, Wayne. *Pioneer Friends Preachers*. Columbus, OH: Brentwood Christian Press, 1996.

Al-Refaie, Abbas and Mohammad Al-Tahat. "Effects of Knowledge Management and Organizational Learning on Firm Performance." *Journal of Nature Science and Sustainable Technology* 8, no. 3 (2014): 369–90.

Alvesson, Mats. "On the Popularity of Organizational Culture." *Acta Sociologica* 33, no. 1 (1990): 31–49.

Anderson, Leith, Don Cousins, and Arthur DeKruyter. *Mastering Church Management*. Portland, OR: Multnomah, 1990.

Anderson, Lynn. *Leadership That Works: Hope and Direction for Church and Parachurch Leaders in Today's Complex World*. Minneapolis: Bethany House, 1999.

———. *They Smell Like Sheep: Spiritual Leadership for the 21st Century*. New York: Columbia University Press, 1997.

Anderson, Ray. *Christians Who Counsel: The Vocation of Wholistic Therapy*. Grand Rapids: Zondervan, 1990.

Angell, Stephen W. "An Early Version of George Fox's 'Letter to the Governor of Barbados.'" *Quaker Studies* 19, no. 2 (March 2015): 277–94.

Anthony, Michael. "Biblical Perspectives of Christian Management." In *Management Essentials for Christian Ministries*, edited by Michael Anthony and James Estep, 13–34. Nashville: B&H, 2005.

Armour, Michael and Don Browning. *Systems-Sensitive Leadership: Empowering Diversity without Polarizing the Church*. Joplin, MO: College Press, 1995.

Audland, John. "Untitled Letter." In *Early Quaker Writings: 1650–1700*, edited by Hugh Barbour and Arthur O. Roberts, 39. Grand Rapids: William B. Eerdmans, 1973.

Aziz, Abdul, Siti Fardaniah, Abu Daud Silong, Kamsuriah Ahmad, Mohd Nasir Selamat, Mohd Reffi Hidayat Roslan, and Mohd Ridhwan Abd Manan. "Developing Organizational Training Impact Scale for Workplace Training: Testing the Malaysian Sample to Determine the Impact of Training on Organizational Effectiveness." *International Journal of Economics and Financial Issues* 6, no. 6 (2016), 142–48.

Backhouse, James. *Memoirs of Francis Howgill: With Extracts from His Writings*. Castlegate: W. Alexander and Son, 1828.

Bacon, Terry. *Elements of Influence: The Art of Getting Others to Follow Your Lead*. New York: AMACOM, 2012.

Banks, John. "An Epistle on Good Order." In *Friends' Library*, edited by William Evans and Thomas Evans, 2:55–56. Philadelphia: Joseph Rakestraw, 1938. http://www.qhpress.org/quakerpages/qwhp/goodorder.htm.

Barbour, Hugh. *The Quakers in Puritan England*. Richmond, IN: Friends United Press, 1964.

Barbour, Hugh and J. William Frost. *The Quakers*. Richmond, IN: Friends United Press, 1988.

Barclay, Robert. *An Apology for the True Christian Divinity Being an Explanation and Vindication of the Principles and Doctrines of the People Called Quakers*. Philadelphia: Friends' Book Store, 1908.

———. "A Catechism and Confession of Faith." In *Quaker Faith*, 9–70. Marion, IN: Paul E. Parker, 1946.

Barker, Eric. *Barking Up the Wrong Tree: The Surprising Science Behind Why Everything You Know about Success Is (Mostly) Wrong*. New York: HarperCollins, 2017.

Barna, George. *Growing True Disciples: New Strategies for Producing Genuine Followers of Christ.* Colorado Springs: Waterbrook, 2001.

Barna, George and Frank Viola. *Pagan Christianity? Exploring the Roots of our Church Practices.* Carol Stream, IL: Tyndale Momentum, 2008.

Bass, Bernard and Ronald Riggio. *Transformational Leadership.* 2nd ed. New York: Psychology Press, 2006.

Bass, Diana Butler. *Christianity for the Rest of Us: How the Neighborhood Church Is Transforming the Faith.* San Francisco: Harper San Francisco, 2006.

Batten, Joe. *Tough-Minded Leadership.* New York: AMACOM, 1989.

Bauman, J. Daniel. *An Introduction to Contemporary Preaching.* Grand Rapids: Baker, 1972.

Bears, Mildred. *Urundi for Christ: A History of the Friends Africa Gospel Mission of Kansas Yearly Meeting, 1933–1940.* Wichita: Kansas Yearly Meeting, 1941.

Becker, Penny. "Understanding Local Mission: Congregational Models and Public Religion in United Methodist Churches." In *Connectionalism: Ecclesiology, Mission and Identity*, edited by Russell Richey, Dennis Campbell, and William B. Lawrence, 267–85. Nashville: Abingdon, 1997.

Beebe, Ralph. *A Garden of the Lord: A History of the Oregon Yearly Meeting of Friends Church.* Newberg, OR: Barclay Press, 1968.

Begley, Sharon. *Can't Just Stop: An Investigation into Compulsions.* New York: Simon & Schuster, 2017.

Belleville, Linda. *Woman Leaders and the Church: Three Crucial Questions.* Grand Rapids: Baker Academic, 2000.

Benjamin, Paul. *The Equipping Ministry: New Testament Methods for Maximum Church Outreach.* Cincinnati: Standard, 1978.

Bennett, Thomas Miles. "Preaching Values in Deuteronomy." *Southwestern Journal of Theology* 7, no. 1 (October 1964): 41–53.

Benson, Clarence. *History of Christian Education.* Chicago: Moody Press, 1943.

Berger, Jonah. *Contagious: Why Things Catch On.* New York: Simon & Schuster, 2013.

Berkner, Randy. *Quantum Ministry: How Pastors Can Make the Leap.* Kansas City: Beacon Hill, 2007.

Berne, Eric. *Games People Play: The Basic Handbook of Transactional Analysis.* New York: Grove Press, 1964.

———. *The Structure and Dynamics of Organizations and Groups.* New York: Grove Press, 1963.

Biech, Elaine. "Learning Eye to Eye: Aligning Training to Business Objectives." *T + D* 63, no. 4 (April 2009): 50–56.

Biffi, Giacomo. *Casta Meretrix: "The Chase Whore"; An Essay on the Ecclesiology of St. Ambrose.* South Bend: Saint Austin, 2001.

Binau, Brad. "Pastoral Theology for the Missional Church: From Pastoral Care to the Care of Souls." *Trinity Seminary Review* 34, no. 1 (Winter/Spring 2014): 11–28.

Birkel, Michael. *Engaging Scripture: Reading the Bible with Early Friends.* Richmond, IN: Friends United Press, 2005.

———. *Silence and Witness: The Quaker Tradition.* Maryknoll, NY: Orbis Books, 2004.

Block, Daniel. "Recovering the Voice of Moses: The Genesis of Deuteronomy." *Journal of the Evangelical Theological Society* 44, no. 3 (September 2001): 385.

Boa, Kenneth. *Conformed to His Image: Biblical and Practical Approaches to Spiritual Formation.* Grand Rapids: Zondervan, 2001.

Bock, Laslo. *Work Rules!: Insights from Inside Google That Will Transform How You Live and Lead.* New York: Twelve, 2015.

Boehme, Ron. *Leadership for the 21st Century.* Seattle: Frontline Communications, 1989.

Boettner, Loraine. *Studies in Theology.* Philadelphia: Presbyterian and Reformed Publishing, 1947.

Bonk, Jonathan, ed. "Beyond Babel: Pentecost and Mission." *International Bulletin of Missionary Research* 30, no. 2 (April 2006): 57–58.

Brace, Laura. *The Idea of Property in Seventeenth-Century England: Tithes and the Individual.* Manchester, UK: Manchester University Press, 1998.

Brachlow, Stephen. *The Communion of Saints: Radical Puritan and Separatist Ecclesiology, 1570–1625.* Oxford: Oxford University Press, 1988.

Braithewaite, William. *The Beginnings of Quakerism.* Cambridge: Cambridge University Press, 1955.

Braithewaite, William Charles. *The Second Period of Quakerism.* London: Macmillan, 1919.

Braithwaite, William and Henry Hodgkin. *The Message and Mission of Quakerism.* Philadelphia: John C. Winston, 1912.

Breazeale, Kathlyn. *Mutual Empowerment: A Theology of Marriage, Intimacy, and Redemption.* Minneapolis: Fortress, 2008.

Briggs, Richard. "Biblical Hermeneutics and Practical Theology: Method and Truth in Context." *Anglican Theological Review* 97, no. 2 (Spring 2015): 201–17.

Brinton, Howard. *Guide to Quaker Practice.* Wallingford, PA: Pendle Hill, 1955.

———. *Prophetic Ministry.* Wallingford, PA: Pendle Hill, 1950.

Brister, C. W. *Pastoral Care in the Church.* San Francisco: Harper San Francisco, 1992.

Bronner, Edwin. *Quakerism and Christianity.* Wallingford, PA: Pendle Hill, 1967.

Brooks, David. *The Road to Character.* New York: Random House, 2015.

———. *The Social Animal: The Hidden Sources of Love, Character, and Achievement.* New York: Random House, 2012.

Brown, Elmer Howard. *The Quaker Queries.* Boston: Penmaen, 1969.

Brown, L. E. "Missional Ecclesiology in the Book of Acts." *Journal of the Grace Evangelical Society* 24, no. 47 (Autumn 2011): 66–88.

Brown, Marjorie Glines. *One Hundred Years in the Promised Land: 1895–1995.* Friendswood, TX: Top Printing, 1995.

Browning, Don. *A Fundamental Practical Theology: Descriptive and Strategic Proposals.* Minneapolis: Fortress, 1996.

———. "Practical Theology and Religious Education." In *Formation and Reflection: The Promise of Practical Theology*, edited by Lewis Mudge and James Poling, 79–102. Minneapolis: Fortress, 2009.

Brunner, Emil. *The Christian Doctrine of God.* Philadelphia: Westminster, 1949.

———. *Dogmatics.* Philadelphia: Westminster, 1960.

Burns, James MacGregor. *Leadership.* New York: HarperPerennial, 1978.

Byars, Ronald. *Christian Worship: Glorifying and Enjoying God.* Louisville: Geneva Press, 2000.

———. *The Future of Protestant Worship: Beyond the Worship Wars.* Louisville: Westminster John Knox, 2002.

———. *Lift Your Hearts on High: Eucharistic Prayer in the Reformed Tradition.* Louisville: Westminster John Knox, 2005.

Byrum, Russell. *Christian Theology: A Systematic Statement of Christian Doctrine.* Rev. ed. Anderson, IN: Warner Press, 1982.

Cadbury, Henry. *The Character of a Quaker.* Wallingford, PA: Pendle Hill, 1959.

Cahalan, Kathleen and Gordon Mikosi, eds. *Opening the Field of Practical Theology: An Introduction.* Lanham, MD: Rowman & Littlefield, 2014.

California Yearly Meeting of Friends. *Friends Worship in a Pastoral Meeting: A Series of Four Lessons for Elders, Pastors, Young People and Others*. Whittier: California Yearly Meeting of Friends, 1960.

Callahan, Kennon. *Dynamic Worship: Mission, Grace, Praise, and Power.* San Franciso: Jossey-Bass, 1994.

Cameron, Euan. *The European Reformation*. Oxford: Clarendon, 1991.

Campbell, Alastair, ed. "Pastoral Care, Nature of." In *A Dictionary of Pastoral Care*, 188–90. New York: Crossroad, 1987.

Carson, D. A. "Matthew." In *The Expositor's Bible Commentary: Volume 8*, edited by Frank Gaebelein and J. D. Douglas, 3–599. Grand Rapids: Zondervan, 1984.

Cartledge, Mark. "Practical Theology." In *Studying Global Pentecostalism: Theories and Method*, edited by Allan Anderson, Michael Bergunder, Andre Droogers, Cornelis Van Der Laan, 268–85. Berkeley: University of California Press, 2010.

Central Yearly Meeting of Friends. *Some Distinctive Views of Friends*. Westfield, IN: Union Bible Seminary, 1957.

Chaffee, Paul. *Accountable Leadership: Resources for Worshipping Communities; A Guide Through Legal, Financial, and Ethical Issues Facing Congregations Today.* San Francisco: ChurchCare, 1993.

Chapell, Bryan. *The Hardest Sermons You'll Ever Have to Preach.* Grand Rapids: Zondervan, 2011.

Chapman, Raymond, ed. *Godly and Righteous, Peevish and Perverse: Clergy and Religions in Literature and Letters; An Anthology*. Grand Rapids: Eerdmans, 2002.

Charles, J. Daryl. "Garnishing with the 'Greater Righteousness': The Disciple's Relationship to the Law (Matthew 5:17)." *Bulletin for Biblical Research* 12, no. 1 (2002): 1–15.

Cherry, Constance. *The Worship Architect: A Blueprint for Designing Culturally Relevant and Biblically Faithful Services*. Grand Rapids: Baker Academic, 2010.

Christensen, Duane. *Word Biblical Commentary.* Vol. 6A, *Deuteronomy 1–11*. Dallas: Word Books, 1991.

Christianity Today. "The Women in Paul's Life: Two Competing Bibles for Women Highlight the Human Component of Bible Translation and Interpretation." *Christianity Today* 41, no. 12 (October 27, 1997): 74–75.

Clarkson, Thomas. *A Portraiture of Quakerism . . . and Character of the Society of Friends*. Indianapolis: Merril & Field, 1870.

Clinebell, Howard. *Basic Types of Pastoral Counseling*. Rev. ed. Nashville: Abingdon, 1992.

Coffin, Charles. "Establishment of Western Yearly Meeting." *Bulletin of Friends Historical Society of Philadelphia* 2, no. 1 (1908): 9–11.

Coffin, Elijah. *The Mother's Catechism of Christian Doctrine and Practice: Designed for the Use of Families and Schools.* Richmond, IN: Central Book and Tract Committee of Friends, 1859.

Collier, Howard. *The Quaker Meeting.* Wallingford, PA: Pendle Hill, 1944.

Collins, Jim. *Good to Great: Why Some Companies Make the Leap . . . and Others Don't.* New York: Harper Business, 2001.

Collins, Peter. "The Practice of Discipline and the Discipline of Practice." In *Exploring Regimes of Discipline*, edited by Noel Dyck, 85–97. New York: Berghahn Books, 2008.

———. "The Problem of Quaker Identity." *Quaker Studies* 13, no. 2 (2009): 205–19.

Collins, Raymond. *The Many Faces of the Church: A Study in New Testament Ecclesiology*. New York: Crossroad, 2003.

Coloe, Mary. *Dwelling in the Household of God: Johannine Ecclesiology and Spirituality*. Collegeville, MN: Liturgical Press, 2007.

Colson, Charles. "Building the Church for Those in Prison." In *Setting the Captives Free: Relevant Ideas in Criminal Justice and Prison Ministry*, edited by Don Smarto, 207–20. Grand Rapids: Baker, 1993.

Comfort, William Wistar. *Just Among Friends: The Quaker Way of Life*. New York: MacMillan, 1941.

Conner, Walter. *Christian Doctrine*. Nashville: Broadman, 1937.

Cooper, Wilmer. *A Living Faith: An Historical and Comparative Study of Quaker Beliefs*. 2nd ed. Richmond, IN: Friends United Press, 2001.

Cooper-White, Pam and Michael Cooper-White. *Exploring Practices of Ministry*. Minneapolis: Fortress, 2014.

Cope, Jackson. "Seventeenth-Century Quaker Style." *PMLA* 71, no. 4 (1956): 725–54.

Cornell, John. *The Principles of the Religious Society of Friends*. Baltimore: Isaac Walker, 1896.

Cosgrove, Francis. *Essentials of Discipleship: Practical Help on How to Live as Christ's Disciple*. Colorado Springs: NavPress, 1980.

Craddock, Fred. *Preaching*. Nashville: Abingdon, 1985.

Crouch, William. "Posthuma Christiana." In *Early Quaker Writings: 1650–1700*, edited by Hugh Barbour and Arthur O. Roberts, 83–90. Grand Rapids: William B. Eerdmans, 1973.

Cully, Iris. *Education for Spiritual Growth*. San Francisco: Harper & Row, 1984.

Daft, Richard. *Organization Theory and Design*. 9th ed. Mason, OH: South-Western, 2007.

Dandelion, Pink. *An Introduction to Quakerism*. Cambridge: Cambridge University Press, 2007.

———. *The Liturgies of Quakerism*. Burlington, VT: Ashgate, 2005.

Daniel, Eleanor, John Wade, and Charles Gresham. *Introduction to Christian Education*. Cincinnati: Standard, 1980.

Daniels, C. Wess. "A Convergent Model of Hope: Remixing the Quaker Tradition in a Participatory Culture." PhD diss., Fuller Theological Seminary, 2013.

Davies, Horton. *Christian Worship: Its History and Meaning*. Nashville: Abingdon, 1957.

Davis, Jud. "Acts 2 and the Old Testament: The Pentecost Event in Light of Sinai, Babel, and the Table of Nations." *Criswell Theological Review* 7, no. 1 (September 2009): 29–48.

Dayton, Edward and Ted Engstrom. *Strategy for Leadership*. Old Tappan, NJ: Revell, 1979.

DeKruyter, Arthur. "Overseeing Church Finances." In *Mastering Church Management*, edited by James Berkley, 85–97. Portland, OR: Multnomah, 1990.

Demerest, B. A. "Systematic Theology." In *Evangelical Dictionary of Theology*, edited by Walter Elwell, 1064–66. Grand Rapids: Baker, 1984.

Devan, S. Arthur. *Ascent to Zion*. New York: Macmillan, 1942.

Dickson, John. *Humilitas: A Lost Key to Life, Love, and Leadership*. Grand Rapids: Zondervan, 2011.

Dingemans, Gisjbert. "Practical Theology and the Academy: A Contemporary Overview." *The Journal of Religion* 76, no. 1 (January 1996): 82–96.

Ditzen, Lowell. *Handbook of Church Administration*. New York: Macmillan, 1962.

Doherty, Robert. *The Hicksite Separation: A Sociological Analysis of Religious Schism in Early Nineteenth-Century America*. New Brunswick: Rutgers University Press, 1967.

Douglas, Eileen. *George Fox: Red Hot Quaker*. London: Salvationist, 1895.

Duff, Nancy J. "The Ordination of Women: Biblical Perspectives." *Theology Today* 73, no. 2 (July 2016): 94–104.

Duhigg, Charles. *The Power of Habit: Why We Do What We Do in Life and Business*. New York: Random House, 2012.

Dunn, Mary, Richard Dunn, Richard Ryerson, Scott Wilds, and Jean Soderlund, eds. *The Papers of William Penn: 1644–1679*. Philadelphia: University of Pennsylvania Press, 1981.

Dyer, Lillian and Evelyn Hoch. *Alva Friends Meeting: 1901–1961*. Alva, OK: Alva Friends Meeting, 1961.

Eccles, Solomon. *The Art of Musick (That Is So Much Vindicated In Christendome)*. . . . (1667). Retrieved from http://www.qhpress.org/texts/eccles.html.

Eims, Leroy. *The Lost Art of Disciple Making*. Grand Rapids: Zondervan, 1978.

———. *Be a Motivational Leader*. Wheaton: Victor Books, 1980.

Ekpel, Ekpe, Sunday Enehl, and Benjamin J. Inyang. "Leveraging Organizational Performance through Effective Mission Statement." *International Business Research* 8, no. 9 (2015): 139.

Elashmawi, Farid and Phillip Harris. *Multicultural Management: New Skills for Global Success*. Houston: Gulf, 1993.

Elder, James. "Making the Contact: Pastoral Visitation and Counseling." In *An Introduction to Pastoral Counseling*, edited by Wayne Oates, 69–80. Nashville: Broadman, 1959.

Elliot, Elisabeth. *The Liberty of Obedience*. Waco, TX: Word Books, 1968.

Elliot, Errol. *Whither Bound Quakers*. Wichita, 1970.

Ellor, James and Sheldon Tobin. "Beyond Visitation: Ministries with the Homebound Elderly." *The Journal of Pastoral Care* 39, no. 1 (1985): 12–21.

Emmot, Elizabeth. *The Story of Quakerism*. London: Headley Brothers, 1908.

Engstrom, Ted. *Your Gift of Administration: How to Discover and Use It*. Nashville: Thomas Nelson, 1983.

Erickson, Millard. *Christian Theology*. Grand Rapids: Baker, 1985.

———. *Introducing Christian Doctrine*. 2nd ed. Grand Rapids: Baker Academic, 2001.
Espinoza, Benjamin, and Beverly Johnson-Miller. "Catechesis, Developmental Theory, and a Fresh Vision for Christian Education." *Christian Education Journal* 11, no. 1 (2014): 8–23.
Estep, James, Jr. "Decision Making and Communication within the Organization." In *Management Essentials for Christian Ministries*, edited by Michael Anthony and James Estep, 222–39. Nashville: B&H, 2005.
Eswine, Zack. *Preaching to a Post-Everything World: Crafting Biblical Sermons That Connect with Our Culture*. Grand Rapids: Baker, 2008.
Evangelical Friends Church—Eastern Region. *Faith and Practice: Book of Discipline*. Canton: Evangelical Friends Church—Eastern Region, 2013.
Evangelical Friends Church—Mid America Yearly Meeting. *Faith and Practice: The Book of Discipline*. Wichita: EFC-MAYM, 2011. http://www.efcmaym.org/faith-and-practice.
Evangelical Friends Church—Southwest. *Faith and Practice*. Yorba Linda: EFC—Southwest, 2011.
Evans, Charles. *Friends in the Seventeenth Century*. Philadelphia: Friends' Bookstore, 1885.
Evans, Thomas. *A Concise Account of the Religious Society of . . . Doctrines and Practices*. Philadelphia: Friends' Bookstore, n.d.
Farley, Edward. "Interpreting Situations: An Inquiry into the Nature of Practical Theology." In *Formation and Reflection: The Promise of Practical Theology*, edited by Lewis Mudge and James Poling, 1–26. Philadelphia: Fortress, 1987.
Farrow, Douglas. *Ascension and Ecclesia: On the Significance of the Doctrine of Ascension for Ecclesiology and Christian Cosmology*. Grand Rapids: William B. Eerdmans, 1999.

Fawcett, Cheryl. *Understanding People: Ministry to All Stages of Life.* Wheaton: Evangelical Training Association, 2000.

Feinzig, Sheri and Louise Raisbeck. "If You Listen, They Will Speak: Active Employee Listening for Organizational Success." *Workforce Solutions Review* 8, no. 2 (April 2017): 17–21.

Fell, Margaret. "An Epistle to Friends." In *Quaker Writings: An Anthology, 1654–1920*, edited by Thomas Hamm, 47–49. London: Penguin Classics, 2010.

———. *Women's Speaking Justified, Proved, and Allowed of by The Scriptures. . . . 1666.* Reprint, Amherst, MA: Mosher Book & Tract Committee, New England Yearly Meeting of Friends, 1980.

Fendall, Lon, Jan Wood, and Bruce Bishop. *Practicing Discernment Together: Finding God's Way Forward in Decision Making.* Newberg, OR: Barclay Press, 2007.

Fiddes, Paul. "Christian Doctrine and Free Church Ecclesiology: Recent Developments Among Baptists in the Southern United States." *Ecclesiology* 7, no. 2 (2011): 195–219.

Finger, Reta Halteman. "A Theology of Welcome: The Hospitable Hidden Women of Acts 2, 4, and 6." *The Conrad Grebel Review* 23, no. 1 (2005): 30–41.

Fisher, Sydney G. *The Quaker Colonies: A Chronicle of the Proprietors of the Delaware.* 1919. Reprint, London: Forgotten Books, 2013.

Five Years Meeting of Friends in America. *Lessons in Friends History and Belief.* Richmond, IN: G. O. Ballinger, 1923.

———. *The Message of Christ for Today—Through Friends.* Richmond, IN: Friends in America, 1945.

Forrester, Duncan. *Truthful Action: Explorations in Practical Theology.* Edinburgh: T & T Clark, 2000.

Forsyth, Donelson. *An Introduction to Group Dynamics.* Monterrey: Brooks/Cole, 1983.

Foss, Michael. "Preaching for Discipleship." In *Great Preaching: Practical Advice from Powerful Preachers*, edited by Paul Woods, 161–72. Loveland, CO: Group Publishing, 2003.

Foster, Richard and James Smith. *Devotional Classics: Selected Readings for Individuals and Groups*. New York: HarperOne, 1993.

Fowler, Gene. "Pastoral Care and the Church." In *Turning Points in Pastoral Care: The Legacy of Anton Boisen and Seward Hiltner*, edited by Leroy Aden and J. Harold Ellens, 187–204. Grand Rapids: Baker, 1990.

Fox, George. "Epistle 267—To Ministering Friends." In *A Collection of Many Select and Christian Epistles, Letters and Testimonies, Written on Sundry Occasions by that Ancient, Eminent, Faithful Friend, and Minister of Christ Jesus, George Fox*. Vol. 2. Lexington: BiblioBazaar, 2014.

———. *The Journal*. Edited by Nigel Smith. New York: Penguin Books, 1998.

———. *Journal of George Fox*. Edited by Rufus Jones. Richmond, IN: Friends United Press, 1976.

———. *Journal of George Fox*. Edited by John Nickalls. Philadelphia: Philadelphia Yearly Meeting of the Religious Society of Friends, 2005.

———. *Some Principles of the Elect People of God Who in Scorn Are Called Quakers*. Lexington: Wildside Press, 2009.

———. *The Works of George Fox*. 8 vols. Memphis, TN: General Books, 2012.

Frame, Nathan and Esther Frame. *Reminiscences of Nathan T. Frame and Esther G. Frame*. Cleveland: Brinton, 1907.

Friends United Meeting. *Foundations for Membership in a Friends Meeting: A Membership Training Manual*. Richmond, IN: Friends United Meeting, 1967.

Fry, A. Ruth. *Quaker Ways: An Attempt to Explain Quaker Beliefs and Practices and to Illustrate Them by the Lives and Activities of Friends of Former Days*. London: Cassell, 1933.

Fry, Brian and J. S. Griswold. "Defining and Implementing the Learning Organization: Some Strategic Limitations." *Public Administration Quarterly* 27, no. 3 (Fall 2003): 311–35.

Frye, John. *Jesus the Pastor*. Grand Rapids: Zondervan, 2002.

Frye, Willie R. *What Can I Believe?* Richmond, IN: Friends United Meeting, 1967.

Gallagher, Carol. *Family Theology: Finding God in Very Human Relationships*. New York: Morehouse, 2012.

Gamertsfelder, S. J. *Systematic Theology*. Cleveland: Evangelical Publishing House, 1921.

Gangel, Kenneth. *Church Education Handbook*. Wheaton: Victor Books, 1985.

———. "The Meaning of Leadership." In *Leadership Handbook of Management and Administration*. Edited by James Berkley, 177–84. Grand Rapids: Baker, 2007.

Gatewood, Tee. "All Who Follow Jesus? The Trouble with Peterson and the Wider Church." In *Pastoral Work: Engagements with the Vision of Eugene Peterson*, edited by Jason Byassee and L. Rogers Owens, 41–52. Eugene: Cascade Books, 2014.

George, Carl F. and Robert Logan. *Leading and Managing Your Church*. New York: Fleming H. Revell, 1987.

Getz, Gene. *Sharpening the Focus of the Church*. Chicago: Moody, 1974.

Giesecke, Joan and Beth McNeil. "Transitioning to the Learning Organization." *Library Trends* 53, no. 1 (Summer 2004): 54–67.

Gill, Catie. "Evans and Cheevers's *A Short Relation* in Context: Flesh, Spirit, and Authority in Quaker Prison Writings,

1650–1662." *Huntington Library Quarterly* 72, no. 2 (June 2009): 257–72.

Glaser, Judith. *Conversational Intelligence: How Great Leaders Build Trust and Get Extraordinary Results.* New York: Routledge, 2016.

Glines, Elsa F., ed. *Undaunted Zeal: The Letters of Margaret Fell.* Richmond, IN: Friends United Press, 2003.

Godin, Seth. *Linchpin: Are You Indispensable.* New York: Portfolio, 2010.

Goldhaber, Gerald. *Organizational Communication.* 5th ed. Dubuque: W. C. Brown, 1990.

Goleman, Daniel. *Focus: The Hidden Driver of Excellence.* New York: HarperCollins, 2013.

Goleman, Daniel, Richard Boyatzis, and Anne Mckee. *Primal Leadership: Learning to Lead with Emotional Intelligence.* Boston: Harvard Business School Press, 2002.

Gowan, Donald. *Theology of the Prophetic Books: The Death and Resurrection of Israel.* Louisville: Westminster John Knox, 1998.

Gragg, Larry. "A Heavenly Visitation." *History Today* 52, no. 2 (2002): 46–51.

Grant, Rhiannon. "Understanding Quaker Religious Language in Its Community Context." *Quaker Studies* 19, no. 2 (2015): 260–76.

Graves, Michael. "Ministry and Preaching." In *The Oxford Handbook of Quaker Studies*, edited by Steven Angell and Pink Dandelion, 277–91. Oxford: Oxford University Press, 2013.

———. *Preaching the Inward Light: Early Quaker Rhetoric.* Waco: Baylor University Press, 2009.

Green, Joel. "'In Our Own Languages': Pentecost, Babel, and the Shaping of Christian Community in Acts 2:1–13." In *Word Leaps the Gap: Essays on Scripture and Theology in Honor* of *Richard B. Hays*, edited by J. Ross Wagner, C. Kavin Rowe, and Katherine Grieb, 198–213. Grand Rapids: William B. Eerdmans, 2008.

Greer, Peter and Chris Horst. *Mission Drift: The Unspoken Crisis Facing Leaders, Charities, and Churches*. Bloomington: Bethany House, 2014.

Grethlein, Christian. *An Introduction to Practical Theology: History, Theory, and the Communication of the Gospel in the Present*. Waco: Baylor University Press, 2016.

Grubb, Edward. *What Is Quakerism? An Exposition of the Leading Principles and Practices of the Society of Friends, as Based on the Experience of "The Inward Light."* London: Headley Brothers, 1940.

Gurney, Joseph. *Observations on the Distinguishing Views and Practices of the Society of Friends.* 1860. Reprint, London: Forgotten Books, 2012.

———. *A Peculiar People: The Rediscovery of Primitive Christianity.* Richmond, IN: Friends United Press, 2012.

Gwyn, Douglas. *Apocalypse of the Word: The Life and Message of George Fox (1624–1691)*. Richmond, IN: Friends United Press, 1986.

———. *Unmasking the Idols: A Journey among Friends*. Richmond, IN: Friends United Press, 1989.

Habecker, Eugene. *Leading with a Follower's Heart: Practicing Biblical Obedience and Humility in the Workplace*. Wheaton: Victor Books, 1990.

Hagglund, Betty. "Quakers and Print Culture." In *The Oxford Handbook of Quaker Studies*, edited by Stephen Angell and Pink Dandelion, 477–91. Oxford: Oxford University Press, 2013.

Hagner, Donald. *Word Biblical Commentary.* Volume 33B, *Matthew 14–28*. Dallas: Word Books, 1995.

Hall, Christopher. *Learning Theology with the Church Fathers*. Downers Grove, IL: IVP Academic, 2002.

Hallett, Tim. "Symbolic Power and Organizational Culture." *Sociological Theory* 21, no. 2 (2003): 128–49.

Halloran, Brian. "Spirited Scottish Students: The Scots College Paris in 1639." *Innes Review* 45, no. 2 (1994): 171–77.

Hamm, Thomas. "Chipping at the Landmarks of Our Fathers: The Decline of the Testimony Against Hireling Ministry in the Nineteenth Century." *Quaker Studies* 13, vol. 2 (2009): 136–59.

———. *The Quakers in America*. New York: Columbia University Press, 2003.

———. *The Transformation of American Quakerism: Orthodox Friends, 1800–1907*. Bloomington: Indiana University Press, 1988.

Hansen, David. *The Art of Pastoring: Ministry Without All the Answers*. Downers Grove, IL: IVP, 1994.

Harold, Henry. "Early Activities." In *Life and Works of Amos M. Kenworthy*, edited by Lydia Williams-Cammack and Truman Kenworthy, 1–4. Richmond, IN: Nicholson, 1918.

Harvey, Thomas. *The Rise of the Quakers*. London: National Council of Evangelical Free Churches, 1905.

Hatch, Mary Jo. "The Dynamics of Organizational Culture." *The Academy of Management Review* 18, no. 4 (October 1993): 657–93.

Haworth, Sara. *Springfield 1773–1940: A History of the Establishment and Growth of the Springfield Monthly Meeting of Friends*. High Point, NC: Barber-Hall, 1940.

Hayden, Judith. *In Search of Margaret Fell*. London: Quaker Books, 2002.

Hayes, Edward. "Theological Foundations for Adult Education." In *The Christian Educator's Handbook on Adult Education*, edited by Kenneth Gangel and James Wilhoit, 31–50. Wheaton: Victor Books, 1993.

Healey, Robynne. *From Quaker to Upper Canadian: Faith and Community among Yonge Street Friends, 1801–1850*. Kingston, ON: McGill-Queen's University Press, 2006.

Heath, Chip and Dan Heath. *Decisive: How to Make Better Choices in Life and Work*. New York: Crown Business, 2013.

Heil, John Paul. *The Letters of Paul as Rituals of Worship*. Cambridge, UK: James Clark, 2011.

Hendriksen, William. *New Testament Commentary: Exposition of the Gospel According to Matthew*. Grand Rapids: Baker, 1973.

Henry, Todd. *The Accidental Creative: How to Be Brilliant at a Moment's Notice*. New York: Portfolio, 2011.

Hensley, Adam. "Σιγάω, λαλέω, and ὑποτάσσω in 1 Corinthians 14:34 in Their Literary and Rhetorical Context." *Journal of the Evangelical Theological Society* 55, no. 2 (June 2012): 343–64.

Hershey, Paul and Kenneth Blanchard. *Management and Organizational Behavior: Utilizing Human Resources*. 5th ed. Englewood Cliffs: Prentice Hall, 1988.

Heusel, Lorton. *The Quaker Pastorate*. Richmond, IN: Indiana Yearly Meeting, 1956.

Hieronimus, Dorothy. *Friends in Tennessee*. Richmond, IN: American Friends Board of Missions, 1920.

Hills, A. M. *Homiletics and Pastoral Theology*. Kansas City: Nazarene Publishing House, 1929.

Hiltner, Seward and Lowell Colston. *The Context of Pastoral Counseling*. Nashville: Abingdon, 1961.

Hilty, Hiram. *Friends in Cuba*. Richmond, IN: Friends United Press, 1977.

Hinshaw, Greg. "Five Years Meeting and Friends United Meeting, 1887–2010." In *The Oxford Handbook of Quaker Studies*, edited by Stephen Angell and Pink Dandelion. Oxford: Oxford University Press, 2013.

———. *Indiana Friends Heritage: 1821–1996*. Muncie: Indiana Yearly Meeting of Friends, 1996.

Hinshaw, Seth. *The Carolina Quaker Experience*. Greensboro: North Carolina Friends Historical Society, 1984.

———. *Carolina Quakers: Three Hundred Years 1672–1972: Glimpses of Our Quaker Heritage; History in the Making; A Study Unit for Young Friends*. Greensboro: North Carolina Yearly Meeting, 1971.

———. *The Message and Mission of Friends*. Richmond, IN: Five Years Meeting, 1960.

———. *The Spoken Ministry Among Friends: Three Centuries of Progress and Development*. Greensboro: North Carolina Yearly Meeting of Friends, 1987.

Hinson, Glenn. "Persistence in Prayer in Luke-Acts." *Review & Expositor* 104, no. 4 (September 2007): 721–36.

Hobart, John. *Can Quakerism Speak to the Times?* Wallingford, PA: Pendle Hill, 1954.

Holden, David. *Friends Divided: Conflict and Division in the Society of Friends*. Richmond, IN: Friends United Press, 1988.

Holloran, Brian. "Spirited Scottish Students: The Scots College Paris in 1639." *Innes Review* 45, no. 2 (1994): 171–77.

Holmås, Geir Otto. "'My house shall be a house of prayer': Regarding the Temple as a Place of Prayer in Acts within the Context of Luke's Apologetic Objective." *Journal for the Study of the New Testament* 27, no. 4 (June 2005): 393–416.

Hoover, J. Y. *History of the Life and Labors of J. Y. Hoover: A Minister of the Gospel of Our Lord Jesus Christ*. West Branch, IA, 1901.

Horn, Matthew. "Texted Authority: How Letters Helped Unify the Quakers in the Long Seventeenth Century." *The Seventeenth Century* 23, no. 2 (October 2008): 290–314.

Horsthuis, Jim. "Beyond Theodicy: Moving Toward a Trinitarian and Participative Spirituality of Care." *Didaskalia* 26, (2016): 85–108.

Hovorun, Cyril. *Meta-Ecclesiology: Chronicles of Church Awareness.* New York: MacMillan, 2015.

Hull, Bill. *The Disciple-Making Church.* Grand Rapids: Fleming H. Revell, 1990.

Humphrey, Vernon. "Training the Total Organization." *Training and Development Journal* 44, no. 10 (1990): 57.

Hurst, David. *Crisis and Renewal: Meeting the Challenge of Organizational Change.* Boston: Harvard Business Review Press, 2002.

Hybels, Bill, Stuart Briscoe, and Haddon Robinson. *Mastering Contemporary Preaching.* Portland, OR: Multnomah, 1989.

Hybels, Bill and Valerie Bell. "Communicating Vision by Going Public." In *Great Preaching: Practical Advice from Powerful Preachers*, edited by Paul Woods, 33–41. Loveland, CO: Group, 2003.

Ibarra, Herminia. *Act Like a Leader, Think Like a Leader.* Boston: Harvard Business Review Press, 2015.

Indiana Yearly Meeting of the Religious Society of Friends. *Discipline of the Indiana Yearly Meeting.* Richmond, IN: Nicholson Press, 1905.

———. *The Discipline of the Society of Friends of Indiana Yearly Meeting.* Cincinnati: A. Pugh, 1854.

———. *Discipline of the Society of Friends of Indiana Yearly Meeting.* Richmond, IN: E. Morgan & Sons, 1864.

———. *Faith and Practice of Indiana Yearly Meeting of the Religious Society of Friends.* Muncie: Indiana Yearly Meeting of the Religious Society of Friends, 2015.

———. *Rules of Discipline of Indiana Yearly Meeting of the Religious Society of Friends.* Richmond, IN: M. Cullaton, 1892.

Ingle, H. Larry. *First Among Friends: George Fox & the Creation of Quakerism.* New York: Oxford University Press, 1994.

———. "A Quaker Woman on Women's Roles: Mary Penington to Friends, 1678." *Signs: Journal of Women in Culture and Society* 16, no. 3 (1991): 587–96.

———. *Quakers in Conflict: The Hicksite Reformation.* Knoxville: University of Tennessee Press, 1986.

Ingram, Larry. "Leadership, Democracy, and Religion: Role Ambiguity Among Pastors in Southern Baptist Churches." *Journal for the Scientific Study of Religion* 20, no. 2 (1981): 119–29.

Iowa Yearly Meeting of Friends. *Book of Discipline.* Oskaloosa: Oskaloosa Herald Print, 1891.

———. *Discipline of Iowa Yearly Meeting of Friends.* Oskaloosa: Iowa Yearly Meeting of Friends, 2016.

———. *Friends' Graded Bible School Lessons: Junior, Third Year, Part One, Teacher's Book.* Oskaloosa: Iowa Yearly Meeting, 1934.

———. *Friends' Graded Bible School Lessons: Second Year, Part Four, Pupil's Book.* Oskaloosa: Iowa Yearly Meeting, 1933.

Ivey, Allen, Mary-Bradford Ivey, and Carlos Zalaquett. "The Neuroscience of Listening, Microskills and Empathy." *Counseling Today* 59, no. 2 (August 2016): 18–21.

Jackson, Sheldon. *Quaker Preachers on the Prairie: The Life and Times of Ralph and Marva Jackson.* Glendora, CA: Citrus Press, 1985.

Jacob, Caroline. *Builders of the Quaker Road: 1652–1952.* Chicago: Henry Regnery, 1953.

Jagerson, Jennifer. "Harnessing the Power of Narrative: Literacy and Orality in Christian Education." *Christian Education Journal* 11, no. 2 (September 2014): 259–75.

Janzen, Marshall. "Orderly Participation or Silenced Women?: Clashing Views on Decent Worship in 1 Corinthians 14." *Direction* 42, no. 1 (2013): 55–70.

Jashapara, Ashok. "The Competitive Learning Organization: A Quest for the Holy." *Management Decision* 31, no. 8 (1993): 52.

Jenkins, Michael. *The Church Faces Death: Ecclesiology in a Post-Modern Context*. New York: Oxford University Press, 1999.

Johansson, Frans. *The Click Moment: Seizing Opportunity in an Unpredictable World*. New York: Portfolio, 2012.

Johnson, David and Frank Johnson. *Joining Together: Group Theory and Group Skills*. Boston: Allyn & Bacon, 1997.

Johnson, Orien. *Recovery of Ministry: A Guide for the Laity*. Valley Forge, PA: Judson Press, 1972.

Johnson, Rosalind. "The Case of the Distracted Maid: Healing and Cursing in Early Quaker History." *Quaker Studies* 21, no. 1 (2016): 33–47.

Jones, Louis Thomas. *The Quakers of Iowa*. Iowa City: State Historical Society of Iowa, 1914.

Jones, Rufus. *The Faith and Practice of the Quakers*. Richmond, IN: Friends United Press, n.d.

———s. *The Later Periods of Quakerism*. London: Macmillan, 1921.

———. *The Life and Message of George Fox 1624–1924*. New York: Macmillan, 1924.

———. *Practical Christianity*. Philadelphia: John C. Winston, 1899.

———. "Quietism." *The Harvard Theological Review* 10, no. 1 (1917): 1–51.

Junior, J. A. *Monthly Meeting Chronicle*. Richmond, IN: Friends Publication Board, 1914.

Kang, Steve, and Michael Feldman. "Transformed by the Transfiguration: Reflections on a Biblical Understanding of Transformation and Its Implications for Christian Education." *Christian Education Journal* 10, no. 2 (September 2013): 365–77.

Kansas Yearly Meeting of Friends. *Discipline*. Medford, OR: Medford Printing, 1940.

———. *Discipline of the Society of Friends of the Kansas Yearly Meeting*. Richmond, IN: Nicholson & Bro., 1892.

———. *Minutes of Kansas Yearly Meeting of Friends.* Lawrence, KS: Journal Steam Book and Job, 1873.

———. *Minutes of Kansas Yearly Meeting of Friends.* Lawrence, KS: Journal Steam Book and Job, 1874.

———. *Minutes of Kansas Yearly Meeting of Friends.* Lawrence, KS: Journal Steam Book and Job, 1875.

———. *Minutes of Kansas Yearly Meeting of Friends.* Lawrence, KS: Journal Steam Book and Job, 1883.

———. *Minutes of Kansas Yearly Meeting of Friends*. Lawrence, KS: P. T. Foley, Book and Job, 1884.

———. *Minutes of Kansas Yearly Meeting of Friends*. Columbus, OH: William G. Hubbard, 1886.

———. *Minutes of Kansas Yearly Meeting of Friends*. Columbus, OH: William G. Hubbard, 1887.

———. *Minutes of Kansas Yearly Meeting of Friends.* Lawrence, KS: Journal Steam Book and Job, 1888.

———. *Minutes of Kansas Yearly Meeting of Friends*. Lawrence, KS: Journal Steam Book and Job, 1890.

———. *Minutes of Kansas Yearly Meeting of Friends*. Lawrence, KS: Journal Books and Job, 1891.

———. *Minutes of Kansas Yearly Meeting of Friends*. Wichita: Eagle Press, 1900.

———. *Minutes of Kansas Yearly Meeting of Friends*. Wichita: Eagle Press, 1914.

———. *Minutes of Kansas Yearly Meeting of Friends*. Wichita: Lassen Printery, 1921.

———. *Minutes of Kansas Yearly Meeting of Friends.* Wichita: Kansas Yearly Meeting of Friends, 1925.

———. *Minutes of Kansas Yearly Meeting of Friends.* Wichita: Kansas Yearly Meeting of Friends, 1930.
———. *Minutes of Kansas Yearly Meeting of Friends.* Wichita: Kansas Yearly Meeting of Friends, 1936.
———. *Minutes of Kansas Yearly Meeting of Friends.* Wichita: Kansas Yearly Meeting of Friends, 1952.
———. *Minutes of Kansas Yearly Meeting of Friends.* Wichita: Kansas Yearly Meeting of Friends, 1954.
———. *Minutes of Kansas Yearly Meeting of Friends.* Wichita: Kansas Yearly Meeting of Friends, 1955.
———. *Minutes of Kansas Yearly Meeting of Friends.* Wichita: Kansas Yearly Meeting of Friends, 1956.
———. *Minutes of Kansas Yearly Meeting of Friends.* Wichita: Kansas Yearly Meeting of Friends, 1957.
———. *Minutes of Kansas Yearly Meeting of Friends.* Wichita: Kansas Yearly Meeting of Friends, 1958.
———. *Minutes of Kansas Yearly Meeting of Friends.* Wichita: Kansas Yearly Meeting of Friends, 1959.
———. *Minutes of Kansas Yearly Meeting of Friends.* Wichita: Kansas Yearly Meeting of Friends, 1962.
———. *Minutes of Kansas Yearly Meeting of Friends.* Wichita: Kansas Yearly Meeting of Friends, 1965.
———. *Minutes of Kansas Yearly Meeting of Friends.* Wichita: Kansas Yearly Meeting of Friends, 1968.
———. *Minutes of Kansas Yearly Meeting of Friends.* Wichita: Kansas Yearly Meeting of Friends, 1969.
———. *Minutes of Kansas Yearly Meeting of Friends.* Wichita: Kansas Yearly Meeting of Friends, 1978.
Kao, John. *Jamming: The Art and Discipline of Business Creativity.* New York: HarperBusiness, 1996.
Kaplan, Robert. *Warrior Politics: Why Leadership Demands a Pagan Ethos.* New York: Random House, 2002.

Kapp, K. M. "Transforming Your Manufacturing Organization into a Learning Organization." *Hospital Materiel Management Quarterly* 20, no. 4 (1999): 46–54.

Kaur, Lovleen and Ambika Bhatia. "Involvement of Stakeholders in Evaluation: A Prerequisite for Success of Training Programs." *International Journal of Management Research and Reviews* 3, no. 8 (August 2013): 3229–37.

Keener, Craig. *The Gospel of Matthew: A Socio-Rhetorical Commentary.* Grand Rapids: William B. Eerdmans, 2009.

———. "Matthew's Missiology: Making Disciples of the Nations (Matthew 28:19–20)." *Asian Journal of Pentecostal Studies* 12, no. 1 (January 2009): 3–20.

Kent, Homer. *The Pastor and His Work.* Chicago: Moody, 1963.

Kenworthy, Leonard. *Toward a Fourth Century of Quakerism.* Philadelphia: Friends' Book Store, 1952.

Kesler, Jay. *Being Holy, Being Human: Dealing with the Expectations of Ministry.* Carol Stream, IL: CTI, 1988.

Klaus, Peggy. *Brag! The Art of Tooting Your Own Horn without Blowing It.* New York: Warner Business, 2003.

Kohles, Mary, William Baker, and Barbara Donaho. *Transformational Leadership: Renewing Fundamental Values and Achieving New Relationships in Health Care.* Chicago: American Hospital, 1995.

Kramlinger, Tom. "Training's Role in a Learning Organization." *Training* 29, no. 7 (July 1992): 46.

Kuhne, Gary. "Developing a Meaningful Relationship." In *Discipleship: The Best Writings from the Most Experienced Disciple Makers,* edited by Billie Hanks and William Shell, 131–45. Grand Rapids: Zondervan, 1981.

Kuo-Chien, Chang, Chen Mu-Chen, Hsu Chia-Lin, and Nien-Te Kuo. "The Effect of Service Convenience on Post-Purchasing Behaviours." *Industrial Management & Data Systems* 110, no. 9 (2010): 1420–43.

Kuyper, Neal. "Are Pastors 'Called' to Home Visitation?" *Christianity Today* 24, no. 20 (November 1980): 38.

LaMothe, Ryan. "Broken and Empty: Pastoral Leadership as Embodying Radical Courage, Humility, Compassion, and Hope." *Pastoral Psychology* 61, no. 4 (2012): 451–66.

Landes, Jordan. *London Quakers in the Trans-Atlantic World: The Creation of an Early Modern Community*. New York: Palgrave Macmillan, 2015.

Langford, Mary. *The Fairest Isle: History of Jamaica Friends*. Richmond, IN: Friends United Press, 1997.

Larsen, David. *Caring for the Flock: Pastoral Ministry in the Local Congregation*. Wheaton: Crossway Books, 1991.

Lavoie, Catherine. "Reunified, Rebuilt, Enlarged, or Rehabilitated: Deciphering Friends' Complex Attitudes toward Their Meeting Houses." *Buildings & Landscapes: Journal of the Vernacular Architecture Forum* 3, no. 2 (Fall 2012): 20–52.

Leach, William. *Handbook of Church Management*. Englewood Cliffs: Prentice-Hall, 1958.

Lee, Bill. "Marketing Is Dead." *Harvard Business Review* (August 2012). https://hbr.org/2012/08/marketing-is-dead.

Lehrer, Jonah. *Imagine: How Creativity Works*. Boston: Houghton Mifflin, 2012.

Leithart, Peter. "The Pastor Theologian as Biblical Theologian: From the Church for the Church." In *Becoming a Pastoral Theologian: New Possibilities for Church Leadership*, edited by Todd Wilson and Gerald Hiestand, 7–22. Downers Grove, IL: IVP Academic, 2016.

Le Shana, David. *Quakers in California: The Effects of 19th Century Revivalism on Western Quakerism*. Newberg, OR: Barclay Press, 1969.

Lewis, Phillip. *Transformational Leadership: A New Model for Total Church Involvement*. Nashville: Broadman & Holman, 1996.

Li, Charlene. *Open Leadership: How Social Technology Can Transform the Way You Lead*. San Francisco: Jossey-Bass, 2010.

Liston, Gregory. *The Anointed Church: Toward a Third Article Ecclesiology*. Minneapolis: Fortress, 2015.

Lloyd, Arnold. *Quaker Social History: 1669–1738*. Westport, CT: Greenwood, 1950.

Loehr, Jim and Tony Schwartz. *The Power of Full Engagement: Managing Energy, Not Time, Is the Key to High Performance and Personal Renewal*. New York: Free Press, 2003.

London Yearly Meeting of Friends. *A Selection from the Christian Advices Issued by the Yearly Meeting of the Society of Friends, Held in London*. Cincinnati: E. Morgan, 1849.

London Yearly Meeting of the Religious Society of Friends. *Christian Faith and Practice in the Experience of the Society of Friends*. Richmond, IN: Friends United Press, 1973.

Long, Kimberly. "The Shepherd Jesus." *Journal for Preachers* 29, no. 3 (2006): 51–54.

Longenecker, Richard. "The Acts of the Apostles." In *The Expositor's Bible Commentary*. Vol. 9, *John-Acts*, 206–573. Grand Rapids: Regency Reference Library, 1981.

Lord, Jennifer. *Finding Language and Imagery: Words for Holy Speech*. Minneapolis: Fortress, 2010.

Loscalzo, Craig. *Preaching Sermons that Connect: Effective Communication through Identification*. Downers Grove, IL: InterVarsity, 1992.

Lose, David. *Confessing Jesus Christ: Preaching in a Postmodern World*. Grand Rapids: Eerdmans, 2003.

Lovin, Robin. "The Real Task of Practical Theology." *The Christian Century* 109, no. 5 (February 1992): 125–28.

Lowney, Chris. *Heroic Leadership: Best Practices from a 450-Year-Old Company That Changed the World*. Chicago: Loyola, 2005.

Lowry, Eugene. *The Homiletical Plot: The Sermon as Narrative Art Form*. Atlanta: John Knox, 1980.

Lucas, Sidney. *The Quaker Message*. Wallingford, PA: Pendle Hill, 1948.

———. *The Quaker Story*. New York: Harper & Row, 1949.

Luthans, Fred. *Organizational Behavior*. New York: McGraw Hill, 1977.

Macarthur, John. *The Book on Leadership*. Nashville: Thomas Nelson, 2004.

Macchia, Frank. "Unity and Otherness: Lessons from Babel and Pentecost." *The Living Pulpit* 13, no. 4 (October 2004): 5–7.

MacCulloch, Diarmaid. *Christian History: An Introduction to the Western Tradition*. Werrington, UK: Epworth Press, 2006.

Mack, Phyllis. *Visionary Women: Ecstatic Prophecy in Seventeenth-Century England*. Berkeley: University of California Press, 1992.

MacMullen, Ramsay. *Christianizing the Roman Empire: (A.D. 100–400)*. New Haven: Yale University Press, 1984.

Macnair, Donald. *The Birth, Care, and Feeding of the Local Church*. Washington, DC: Canon, 1971.

Macquarrie, John. *Faith of the People of God: Lay Theology*. New York: Charles Scriber's Sons, 1972.

Macy, Howard. *Stepping in the Light: Life in Joy and Power*. Richmond, IN: Friends United Press, 2007.

Malphurs, Aubrey. *Values-Driven Leadership: Discovering and Developing Your Core Values for Ministry*. 2nd ed. Grand Rapids: Baker, 2004.

Manjoo, Farhad. *True Enough: Learning to Live in a Post-Fact Society*. Hoboken, NJ: Wiley, 2008.

Mardock, Hubert. *Adventures in Soul Winning*. Los Angeles: Peniel Herald, 1952.

Marmon, Ellen L. "Transformative Learning Theory: Connections with Christian Adult Education." *Christian Education Journal* 9, no. 2 (September 2013): 424–31.

Marquardt, Steven Aaron. "The Peculiar Use of ἐκκλησία in 1 Corinthians 14:34–35." *Conversations with the Biblical World* 35, no. 1 (2015): 289–303.

Marsh, Josiah. *A Popular Life of George Fox the First of the Quakers.* . . . Philadelphia: Henry Longstreth, n.d.

Marshall, Charles. "Testimony Concerning John Camm and John Audland." In *Early Quaker Writings: 1650–1700*, edited by Hugh Barbour and Arthur O. Roberts, 79–82. Grand Rapids: William B. Eerdmans, 1973.

Martin, Ralph. *Worship in the Early Church*. Grand Rapids: William B. Eerdmans, 1964.

Mason, Robert, Carol Currier, and John Curtis. *The Clergymen and the Psychiatrist: When to Refer*. Chicago: Nelson-Hall, 1978.

Mathewson, Steven. *The Art of Preaching Old Testament Narrative*. Grand Rapids: Baker Academic, 2002.

Mawhinney, Bruce. *Preaching with Freshness*. Eugene, OR: Harvest House, 1991.

Maxwell, John. *Developing the Leader within You*. Nashville: Thomas Nelson, 1993.

Mayers, Marvin. *Christianity Confronts Culture*. Rev. ed. Grand Rapids: Zondervan, 1987.

McBrien, Richard. *Catholicism*. Vol. 2. Minneapolis: Winston, 1980.

McClure, John. "Collaborative Preaching and the Bible: Toward a Practical Theology of Memory." In *Preaching and the Personal*, edited by J. Dwayne Howell, 56–70. Eugene, OR: Wipf and Stock, 2013.

McCracken, Brett. *Hipster Christianity: When Church and Cool Collide*. Grand Rapids: Baker, 2010.

McCracken, Robert J. *The Making of the Sermon*. New York: Harper & Brothers, 1956.

McGonigal, Kelly. *The Willpower Instinct: How Self-Control Works, Why It Matters, and What You Can Do to Get More of It*. New York: Penguin, 2012.

McKenzie, Leon. *The Religious Education of Adults*. Birmingham: Religious Education, 1982.

McKim, Donald. *Westminster Dictionary of Theological Terms*. Louisville: Westminster John Knox, 1996.

Meeks, Wayne, ed. *The Writings of St. Paul: A Norton Critical Edition*. New York: W. W. Norton, 1972.

Middendorf, Jesse. "Pastoral Leadership and Administration." In *The Pastor's Guide to Effective Ministry*, edited by William Willimon, 87–98. Kansas City: Beacon Hill, 2002.

Milavec, Aaron. "Modern Exegesis, Doctrinal Innovations, and the Dynamics of Discipleship." *Anglican Theological Review* 60, no. 1 (January 1978): 55–74.

Miller, Calvin. *Preaching: The Art of Narrative Exposition*. Grand Rapids: Baker, 2006.

Miller, R. Scot. *Friends and Their Beliefs*. Philadelphia: Philadelphia Yearly Meeting, 1953.

Miller-McLemore, Bonnie. "Also a Pastoral Theologian: In Pursuit of Dynamic Theology." *Pastoral Psychology* 59, no. 6 (2010): 813–28.

Milstein, Glen, Martha Bruce, Nina Gargon, Ellen Brown, Patrick Raue, and Gail McAvay. "Religious Practice and Depression among Geriatric Home Care Patients." *International Journal of Psychiatry in Medicine* 33, no. 1 (2003): 71–83.

Milton, Michael. "So What Are You Doing Here? The Role of a Minister of the Gospel in Hospital Visitation, or a Theological Cure for the Crisis in Evangelical Pastoral Care." *Journal of the Evangelical Theological Society* 46, no. 3 (2003): 449–63.

Minear, Mark. *Richmond, 1887*. Richmond, IN: Friends United Press, 1987.

Mintzberg, Henry. *Power In and Around Organizations*. Englewood Cliffs, NJ: Prentice Hall, 1983.

Mitchell, Margaret. *Paul and the Rhetoric of Reconciliation: An Exegetical Investigation of the Language and Composition of 1 Corinthians*. Louisville: Westminster John Knox, 1991.

Molina-Markham, Elizabeth. "Being Spoken Through: Quaker 'Vocal Ministry' and the Premises of Personhood." *Journal of Communication and Religion* 36, no. 3 (2013), 127–48.

Montoya, Alex. "Leading." In *Rediscovering Pastoral Ministry: Shaping Contemporary Ministry with Biblical Mandates*, edited by John MacArthur, 281–304. Dallas: Word, 1995.

Morgan, Angie, Courtney Lynch, and Sean Lynch. *Spark: How to Lead Yourself and Others to Greater Success*. New York: Houghton Mifflin Harcourt, 2017.

Morrow, Jonathan. "Introducing Spiritual Formation." In *Foundations of Spiritual Formation*, edited by Paul Pettit, 31–50. Grand Rapids: Kregel, 2008.

Mudge, Lewis and James Poling, eds. *Formation and Reflection: The Promise of Practical Theology*. Philadelphia: Fortress, 1987.

Myles, Anne G. "From Monster to Martyr: Re-Presenting Mary Dyer." *Early American Literature* 36, no. 1 (2001): 1–30.

Nagel, Norman. "The Twelve and the Seven in Acts 6 and the Needy." *Concordia Journal* 31, no. 2 (April 2005): 113–26.

Nayler, James. *Works of James Nayler*. Vol. 1. Glenside, PA: Quaker Heritage Press, 2003.

Newby, J. Edwin. *Teachings of Evangelical Friends: As Gleaned from George Fox's Journal and Friends Disciplines*. Kokomo, IN: Central Yearly Meeting of Friends, 1952.

Newman, Daisy. *A Procession of Friends: Quakers in America*. Garden City, NY: Doubleday, 1972.

Newman, Steward. *A Free Church Perspective: A Study in Ecclesiology.* Exeter, UK: Stevens Books, 1986.

Niles, Daniel. *The Preacher's Task and the Stone of Stumbling.* New York: Harper & Brothers, 1958.

North Carolina Yearly Meeting of Friends. *Carolina Quakers: Our Heritage, Our Hope: Tercentenary 1672–1972.* Edited by Seth Hinshaw and Mary Hinshaw. Greensboro: North Carolina Yearly Meeting of Friends, 1972.

———. *Faith and Practice: Book of Discipline.* Greensboro: North Carolina Yearly Meeting of Friends, 2012.

Northouse, Peter. *Leadership: Theory and Practice.* 7th ed. Los Angeles: Sage, 2016.

Northwest Yearly Meeting of Friends Church. *Faith and Practice: A Book of Christian Discipline.* Newberg, OR: Northwest Yearly Meeting of Friends Church, 2012.

Nuttall, Geoffrey. *To the Refreshing of the Children of Light.* Wallingford, PA: Pendle Hill, 1959.

Oates, Wayne. *The Christian Pastor.* Philadelphia: Westminster, 1961.

———. *Pastoral Counseling.* Philadelphia: Westminster, 1974.

———. *Protestant Pastoral Counseling.* Philadelphia: Westminster, 1962.

O'Brien, P. T. "Prayer in Luke-Acts." *Tyndale Bulletin* 24, (1973): 111–27.

Oden, Thomas. *The Living God.* Vol. 1, *Systematic Theology.* Peabody, MA: Hendrickson, 2006.

———. *Pastoral Theology: Essentials of Ministry.* San Francisco: Harper San Francisco, 1983.

Odom, Randall, W. Randy Boxx, and Mark Dunn. "Organizational Cultures, Commitment, Satisfaction, and Cohesion." *Public Productivity & Management Review* 14, no. 2 (January 1990): 157–69.

Økland, Jorunn. *Women in Their Place: Paul and the Corinthian Discourse of Gender and Sanctuary Space*. London: T & T Clark, 2004.

Olford, Stephen. *Anointed Expository Preaching*. Nashville: Broadman & Holman, 1998.

Osborn, Charles. *Journal of That Faithful Servant Charles Osborn, Containing an Account of Many of His Travels and Labors*. . . . Cincinnati: Achilles Pugh, 1854.

Osborne, Larry. "Managing Church Government." In *Leadership Handbook of Management and Administration*, edited by James Berkley, 323–35. Rapids: Baker, 1994.

Ott, Ludwig. *Fundamentals of Catholic Dogma*. Rockford, IL: TAN Books, 1960.

Palmer, Russell. "Contextualizing the *Cruel Sufferings (For the Truths Sake) of Katharine Evans and Sarah Cheevers*: A Historical Materialist Perspective." *ANQ: A Quarterly Journal of Short Articles, Notes and Reviews* 31, no. 1 (2018): 11–17. https://www.tandfonline.com/doi/abs/10.1080/0895769X.2017.1340825

Palmer, T. Vail, Jr. "Did William Penn Diverge Significantly from George Fox in His Understanding of the Quaker Message?" *Quaker Studies* 11, no. 1 (September 2006): 59–70.

Palmieri, Brooke. "The Wild, the Innocent, and the Quaker's Struggle." *The Appendix* 2, no. 3 (2014): 98–104.

Pao, David. "Waiters or Preachers: Acts 6:1–7 and the Lukan Table Fellowship Motif." *Journal of Biblical Literature* 130, no. 1 (2011): 127–44.

Paschke, Boris. "Praying to the Holy Spirit in Early Christianity." *Tyndale Bulletin* 64, no. 2 (2013): 299–316.

Patel, Eboo. *Interfaith Leadership: A Primer*. Boston: Beacon, 2016.

Patterson, Kerry, Joseph Grenny, David Maxfield, Ron McMillan, and Al Switzer. *Influencer: The New Science of Leading Change.* 2nd ed. New York: MacGraw-Hill Education, 2013.

Patterson, Kerry, Joseph Grenny, Ron McMillan, and Al Switzler. *Crucial Conversations: Tools for Talking When Stakes Are High.* 2nd ed. New York: McGraw-Hill, 2012.

Pattison, Stephen. *The Challenge of Practical Theology: Selected Essays.* London: Jessica Kingsley, 2007.

Peake, Frank. "Reflections on Anglican Theological Education." *Journal of the Canadian Church Historical Society* 41, no. 2 (Fall 1999): 99–125.

Penington, Isaac. "A Short Catechism for the Sake of the Simple-Hearted." In *The Works of Isaac Penington, a Minister of the Gospel in the Society of Friends.* 1:1167–82. Sherwood, NY: David Heston, 1861.

Penn, William. *A Brief Account of the Rise and Progress of the People Called Quakers.* Charleston: CreateSpace, 2012.

———. *No Cross, No Crown.* Edited by Ronald Selleck. Richmond, IN: Friends United Press, 1981.

Perl, Paul. "Gender and Mainline Protestant Pastors' Allocation of Time to Work Tasks." *Journal for the Scientific Study of Religion* 41, no. 1 (2002): 169–78.

Pfeffer, Jeffrey. *Power: Why Some People Have It and Others Don't.* New York: HarperCollins, 2010.

Phelps, Vergil V. "The Pastor and Teacher in New England." *Harvard Theological Review* 4, no. 3 (1911): 388–99.

Philadelphia Yearly Meeting of Friends. *A Brief Catechism with Scripture Answers.* Philadelphia: Friends' Book Store, 1915.

Phillips, F. Peter. "Ancient and Comely Order: Use and Disuse of Arbitration by New York Quakers Symposium." *Journal of Dispute Resolution* 2016, no. 1 (January 2016): 96.

Pinnock, Clark. *Flame of Love: A Theology of the Holy Spirit.* Downers Grove, IL: IVP Academic, 1996.

Plank, Geoffrey. *John Woolman's Path to the Peaceable Kingdom: A Quaker in the British Empire*. Philadelphia: University of Pennsylvania Press, 2012.

Plant, Helen. "'Subjective Testimonies': Women Quaker Ministers and Spiritual Authority in England; 1750–1825." *Gender & History* 15, no. 2 (2003): 296–318.

Plantinga, Richard, Thomas Thompson, and Matthew Lundberg. *An Introduction to Christian Theology*. Cambridge: Cambridge University Press, 2010.

Plimpton, Ruth. *Mary Dyer: Biography of a Rebel Quaker*. Boston: Branden, 1994.

Plugh, Michael. "Meaning in Silence and the Quaker Tradition." *Et Cetera* 69, no. 2 (Apr 2012): 204–15.

Pohl, Christine. *Making Room: Recovering Hospitality as a Christian Tradition*. Grand Rapids: Eerdmans, 1999.

Polhill, John. *Paul and His Letters*. Nashville: Broadman & Holman, 1999.

Pollard, Beatrce, Francis Pollard, and Robert Pollard. *Democracy and the Quaker Method*. New York: Philosophical Library, 1950.

Pollock, David. "Managing the Church Office." In *Leadership Handbook of Management and Administration*, edited by James Berkley, 337–52. Grand Rapids: Baker, 1994.

Prunty, Kenneth. "Jesus: The Inner Side of Leadership." In *Living Leadership: Biblical Leadership Speaks to Our Day*, edited by Kenneth Hall, 161. Anderson, IN: Warner, 1991.

Prusak, Bernard P. *The Church Unfinished: Ecclesiology Through the Centuries*. New York: Paulist Press, 2004.

Pullin, Naomi. "Providence, Punishment, and Identity Formation in the Late-Stuart Quaker Community, c. 1650–1700." *The Seventeenth Century* 31, no. 4 (2016): 471–94.

Punshon, John. *Patterns of Change: The Quaker Experience and the Challenges of the Contemporary World.* Richmond, IN: Friends United Press, 1987.

———. *Portrait in Grey: A Short History of the Quakers.* London: Quaker Home Service, 1984.

Purcell, Larry. "Recruiting and Screening Volunteers." In *Management Essentials for Christian Ministries*, edited by Michael Anthony and James Estep, 244–57. Nashville: B&H, 2005.

Rainer, Thom and Eric Geiger. *Simple Church.* Nashville: B&H, 2006.

Rapaport, Diane. *The Naked Quaker: True Crimes and Controversies from the Courts of Colonial New England.* Beverly, MA: Commonwealth Editions, 2007.

Reagan, Timothy. *Non-Western Educational Traditions: Indigenous Approaches to Educational Thought and Practice.* 3rd ed. New York: Routledge, 2010.

Reece, G. *Friends and the Holy Spirit.* Richmond, IN: Five Years Meeting of Friends, 1960.

Reinhold, Barbara. *Toxic Work: How to Overcome Stress, Overload, and Burnout and Revitalize Your Career.* New York: Dutton, 1996.

Richards, Lawrence and Clyde Hoeldtke. *Church Leadership: Following the Example of Jesus Christ.* Grand Rapids: Zondervan, 1980.

Richmond, Kent and Dave Middleton. *The Pastor and the Patient: A Practical Handbook for Hospital Visitation.* Nashville: Abingdon, 1992.

Rightmire, David. "Subordination of Ecclesiology and Sacramental Theology to Pneumatology in the Nineteenth-Century Holiness Movement." *Wesleyan Theological Journal* 47, no. 2 (September 2012): 27–35.

Roberts, Arthur O. *The Association of Evangelical Friends: A Story of Quaker Renewal in the Twentieth Century*. Newberg, OR: Barclay Press, 1975.

———. "Evangelical Quakers: 1887–2010." In *The Oxford Handbook of Quaker Studies,* edited by Stephen Angell and Pink Dandelion, 108–25. Oxford: Oxford University Press, 2013.

———. *Tomorrow Is Growing Old: Stories of Quakers in Alaska*. Newberg, OR: Barclay Press, 1978.

Roberts, Wes. *The Leadership Secrets of Attila the Hun*. New York: Business Plus, 1987.

Robinson, Anthony. "It's About God, Stupid: Leadership as a Theological Practice." In *Pastoral Work: Engagements with the Vision of Eugene Peterson*, edited by Jason Byasse and L. Roger Owens, 28–40. Eugene, OR: Cascade, 2014.

Rock, Hugh. "George Fox and Theological Liberalism." *Modern Believing* 58, no. 1 (2017): 29–39.

Rocky Mountain Yearly Meeting of the Friends Church. *The Faith and Practice*. Denver: Rocky Mountain Yearly Meeting of the Friends Church, 2000.

Rosenthal, Norman. *The Gift of Adversity: The Unexpected Benefits of Life's Difficulties, Setbacks, and Imperfections.* New York: Tarcher, 2013.

Rowe, Arthur J. "1 Corinthians 12–14: The Use of a Text for Christian Worship." *The Evangelical Quarterly* 77, no. 2 (April 2005): 119–28.

Rubin, Paul. "Taking Care of the Customer." *Hospital Material Management Quarterly* 16, no. 1, (1994): 62–66.

Rushmore, Jane. *The Quaker Way*. Philadelphia: Philadelphia Meeting of Friends, n.d.

Russell, Elbert. *The History of Quakerism*. New York: Macmillan, 1942.

Ryan, James Emmett. *Imaginary Friends: Representing Quakers in American Culture, 1650–1950.* Madison: University of Wisconsin Press, 2009.

Sanders, Dennis. "Why I Dread Pastoral Visits." *Christian Century* 13, no. 1 (2015): 11–12.

Sanders, J. Oswald. *Spiritual Leadership: Principles of Excellence for Every Believer.* Chicago: Moody, 1994.

Sandy, D. Brent. *Plowshares & Pruning Hooks: Rethinking the Language of Biblical Prophecy and Apocalyptic.* Downers Grove: IVP Academic, 2002.

Salmon, Bruce. *Storytelling in Preaching: A Guide to the Theory and Practice.* Nashville: Broadman, 1988.

Samit, Jay. *Disrupt You!: Master Personal Transformation, Seize Opportunity, and Thrive in the Era of Endless Innovation.* New York: Flatiron Books, 2015.

Sampley, J. Paul. "The First Letter to the Corinthians: Introduction, Commentary, and Reflections." In Vol. 1, *The New Interpreter's Bible.* Edited by Leander Keck. Nashville: Abingdon, 2002.

Scaer, David P. "Was Junias a Female Apostle?: Maybe Not." *Concordia Theological Quarterly* 73, no. 1 (January 2009): 76.

Scherzer, Carl. *Ministering to the Dying.* Englewood Cliffs, NJ: Prentice-Hall, 1963.

———. *Ministering to the Physically Sick.* Englewood Cliffs, NJ: Prentice-Hall, 1963.

Schlafer, David and Michael Graves, eds. *What's the Shape of Narrative Preaching?* Duluth: Chalice, 2008.

Schneider, Jo Anne, Patricia Wittberg, Heidi Unruh, Jill Sinha, and John Belcher. "Comparing Practical Theology across Religions and Denominations." *Review of Religious Research* 52, no. 4 (2011): 405–26.

Schweizer, Eduard. "Service of Worship: An Exposition of 1 Corinthians 14." *Interpretation* 13, no. 4 (October 1959): 400–408.

Schwiebert, Jonathan. "Table Fellowship and the Translation of 1 Corinthians 5:11." *Journal of Biblical Literature* 127, no. 1 (2008): 159–64.

Scott, Janet. "Ecclesiology and Mission: A Quaker Perspective." *International Review of Mission* 40, no. 358 (2001): 317–23.

Scotti, Dennis J., Joel Harmon, and Scott J. Behson. "Structural Relationships Between Work Environment and Service Quality Perceptions as a Function of Customer Contact Intensity: Implications for Human Service Strategy." *Journal of Health and Human Services Administration* 32, no. 2 (Fall 2009): 1–234.

Segler, Franklin and Randall Bradley. *Christian Worship: Its Theology and Practice*. 3rd ed. Nashville: B&H, 2006.

Seidel, Andrew. "Leadership and Spiritual Formation." In *Foundations of Spiritual Formation: A Community Approach to Becoming Like Christ*, edited by Paul Petit, 245–68. Grand Rapids: Kregel, 2008.

Seidman, Dov. *How: Why How We Do Anything Means Everything*. Hoboken, NJ: John Wiley & Sons, 2007.

Self, Doug. "Ministering in the Marketplace." In *Mastering Pastoral Care*, by Bruce Larson, Paul Anderson, and Doug Self, 45–56. Portland, OR: Multnomah, 1990.

Sell, Phillip. "The Seven in Acts 6 as a Ministry Team." *Bibliotheca Sacra* 167, no. 665 (January 2010): 58–67.

Senecal, Patricia and Ellen Burke. "Learning to Listen." *Occupational Hazards* 54, no. 12 (1992): 37–39.

Seymour, Jack. "A Reforming Movement: The Story of the Protestant Sunday School." In *Renewing the Sunday School and the CCD*, edited by D. Campbell Wyckoff, 3–26. Birmingham: Religious Education, 1986.

Sharman, Cecil. *George Fox and the Quakers*. Richmond, IN: Friends United Press, 1991.

Sheeran, Michael. *Beyond Majority Rule: Voteless Decisions in the Religious Society of Friends*. Philadelphia: Philadelphia Yearly Meeting of the Religious Society of Friends, 1983.

Shideler, Emerson. "The Concept of the Church in Seventeenth-Century Quakerism." *Bulletin of Friends Historical Association* 45, no. 2 (1956): 67–81.

Shields, Harry. "Preaching and Spiritual Formation." In *Foundations of Spiritual Formation: A Community Approach to Becoming Like Christ*, edited by Paul Petit, 245–68. Grand Rapids: Kregel, 2008.

Sim, Stuart. "Postmodernism and Philosophy." In *The Routledge Companion to Postmodernism*, edited by Stuart Sim, 3–14. New York: Routledge, 2011.

Sinclair, Amanda. "Approaches to Organisational Ethics." *Journal of Business Ethics* 12, no. 1 (January 1993): 63–73.

Smalley, Stephen S. "Spirit, Kingdom and Prayer in Luke-Acts." *Novum Testamentum* 15, no. 1 (January 1973): 59–71.

Smith, Chuck. *The Philosophy of Ministry of Calvary Chapel*. Diamond Bar, CA: Logos Media, n.d.

Smith, Gary. *The Prophets as Preachers: An Introduction to the Hebrew Prophets*. Nashville: B&H Academic, 1994.

Snodgrass, Klyne. *Stories with Intent: A Comprehensive Guide to the Parables of Jesus*. Grand Rapids: William B. Eerdmans, 2008.

Snow, Shane. *Smartcuts: How Hackers, Innovators, and Icons Accelerate Success*. New York: HarperCollins, 2014.

Spencer, Carole. *Holiness: The Soul of Quakerism; An Historical Analysis of the Theology of Holiness in the Quaker Tradition*. Eugene, OR: Wipf & Stock, 2007.

Spencer, F. Scott. "Neglected Widows in Acts 6:1–7." *Catholic Biblical Quarterly* 56, no. 4 (October 1994): 715–33.

Spitale, Lennie. *Prison Ministry: Understanding Prison Culture Inside and Out*. Nashville: Broadman & Holman, 2002.

Spurgeon, Andrew B. "Pauline Commands and Women in 1 Corinthians 14." *Bibliotheca Sacra* 168, no. 671 (July 2011): 317–33.

Srivastava, Shekhar and Ashish Bhatnagar. "Impact of Customer Care Services on Customer Satisfaction—A Study of Mobile Phone Subscribers of U.P. (East) Circle." *International Journal of Management Research and Reviews* 3, no. 1 (January 2013): 2224–42.

Stafford, Gilbert. *Theology for Disciples*. Anderson, IN: Warner Press, 1996.

Stanger, Frank. *Spiritual Formation in the Local Church*. Grand Rapids: Francis Asbury, 1989.

Steele, Les. *On the Way: A Practical Theology of Christian Formation*. Grand Rapids: Baker, 1990.

Steere, Douglas and Dorothy Steere. *Friends Work in Africa*. London: Friends World Committee for Consultation, 1954.

Steers, Richard. *Introduction to Organizational Behavior*. 4th ed. New York: HarperCollins, 1991.

Stone, Lance. "Word and Sacrament as Paradigmatic for Pastoral Theology: In Search of a Definition via Brueggmann, Hauerwas, and Ricoeur." *Scottish Journal of Theology* 56, no. 4 (2003): 444–63.

Stott, John. *Basic Christian Leadership: Biblical Models of Church, Gospel, and Ministry*. Downers Grove, IL: IVP, 2002.

———. *Between Two Worlds: The Art of Preaching in the Twentieth Century*. Grand Rapids: Eerdmans, 1982.

Stout, Harry. *New England Soul: Preaching and Religious Culture in Colonial New England*. Oxford: Oxford University Press, 2012.

Stramara, Daniel. "Toward a Charismatic Ecclesiology as a Theological Basis for Primacy." *Journal of Ecumenical Studies* 49, no. 2 (2014): 218–46.

Stranahan, Edgar. *History of Friends: An Outline Study*. Richmond, IN: Friends Publication Board, 1930.

Strawbridge, Jennifer. "The Word of the Cross: Mission, Power, and the Theology of Leadership." *Anglican Theological Review* 91, no. 1 (2009): 61–79.

Strong, Augustus. *Systematic Theology*. Old Tappan, NJ: Fleming H. Revell, 1907.

Stuard, Susan. "Women's Witnessing: A New Departure." In *Witnesses for Change: Quaker Women Over Three Centuries*, edited by Elizabeth Potts Brown and Susan Stuard, 3–25. Brunswick: Rutgers University Press, 1989.

Sutton, Robert and Huggy Rao. *Scaling Up Excellence: Getting to More without Settling for Less*. New York: Crown Books, 2014.

Swift, David. *Joseph John Gurney: Banker, Reformer, and Quaker*. Middletown: Wesleyan University Press, 1962.

Thompson, Derek. *Hit Makers: The Science of Popularity in an Age of Distraction*. London: Penguin, 2017.

Thorley, John. "Junia, a Woman Apostle." *Novum Testamentum* 38, no. 1 (January 1996): 18–29.

Tidwell, Charles. *Educational Ministry of a Church: An Introduction to Educational Administration*. Nashville: Broadman, 1982.

Tjørhom, Ola. "Better Together: Apostolicity and Apostolic Succession in Light of an Ecumenical Ecclesiology." *Pro Ecclesia* 23, no. 3 (2014): 282–93.

Tongue, Archer. *The Vocation of Friends in the Modern World*. London: Friends World Conference Committee, 1950.

Trueblood, Elton. *The Incendiary Fellowship*. New York: Harper & Row, 1967.

———. *The People Called Quakers*. New York: Harper & Row, 1966.

———. *Robert Barclay.* New York: Harper & Row, 1968.
———. *Studies in Quaker Worship*. Philadelphia: Young Friends Movement, 1935.
———. *Total Gospel*. Richmond, IN: Friends United Press, 1966.
Tucker, Austin. *The Preacher as Storyteller: The Power of Narrative in the Pulpit*. Nashville: B&H Academic, 2008.
Tunio, Ghazala, Nizammuddin Channa, and Saima Kamran Pathan. "Training Practices and Their Effectiveness in Non-Government Organizations of Pakistan." *International Research Journal of Arts and Humanities* 44, no. 44 (2016): 191–98.
Tyler, Jo. "Reclaiming Rare Listening as a Means of Organizational Re-Enchantment." *Journal of Organizational Change Management* 24, no. 1 (2011): 143–57.
Underhill, Evelyn. *Worship*. New York: Harper, 1937.
Van Edwards, Vanessa. *Captivate: The Science of Succeeding with People*. New York: Portfolio, 2017.
Van Etten, Henry. *George Fox and the Quakers*. New York: Harper Torchbooks, 1959.
VandeCreek, Larry. "The Parish Clergy's Ministry of Prayer with Hospitalized Parishioners." In *Psychological Perspectives on Prayer*, edited by Leslie Francis and Jeff Astley, 207–18. Leominster: Gracewing, 2001.
Vanhoozer, Kevin. *Everyday Theology: How to Read Cultural Texts and Interpret Trends*. Edited by Charles Anderson and Micahel Sleasman. Grand Rapids: Baker Academic, 2007.
Vendantam, Shankar. *The Hidden Brain: How Our Unconscious Minds Elect Presidents, Control Markets, Wage Wars, and Save Our Lives*. New York: Spiegel & Grau, 2010.
Vipont, Elfrida. *George Fox and the Valiant Sixty*. London: Hamish Hamilton, 1975.
———. *The Story of Quakerism: 1652–1952*. London: Bannisdale Press, 1955.

Volf, Miroslav. *After Our Likeness: The Church as the Image of the Trinity*. Grand Rapids: William B. Eerdmans, 1998.

Volz, Carl. *Pastoral Life and Practice in the Early Church*. Minneapolis: Augsburg, 1990.

Von Rad, Gerhard. "Ancient Word and Living Word: The Preaching of Deuteronomy and Our Preaching." *Interpretation* 15, no. 1 (January 1961): 3–13.

Von Wahlde, Urban C. "The Theological Assessment of the First Christian Persecution: The Apostles' Prayer and Its Consequences in Acts 4:24–31." *Biblica* 76, no. 4 (1995): 523–31.

Vowell, Sarah. *Wordy Shipmates*. New York: Riverhead Books, 2008.

Ward, Madeleine. "Transformative Faith and the Theological Response of the Quakers to the Boston Executions." *Quaker Studies* 21, no. 1 (2016): 15–32.

Waters, Guy Prentiss. "Curse Redux?: 1 Corinthians 5:13, Deuteronomy, and Identity in Corinth." *The Westminster Theological Journal* 77, no. 2 (September 2015): 237–50.

Webb, Joseph. *Preaching Without Notes*. Nashville: Abingdon, 2001.

Webb, Maria. *The Fells of Swarthmore Hall*. Philadelphia: Henry Longstreth, 1896.

Webb, Norval. *Fellowship Evangelism: A Workbook for Friends Meetings*. Indianapolis: John Woolman Press, 1964.

Weger, Harry, Gina Castle Bell, and Melissa Robinson. "The Relative Effectiveness of Active Listening in Initial Interactions." *International Journal of Listening* 28, no. 1 (January 2014): 13–31.

Welch, Robert. "Managing Buildings and Grounds." In *Leadership Handbook of Management and Administration*, edited by James Berkley, 367–75. Grand Rapids: Baker, 1994.

Western Yearly Meeting of Friends. *Faith and Practice of Western Yearly Meeting of Friends Church.* Plainfield: Western Yearly Meeting, 2005.

———. *Minutes of the Ministerial Conference of Western Yearly Meeting of Friends.* Indianapolis: Baker & Randolph, 1880.

———s. *Semi-Centennial Anniversary: Western Yearly Meeting of Friends Church.* Plainfield: Publishing Association of Friends, 1908.

Westhelle, Vítor. "The Church's Crucible: Koinonia and Cultural Transcendence." *Currents in Theology and Mission* 31, no. 3 (June 2004): 211–18.

White, James. *A Brief History of Christian Worship.* Nashville: Abingdon, 1993.

———. *Introduction to Christian Worship.* 3rd ed. Nashville: Abingdon, 2000.

Whitmire, Catherine. *Plain Living: A Quaker Path to Simplicity.* Notre Dame: Sorin Books, 2001.

Wilbert, Warren. *Teaching Christian Adults.* Grand Rapids: Baker, 1980.

Wilbur, Henry. *The Life and Labors of Elias Hicks.* London: Forgotten Books, 2012.

Wilder, Amos. *Early Christian Rhetoric: The Language of the Gospel.* Peabody: Hendrickson, 1971.

Wildes, Henry Emerson. *Voice of the Lord.* Philadelphia: University of Pennsylvania Press, 1965.

Wilkes, C. Gene. *Jesus On Leadership: Discovering the Secrets of Servant Leadership from the Life of Christ.* Wheaton: Tyndale, 1998.

Willard, Dallas. *Knowing Christ Today: Why We Can Trust Spiritual Knowledge.* New York: Harper Collins, 2009.

———. *Renovation of the Heart: Putting on the Character of Christ.* Colorado Springs: NavPress, 2002.

Williams, J. Clifton. *Human Behavior in Organizations.* Cincinnati: South-West, 1978.

Williams, Walter. *The Rich Heritage of Quakerism*. Newberg, OR: Barclay Press, 1987.
Willimon, William. "Crisis and Conflict." In *Leadership Handbook of Management and Administration*, edited by James Berkley, 215–34. Grand Rapids: Baker, 1994.
———. *Worship as Pastoral Care*. Nashville: Abingdon, 1979.
Willink, Jocko and Leif Babin. *Extreme Ownership: How US Navy SEALs Lead and Win*. New York: St. Martin's Press, 2015.
Wilmington Yearly Meeting of the Religious Society of Friends. *Faith and Practice of Wilmington Yearly Meeting of the Religious Society of Friends*. Wilmington, OH: Wilmington Yearly Meeting of the Religious Society of Friends, 2008.
Wilson, Kevin and Jennifer Wauson. "Mission Statements." In *The AMA Handbook of Business Documents: Guidelines and Sample Documents That Make Business Writing Easy*, 86–87. New York: AMACOM, 2011.
Witherington, Ben. *Paul's Narrative Thought World: The Tapestry of Tragedy and Triumph*. Louisville: Westminster John Knox, 1994.
Witvliet, John. *Worship Seeking Understanding: Windows into Christian Perspective*. Grand Rapids: Baker Academic, 2003.
Wolters, Albert. "IOYNIAN (Romans 16:7) and the Hebrew Name Yĕḥunnī." *Journal of Biblical Literature* 127, no. 2 (2008): 397–408.
Wood, James. *The Distinguishing Doctrines of the Religious Society of Friends*. New York: Friends' Book and Tract Committee, 1908.
Woodard, Luke. *A Historical Sketch of the Schism in the Friends Church in the Years 1827–1828 Known as the "Hicksite Separation."* Plainfield: Friday Caller Print, 1914.
Woodman, Charles. *Quakers Find a Way: Their Discoveries in Practical Living*. Indianapolis: Bobbs-Merrill, 1950.

Woodward, Walter. *Timothy Nicholson: Master Quaker*. Richmond, IN: Nicholson Press, 1927.
World Evangelical Fellowship. "The Iguassu Affirmation." In *Global Missiology for the 21st Century: The Iguassu Dialogue*, edited by William Taylor, 15–22. Grand Rapids: Baker Academic, 2000.
Worthington, Everett. *Marriage Counseling: A Christian Approach to Counseling Couples*. Downers Grove, IL: InterVarsity, 1989.
Wright, Christopher. *The Mission of God: Unlocking the Bible's Grand Narrative*. Downers Grove: IVP Academic, 2006.
Wright, H. Norman. *The New Guide to Crisis and Trauma Counseling: A Practical Guide for Ministers, Counselors, and Lay Counselors*. Ventura, CA: Regal, 2003.
Wright, John. *Telling God's Story: Narrative Preaching for Christian Formation*. Downers Grove, IL: IVP Academic, 2007.
Yearly Meeting Centennial Committee. *Wilmington Yearly Meeting: 1891–1991*. Sabina, OH: Gaskins, 1991.
Yolen, Jane. *Friend: The Story of George Fox and the Quakers*. New York: Seabury Press, 1972.
Yukl, Gary. *Leadership in Organizations*. 6th ed. Upper Saddle River, NJ: Pearson, 2006.
Zaprometova, Olga. "The Eucharistic Mystery: The Meeting of Pneumatology and Ecclesiology." *Journal of European Baptist Studies* 14, no. 1 (September 2013): 24–39.
Zimmerli, Walter. *The Fiery Throne: The Prophets and Old Testament Theology*. Minneapolis: Fortress, 2003.

www.ingramcontent.com/pod-product-compliance
Lightning Source LLC
Chambersburg PA
CBHW030101170426
43198CB00009B/448